The Literature of Region and Nation

Edited by

R. P. DRAPER

Regius Chalmers Professor of English
University of Aberdeen

MACMILLAN
PRESS

First published 1989

Published by
THE MACMILLAN PRESS LTD
Houndmills, Basingstoke, Hampshire RG21 2XS
and London
Companies and representatives
throughout the world

Printed and bound in Great Britain at
The Camelot Press plc, Southampton

British Library Cataloguing in Publication Data
The literature of region and nation.
1. Regionalism in literature
I. Draper, R. P.
809′.8891   PN56.R3/
ISBN 0–333–43774–8

Contents

Acknowledgements

The editor wishes to acknowledge the help given by various colleagues in the Aberdeen English Department with the preparation of this volume, and particularly Colin Milton, Secretary of the Conference. Thanks are also due to Mrs Anne Robertson for typing and patient help throughout the editorial process. G. J. B. Watson's contribution was first published in *The Yale Review*, copyright © 1986 by Yale University, and appears here by permission.

The editor and publishers would also like to thank the following who have kindly given permission for the use of copyright material:

Basil Blackwell Ltd, for the extracts from *Nations and Nationalism* by Ernest Gellner.

Carcanet Press Ltd and New Directions Publishing Corp., for the extracts from *The Collected Poems of William Carlos Williams*, Volume 1, copyright © 1982 by William Eric Williams and Paul H. Williams.

J. M. Dent Ltd, for the extracts from *Collected Poems* by Dylan Thomas.

Faber and Faber Ltd, for the extracts from *The Silver Darlings* by Neil Gunn.

Faber and Faber Ltd, for the extracts from *The Whitsun Weddings* by Philip Larkin.

Faber and Faber Ltd, and Farrar, Straus and Giroux Inc., for the extracts from *High Windows* by Philip Larkin. Extracts from 'Show Saturday' and 'Going, Going' from *High Windows*, copyright © 1974 by Philip Larkin; reprinted by permission of Farrar, Straus and Giroux Inc.

Grafton Books, a division of the Collins Publishing Group, for the extracts from *Not That He Brought Flowers* and *Song at the Year's Turning* by R. S. Thomas.

New Directions Publishing Corp., for the extracts from *In the American Grain* by William Carlos Williams, copyright © 1933 by William Carlos Williams; *Selected Letters* by William Carlos Williams, copyright © 1957 by William Carlos Williams; *Selected Essays* by William Carlos Williams, copyright © 1954 William Carlos Williams.

Oxford University Press, for the extracts from *The Letters of William and Dorothy Wordsworth*, 2nd edition (1967–).

The Souvenir Press, for the extracts from *The Drinking Well* by Neil Gunn.

A. P. Watt Ltd, on behalf of Michael B. Yeats and Macmillan London Ltd, for the extracts from *Letters to the New Island* by W. B. Yeats.

Notes on the Contributors

J. H. Alexander is Senior Lecturer in English, University of Aberdeen. His publications include *Two Studies in Romantic Reviewing* (1976), books on *The Lay of the Last Minstrel* and *Marmion* (1979, 1981), and *Reading Wordsworth*. He is currently editing *Kenilworth* for the Edinburgh Edition of the Waverley Novels of Scott.

Jean-Pierre Campill is Professor, Centre Universitaire de Luxembourg.

Thomas Crawford has recently retired as Reader in English, University of Aberdeen. He formerly taught at the University of Auckland. His publications include books on *Robert Burns*, *Scott* and editions of Scottish verse.

R. P. Draper is Regius Professor of English, University of Aberdeen. He has previously taught at the Universities of Adelaide and Leicester. He is the author of *D. H. Lawrence* (1964), *D. H. Lawrence: The Critical Heritage* (1970), Casebooks on *Hardy, The Tragic Novels* (1975) and *George Eliot, 'The Mill on the Floss' and 'Silas Marner'* (1977), *Tragedy, Developments in Criticism* (1980), *Lyric Tragedy* (1985) and *'The Winter's Tale': Text and Performance* (1985). He is currently working on Hardy, Lawrence, Philip Larkin and G. S. Fraser.

Robin Gilmour is Senior Lecturer in English, University of Aberdeen. He is the author of *The Idea of the Gentleman in the Victorian Novel* (1981), *Thackeray: 'Vanity Fair'* (1982), *The Novel in the Victorian Age* (1986), and editor of Trollope's *The Warden* and *Barchester Towers*.

Barbara Hardy is Professor of English, Birkbeck College at the University of London. Her publications include books on Jane Austen, Dickens, George Eliot, Thomas Hardy, Thackeray, *The Appropriate Form* (1964), *Tellers and Listeners* (1975) and *The Advantage of Lyric* (1977).

Seamus Heaney is Boylston Professor of Rhetoric and Oratory at

Harvard University. His most recent volumes of poetry are *Station Island* (1984) and *Hard Water* (1987). He is a director of the Field Day Theatre Company and a member of the Irish Academy of Letters.

David Hewitt is Senior Lecturer, University of Aberdeen. He is the author of *Scott on Himself* (1981), *Literature of the North* (with Michael Spiller, 1983) and *Scott and his Influence* (with J.H. Alexander, 1983). He has been Treasurer of the Association for Scottish Literary Studies since 1973, and is editor-in-chief of the Edinburgh Edition of the Waverley Novels of Scott.

Robert Lawson-Peebles is Lecturer in English, University of Aberdeen. He is the author of *The World Turned Upside Down: Landscape and Written Expression in Revolutionary America*.

A. Walton Litz is Professor of English at Princeton University. He is the author of *The Art of James Joyce* (1961), *Jane Austen* (1965), *Introspective Voyager: The Poetic Development of Wallace Stevens* (1972), and has edited works on James Joyce and *Major American Short Stories*.

Mark S. Madoff is Associate Professor at Royal Roads Military College, Victoria, Canada. He has published several articles on Gothic influences, Swift and Sterne.

Michael Millgate is Professor of English at the University of Toronto. He is the author of *William Faulkner* (1961), *American Social Fiction: James to Cozzens* (1964), *The Achievement of William Faulkner* (1966), *Thomas Hardy: His Career as a Novelist* (1971) and *Thomas Hardy: A Biography* (1982). He is editor (with Richard L. Purdy) of *The Collected Letters of Thomas Hardy* and of *The Life and Work of Thomas Hardy*.

Philip Mosley is Lecturer at Glasgow College of Technology. He is the author of *Ingmar Bergman: Cinema as Mistress* (1981), *Teamasters, Teahouses* (trs. 1982) and *Bruges-la-Morte* (trs. 1986).

Norman Page is Professor of Modern English Literature at the University of Nottingham, formerly Professor of English, University of Alberta. Among his publications are *The Language of Jane Austen* (1972), *Speech in the English Novel* (1973), *Thomas Hardy*

(1977), *A. E. Housman* (1983) and *A Dickens Companion* (1984). He is the editor of *Wilkie Collins: The Critical Heritage* (1974), *D. H. Lawrence: Interviews and Recollections* (1984) and *The Thomas Hardy Annuals*.

Bruce Clunies Ross is Associate Professor of English Literature, Copenhagen University. He is the author of many essays on Australian literature, music and cultural history.

Sepp Simon is at the Centre Universitaire de Luxembourg.

Iain Crichton Smith, OBE, has written many novels, poems, and short stories. His books include *Consider the Lilies* (1968), *Selected Poems* (1980) and *Selected Poems* (1985). He is a Fellow of the Royal Society of Literature.

G. J. B. Watson is Senior Lecturer in English, University of Aberdeen. He is the author of *Irish Identity and Literary Revival* (1979) and of two books on drama.

J. R. Watson is Professor of English, University of Durham. Among his publications are *Picturesque Landscape and English Romantic Poetry* (1970), *Wordsworth's Vital Soul: The Sacred and the Profane in Wordsworth's Poetry* (1982) and *English Poetry of the Romantic Period, 1789–1830* (1985). He is the editor of *Victorian Poetry: 'The City of Dreadful Night' and Other Poems* (1974), *Everyman's Book of Victorian Verse* (1982) and *Thomas Hardy: 'The Mayor of Casterbridge'* (1983).

Introduction*

R. P. DRAPER

Seamus Heaney reminds us that the old BBC 'wireless' used to put out a 'Regional Weather Forecast' as a kind of minor prelude to the more exalted and more widely respected 'General Weather Forecast', but that this distinction no longer exists. We are all regionalists now. In letters, as in meteorological forecasts, the implicit subordination of local to national has been eroded: 'We turn on our radios and wait. All around there is good writing, but where,' asks Heaney, 'is the great carrying voice of the definitive centre?'

In Britain at least we seem to have exhausted that Victorian/ Edwardian energy which bound scattered communities together by railway lines and mutual commercial advantage, turning in the process formerly semi-independent towns and counties into 'the provinces' and the wholly independent nation of Scotland into a new territory called 'North Britain'; and we have lost that confident sense of imperial destiny which made it possible to regard London not only as the metropolitan capital, but as the very hub of the universe. The centralising tendency is, of course, as strong as ever

---

*The first International Conference on the Literature of Region and Nation was held at the University of Aberdeen from 19 to 23 August 1986. Speakers, who came from a variety of countries, spoke on topics which were largely of their own choosing; no attempt was made to impose a particular theme or approach. The present volume records the proceedings of the Conference only in the sense that it publishes all the plenary session papers and a selection of the shorter ones. (A complete list is given in the Appendix, pp. 253–4.) This Introduction was not part of the Conference as such: it is a personal view of some of the topics raised, drawing mainly on the papers printed here, but it would not necessarily command the assent of all the contributors. The literature of region and nation provokes controversy, and, though the Conference itself was conducted in the friendliest possible atmosphere, unanimity is hardly to be expected, or perhaps to be desired. I have attempted to trace figures in the Conference carpet which others might not have found there, and though I express views which have been prompted and modified by the wealth of different ideas put forward at the Conference, the responsibility for what follows is entirely my own.

– stronger perhaps since modern technology has created a 'global village' undreamt of in the nineteenth century, and multinational corporations leap boundaries with homogenised products which make the Hiltons of Mayfair and Cairo and Hong Kong scarcely distinguishable one from the other. But in artistic, if not in political and economic, matters there no longer exists the kind of prevalent certainty which stems from the self-assurance of a culturally dominant group whose standards are implicitly accepted even by those who rebel against them. As Robin Gilmour reminds us, Arnold, the urbane propagandist for Hellenism as against Hebraism, believed in a quiet-voiced 'centre' which ideally had no need for brash self-assertion; but D. H. Lawrence, writing in the 1920s, mocks the decline which this Oxonian manner is already suffering by wickedly ventriloquising it:

> We wouldn't insist on it for a moment
> but we are
> we are
> you admit we are
> superior.[1]

Deference, whether conscious or not, willing or reluctant, is the name of this game, and it is deference that is now withheld. The centre may bully and cajole, and through the mass media, and by means of its administrative tentacles, seek to impose a model of conformity; but there is too much energy and variety out there in the regions, and too little assurance of a God-given role at the metropolitan heart, to make such respect any longer viable.

However, this is not to suggest that regionalism is a discovery of the twentieth century, and its rise somehow a counterpart of the decline and fall of the British Empire. It seems to have been a growth of the late eighteenth century – a response to the Industrial Revolution, at first of a pastoral kind, but rapidly countered by a wish not only to do proper justice to threatened rural traditions, but also to 'paint the cot / As truth will paint it, and as bards will not'.[2] Regional consciousness was not so much escapist as critically aware of the dangers of anonymity and desiccation attendant on the new forces; if it was characterised by a regretful recognition of the loss which inevitably accompanies change, it was also prompted to a fuller awareness of the complex reality of what was under threat and a desire to preserve its essentially human value.

This was certainly the case with Wordsworth. In Book VII of *The

Prelude he reacts away from a London which seems to him a 'monstrous ant-hill on the plain / Of a too busy world', and towards the 'order and relation' which he associates with 'the forms / Perennial of the ancient hills'. His most profound experience, however, in the city is his encounter with a blind beggar. This is an experience which has its counterpart in poems like 'Resolution and Independence' and 'The Old Cumberland Beggar' in which the outcasts of society – or rather, those who would be outcasts in the context of the turbulent city – find a justification and an integrated role in the more humane economy of the rural world. It is true that in terms of the poetry they excite the role they play is still more noticeably a visionary one (this is certainly the case with the old leech-gatherer in 'Resolution and Independence'), but that exists in relation to, and arises out of, their essentially communal, though apparently isolated, function. The business of the Wordsworthian narrator is both to receive their full imaginative impact on his poetic consciousness and to record and celebrate, without idealisation, their more commonplace, day-to-day existence. Nor, as Ian Alexander shows, is this recourse to the solidity of provincial values a merely literary creation. From his letters, too, Wordsworth emerges as 'universal regional poet', without 'any provincial inferiority complex'. He prefers the contemplative quietness of Grasmere to the distractions of London, and reads old, established classics rather than the latest fashionable literature; but he is also aware of the need to make frugal economies, and, above all, he is in contact with his local community, which he defends as 'much more intellectual than a careless observer would suppose'.

This affirmation of regional values is echoed in the work of Scott, and continues in the work of Mrs Gaskell, the Brontës and George Eliot, culminating in the novels (and also the poems) of Thomas Hardy. Though the 'centre' prospered and became increasingly powerful in the nineteenth century, writers such as these resisted its pressures and helped to cultivate in the minds of their readers the notion of a regional/provincial counterbalance to its homogenising influence. And there is continuity, too, in the work of twentieth-century writers: an essential element in the work of Philip Larkin, for example – as I have tried to show in my own discussion of him as 'provincial poet' – is the rediscovery of a positive virtue in English provinciality. Both Wordsworth and Hardy also brought fame to the regions in which they lived, and where residence seemed to be almost a necessary condition of their inspiration (future biographers may perhaps say something similar of 'the Hermit of Hull'[3]); but Hardy went still further, not merely defending provincial values, but also creating a geographical, mapped regionalism which scarcely exists as such in the work of Wordsworth.

'Provincial' is a term which is often used slightingly (though Wordsworth, Hardy and Larkin all seek to represent the life and customs of their native areas as preferable to the metropolis), but 'regional' seems to attract no such derogatory usage. This is perhaps because it carries with it none of the hierarchically subordinate implications of 'provincial'. 'Regional' suggests a division of a larger unit, but without the larger being necessarily dominant. It is at once a more neutral term and a more welcome one than 'provincial', and is generally free from the imputation of narrowness which is often implicit in the use of 'provincial'. As applied to Hardy's work it is inseparable from his development of the notion of 'Wessex' to cover that 'partly real, partly dream-country' which became the setting for most of his fiction.[4] As Michael Millgate suggests, Hardy may not have devised and exploited this idea with such deliberation as the later regional novelist, Faulkner, did in his creation of Yoknapatawpha County, but he gave his Wessex enough imaginative realisation and peopled it with enough distinctively local inhabitants, possessing their own speech and their own 'customs of the country',[5] for it to become in his readers' minds an autonomous artistic territory with its own entirely credible way of life. The way was prepared by his forebears, but it was Hardy who promoted regionalism to its special position in the English imagination. The secret, of course, lies in his unique relationship to the region – born and bred in it, but becoming intellectually detached from it, and thus both feeling it on his pulse, and yet recreating it as an imaginative counterpoise to what he had experienced of the modern, extra-regional world. Hardy, in fact, is a watershed; after him Lawrence, Faulkner, Grassic Gibbon and Neil Gunn can also work with a feeling for region that is deeply rooted in personal experience, while recognising that the integration of such experience with a culture and a community which is facing a spiritual crisis endows the created region with a paradoxically immediate and transcendent significance. Region is thus able to acquire, as Tom Crawford suggests, the resonance of myth; it becomes almost a kind of religion.

Barbara Hardy adds a further dimension to the argument by suggesting that regional literature, or more specifically poetry, 'does not become a genre unless it also becomes nationalist poetry, as frequently happens in war, conquest, or revolution'. And whereas regionalism may be either neutral or benign, nationalism tends to generate an aggressiveness which deforms the culture it seeks to protect. This is illustrated by a comparison of the two Welsh Thomases. R. S. Thomas (born outside Wales, and with something of the fervour of a convert) writes 'a sour pastoral' directed not only against English intruders, but often against the Welsh themselves; while the poetry of Dylan Thomas, though steeped in childhood regional associations, employs those associations for a wider purpose which transcends merely local reference: 'It metamorphoses the objects of Thomas's known and familiar landscape, using the region for more than regional poetry'.

Such a view of region and nation is perhaps open to the objection that it generalises too much from particular examples, and that it does not sufficiently distinguish political nationalism from cultural nationalism, but it usefully highlights a problem which is often encounterd in the literature of the minority nations within Britain, and which is echoed in colonial, and post-colonial, contexts. Barbara Hardy deals with contrasting forms of Welshness; other contributors to this volume reflect the Scottish and Irish experiences. David Hewitt, for example, takes up the theme, frequently debated in Scotland, of the cultural dominance, consequent on economic and political dominance, which is attributed to the influence of England and the English language. Hewitt's specific theme is the 'colonisation' or 'take-over' of the Scots language by English after the Union of the two countries in 1707, but, unusually – and with an 'enlightenment' which is appropriate to the period, though rarely met with in such discussions – he shows that there were beneficial as well as harmful results. The threat to their native speech produced a heightened language consciousness among Scottish writers which helped to preserve and reinvigorate the national character of the literature, and – a benefit which anyone living in Scotland can observe as still the inheritance of its present-day inhabitants – led to the acquisition of a second language rather than the loss of a first.

Whether Scots is a distinct and separate language, or a dialect of English, is a vexed and hoary subject of debate. Whichever answer may be preferred, it is near enough to English in syntax, and even in lexis, for doubt to remain inevitable. Gaelic, however, is certainly another tongue, and a contemporary poet like Iain Crichton Smith, who has to make the transition from first to second language for even more pressing bread-and-butter reasons, finds it a more profoundly disturbing process. He feels himself 'a double man riddled with guilt' who cannot get all of himself into what he writes. In a sense he must be judged unnecessarily guilty, since it is clearly a different self which has emerged from this linguistic crux, and that self at least is finding expression. But the authenticity of his feeling 'that the Gaelic world is not getting into [his] English, that some deep emotional power is missing' cannot, of course, be questioned, especially by a non-Gaelic outsider.

The Gaelic area of Scotland shares a cultural inheritance with Ireland, and the sense of a lost language is also an important theme in much Irish writing. Here the attitude to English and England is still further complicated. Seamus Heaney, for example, treats the problem of deference in the literary relations between the two countries, but finds in James Joyce a model for minority defensiveness which successfully combines 'resolution' and 'presumption of a salutary kind'. If English hegemony is bypassed it is by implicit reference to a European rather than a parochial court of appeal. On the other hand, another Irish contributor to this volume, G. J. B. Watson, born in Northern Ireland of Catholic parents who migrated from Eire, educated at Queen's University, Belfast, and at Oxford, and now a teacher of English at a Scottish university, writes of his personal sense of England as essentially 'a country of the mind'.

The modern English-speaking world has become so numerous and diverse that speakers and writers of the language (and receivers of the image of Englishness as well, since the problem is not merely linguistic) who were not born in England, vastly outnumber those who were. As a result, England is increasingly what it is perceived to be; in a richly confused, cross-cultural situation its mythical dimension, as George Watson's experience suggests, is something which looms larger than the reality. In such a context the title of Norman Page's contribution, 'The Most Wonderful Foreign Land I Have Ever Been In: Kipling's England', is less startling than it might otherwise appear. In popular opinion Kipling is the most fervently nationalistic of all English writers, but, as Page remarks, the England he celebrates is 'partly observed, partly recreated from the historical past, but also to an important extent idealized or invented'. He was an outsider who emotionally adopted Sussex; and it is interesting to note that Page detects in Kipling's evocation of his adopted land 'a sense of being simultaneously inside and outside the English scene'. (This is further confirmation perhaps of that dual condition of belonging and not-belonging which seems to be the hallmark of literary regionalism.)

The Australian Les Murray is yet another non-English English-speaking writer who shares with Scottish, Welsh, Irish or Anglo-Indian this ambiguous relationship between language and country. He asserts that 'I am not European. Nor is my English.' He is an exile in his own land, but, unlike Kipling, he does not try to repatriate himself to a recreated regional England which will satisfy his need for acceptance. Instead he tries to adapt his expression to the real Australian landscape. As Bruce Clunies Ross expresses it, he tries 'to assimilate the environment imaginatively and create a regional ... literature through which Australians can establish an harmonious sense of place and resolve their sense of exile'.

The reality of modern Australia, however, is urban rather than rural, and the anxiety betrayed in this effort to shake off the influence of an English tradition which seems to drive a wedge between language and experience is unlikely to be exorcised by a mystique of 'the bush'. America is probably a more relevant and more hopeful model than anti-Englishness, or reaction from images of England, can provide. In its early, colonial days America also felt the inhibiting influence of an English establishment culture, but its subsequent acquisition of wealth and the sheer weight of its population has made the United States rather than England the twentieth-century base for that cultural take-over bidding which created such anxiety in the late eighteenth and nineteenth centuries. Yet, curiously enough, the result has not been the development of a neo-Arnoldian transatlantic 'centre'. New York, Boston, Chicago, New Orleans, San Francisco, *et alia*, are rival centres, to some extent neutralising each other. And it may be more exact to say 'North America' rather than the USA, since Montreal, Toronto and Vancouver make their own separate bids as well. America is a nation of regions rather than a land in which region and nation are polarised. As Walton Litz and Bob

Lawson-Peebles demonstrate in their respective papers, 'the local is the universal' in the distinctively American poetry which the school of Wallace Stevens and William Carlos Williams cultivate; while Mark Madoff, in an interesting comment on the work of writers such as Lillard and Bowering, further suggests that a special sense of locality is developing along the Pacific seaboard which is bringing to birth a new 'west coast' region that ignores the artificiality of political boundaries.

The new world thus seems to be redressing the balance of the old, evolving a new regionalism which transcends the limitations of the past. It remains to be seen, however, whether it will be capable of matching the achievements of the old regionalism which grew out of the tension between 'centre' and province, and reached its peak in the work of Hardy and Lawrence. For that matter, the European old world can also demonstrate regional affiliations which spill across state borders; and further complexity is added by the existence of linguistic differences which both transcend those borders and create alternative allegiances within them. The Luxembourg–Belgium area is especially fraught with such problems. As the comments of Philip Mosley, Jean-Pierre Campill and Sepp Simon suggest, regionalism here interacts with the influence of powerful neighbours whose languages dominate the mass media so as to produce a situation not unlike that which Crichton Smith finds in the Gaelic-speaking areas of Scotland. On the other hand, the 'Walloon' dialect and literature of Belgium and the 'Lëtzebuergesch' of Luxembourg also disregard frontiers in a way that partly anticipates Madoff's 'west coast' culture.

Such glimpses of the complexity inherent in questions of region and nation remind us that it is a subject on which dogmatism is invariably inappropriate. Of course, the political dimension is one that it is never safe to neglect, and in the latter part of the twentieth-century (to the surprise and dismay of many middle-of-the-road liberals who had come to believe that nationalism was 'old hat') this dimension has reasserted itself in ways that are both violent and bigoted; and there have been poets who have regrettably contributed to this extremism. Even Yeats wondered if that play of his, *Cathleen ni Hoolihan*, 'sent out / Certain men the English shot'.[6] Yet the literature of region and nation more characteristically contributes to the dissolving of simple-minded views rather than the reinforcement of prejudice. As J. R. Watson puts it, the most significant regional literature is 'that which most effectively remains open to indeterminacy, variety, vision, and revision'.

That statement comes at the conclusion of a discussion of Wordsworth which, it must be admitted, is distinctly non-political in its treatment of region. (It is an original and highly sensitive examination of the endlessly shifting variability of viewpoint in a body of poetry which is 'regional' by virtue of its dedication to landscape rather than community; and it is influenced in its approach by critical movements which focus on the peculiar nature of the relationship between reader and text rather than author and his personal experience.) But Professor Watson's emphasis on the subjective nature of Wordsworth's vision and its relation to the changing vantage points, or 'stations', from which landscape is viewed, is nevertheless a relevant comment on the subjectivity underlying all regional issues, literary and political as well. The very preoccupation with region is a tacit acknowledgement of the importance of those controlling influences in environment and community which cause us to see the world in particular local perspectives. And if these may seem limitingly conditional influences, they are also, as the literature of region and nation testifies, potential sources of authenticity and strength. The intensity of what the writer feels, albeit 'subjectively', for his native – or adopted, or it may even be, invented – region enables him to create; and in so doing he converts his seemingly 'airy nothing' into something which has the magic specificity of 'a local habitation and a name'.

NOTES

1. 'The Oxford Voice', *The Complete Poems of D. H. Lawrence*, ed. Vivian de Sola Pinto and Warren Roberts (London, 1964) p. 343.
2. George Crabbe, 'The Village', I, ll. 53–4.
3. Quoted by Anthony Thwaite, Foreword to *Philip Larkin: His Life and Work*, catalogue of an exhibition held in the Library, University College, London, 4 November to 5 December 1986 (Brynmor Jones Library, University of Hull, 1986) p. 3.
4. Thomas Hardy, Preface to *Far From the Madding Crowd*, Wessex Edition (1912); reprinted in *Thomas Hardy's Personal Writings*, ed. Harold Orel (London, 1967) p. 9.
5. 'The Custom of the Country' is the title of Book First, Chapter 3 of *The Return of the Native*.
6. 'The Man and the Echo', W. B. Yeats, *Collected Poems* (London, 1956) p. 393.

1

The Regional Forecast

SEAMUS HEANEY

'The Regional Forecast' was the name of a service broadcast until relatively recently in Britain by the Meteorological Office and the BBC. It followed, supplemented and was presented as ancillary to another weather report named, with superb neutrality, 'The General Forecast'. Yet in what the BBC regarded as 'the regions' this general survey of the overall conditions functioned as a mere precursor, a kind of flourish heralding the main event. Once it ended, in farmhouse kitchens inhabited by people who already knew in their bones what the weather was going to do next anyhow, a silence was commanded. Under the fretworked gaze of wirelesses that broadcast resonantly above their heads, children would be peremptorily hushed. For a moment, like the scullions and footmen in the tale of the Sleeping Beauty, our elders stilled themselves in mid-gesture, obedient, attentive, uncharacteristically drained of presence. Something was temporarily relinquished, a harking towards an elsewhere occurred, personality conceded its autocracy, if only fleetingly, and one sensed a weak link in the chain of the usual.

If an angel had passed or a mighty wind had arisen or tongues of flame descended, the occasion could not have been more prepared for or more expectant. Instead, in a tone so authoritative it verged upon the tyrannical, another BBC announcer from the Northern Ireland Home Service (or the Scottish Home Service or the Welsh Home Service) uttered into his microphone and made official what we already knew by instinct. There was talk of bright intervals and cold fronts, maximum temperatures and moderate visibility. A drying day or a growthy day was never mentioned. You never heard of a ring around the moon or of how close the mountain was – a vital consideration in our part of the world where the propinquity of the mountain was as crucial to our perception of the weather conditions as the position of the hand on the barometer. Certainly the way we talked was not the way the announcer talked.

And yet, by our own admission, this announcer 'gave the weather'. How often, on a perfectly clear morning, did you not hear from an informant wavering between puzzlement and satisfaction that 'rain was giv' by the wireless' for that particular day. If our forecasters had not then advanced as deeply into certitude and as far beyond the linguistic pale as the ones I have heard since in the United States saying that 'Today our forecast calls for snow', they had nevertheless begun to interpose between ourselves and the evidence of our senses a version of the meteorological reality which weakened the sureness of our grip on our own experience.

The weather forecast succeeded in establishing itself in competition with the actual weather. It was not relied upon as prediction and yet it was not regarded as dispensible. That tone of authority was oddly ungainsayable. Even for those fearful and recalcitrant souls who refused for years to have a radio in the house in case it would blow up or weaken them by malign, invisible discharges, even they eventually caved in to its canonical version of things, no matter how that version might differ from what was happening in the sky above them. In other words, when it came to weather forecasts everybody was a weather catholic. The radio pronounced infallible dogma and when that dogma came into collision with the actual facts of the matter, the orthodox mind simply took shelter in the acknowledgement of a mystery. And so matters stood for a few years during what might be thought of as the high middle ages of the weather forecasting service.

It is easy, of course, to draw an analogy between all this and the imprinting of consciousness by the forms and categories of literary imagining derived from a dominant literary tradition. In the same way that the forecaster's fiction was a lens in spite of which the actual wind and rain had to be recognised, so the existing fictions of human reality tend to exert an influence upon the writer's vision stronger, arguably, than the unmediated experience which is being lived through. Life imitates art, not vice versa. By now we have become well versed in the ways our language (which constitutes our world) is usually somebody else's language. We who once thought of ourselves as speakers are only too ready to concede ourselves to be, instead, the spoken.

Even so, as readers and writers, we continue to regard with admiration those who would resist this situation, who refuse to accede to what the forecast calls for and persist in an effort to invent an idiom that will expose us to what exactly it was we experienced. When this happens, the conventional signals are jammed by a note whose pitch and frequency we recognise as our own. We have then raised our subcultural status to cultural power, and by bringing what is proper to us into alignment with what is potential in us, have achieved a truer, more self-enabling image.

Obviously there is a political as well as a literary meaning to this phenomenon. National independence, national identity, national distinctiveness are usually conceived in books before they are carried by the ballot. Yet it is necessary to beware of too easy an assumption that the breaking of political bonds necessarily and successfully issues in the forging of a new literary idiom: in such enterprises of renewal, it is likely that a conflict of interest will arise between the imaginative and the activist wings. The identity which seeks autonomous political status or some sort of independent condition is usually posited on archetypes, images of the ideal community which are nevertheless envisaged with reference to the idealised past. There tends to be an element of Eden in the plan of campaign and if independence is gained or the revolution is successful, that Edenic prototype is going to be the one which the political wing will characteristically attempt to impose.

Now the forecast will certainly be broadcast in local accents but the message may remain equally puzzling and askew. 'Our forecast calls for the Irish language, hydroelectric power and knee-length gym-frocks.' 'Our forecast calls for communal farms and wedding parties at the mausoleum.' Many writers will of course be ready to massage the political programme and continue to discern lineaments of the old dream in the new conditions. At its most reprehensible, this is party hack-work and betrayal; at its most understandable it is lack of talent and pure cliché. The writers of greatest integrity, however, will respond to the new conditions themselves and stay as alive to the shifts of consciousness engendered by the new society as they were alive to the exacerbations of the old. They will register how it is rather than how it ought to be. In prose the result may be satire, irony and parodic fantasy rather than utopian fables and programmatic realism. In poetry it may be hermetic allusiveness and private vision rather than party tunes and national solidarity. One need only think of Joyce and Mandelstam; Milan Kundera and Zbigniew Herbert; Samuel Beckett and Flann O'Brien.

Paradoxically, of course, it is their grasp of political reality which deepens the specifically artistic passion of such writers. They choose to remove themselves from the consensus; they withdraw assent before they can be marginalised. They may indeed be deeply involved with their country's memory and heritage but they tend not to make 'the national character' part of their concern. None of them is 'typical' in the way that, say, Dylan Thomas is typical.

It struck me recently just how clear a case of marginalisation Dylan Thomas now appears to be; a case of somebody who accepted the regional forecast even as he seemed to be totally involved with his own weather. His contributions to the BBC, even those delightful reminiscences like 'A Child's Christmas in Wales' – even, indeed, *Under Milk Wood* – are symptomatic of a not irreprehensible collusion with the stereotype of the voluble Taffy. His purely lyric gift was in the keeping of an intelligence insufficiently wary; indeed his was a clear case of a provincial imagination as defined by Patrick Kavanagh: always looking over its shoulder to see if the metropolis was in favour of its subjects and procedures. I do not wish to impugn Thomas's gifts as a lyric poet, since I also believe that his nerve and panache have been undervalued in the last couple of decades; I merely wish to suggest that in situations outside the centre, talent can rarely afford to be its own reward. For its survival, it has to take thought and be born again, responsible and independent, exposed to the knowledge that while a literary scene in which the provinces revolve around the centre is demonstrably a Copernican one, the task of talent is to reverse things to a Ptolemaic condition. The writer must re-envisage the region as the original point. Stephen Dedalus, naturally, got it right from the very beginning when he inscribed his name and address with all the placidity of his own creator inscribing himself into the cosmic scheme of things: *Stephen Dedalus, Class of Elements, Clongowes Wood College, Sallins, Co. Kildare, Ireland, Europe, The World, The Universe.*

When it comes to seeking the regional redeemer, Joyce is crucial. Just how indispensable his achievement was and how corroborating it continues to be is demonstrable in a thousand ways. But, in the context of a conference on region and nation, I hope it will be instructive to juxtapose a famous passage from his correspondence of 1906 with passages from some letters by James Stephens written in 1912. At the time of writing, that would make Stephens 30 years old and Joyce 24. Stephens had already published his first book of poems in Dublin, Macmillan was in the process of bringing out *The Charwoman's Daughter* and his agent was currently negotiating terms for *The Crock of Gold*. Stephens was also the friend of many of the figures of the Irish Literary Revival and was capable of forthright and interesting judgements, such as this one on the young poet Francis Ledwidge:

> His promise is, I think, greater than any young poet now writing. I do not believe, however, that he will ratify his promise by any almighty performance.... I am inclined to think that when he has published another book of verse he will have delivered (should one say 'reaped') the entire harvest, and will issue only stubble thereafter. A man is a mind and so is a poet and they are man and poet only to the extent of that.... I do not know Ledwidge at all well. I met him twice and then only for a few minutes. He is what we call here 'a lump of a lad' and he was panoplied in all the protective devices, or disguises, which a countryman puts on when he meets a man of the town – country people and children are all great playactors.   [*sic*]

This comes from a letter to Edward Marsh in London, yet Stephens might as well be talking to his Dublin contemporaries. There is no sense of forelock-tugging in the style. His humour is self-possessed and tuned to his own scale; he is prepared to play a bit with the local idiom – 'a lump of a lad' – but he does so with a nice sureness of tone. There is manifest relish and pride in the dialect rather than any insecure flashing of local/yokel knowingness. And to match the security of the tone, there is a sympathetic readiness to speak his mind. The whole passage contrasts significantly with the two which I consider more instructive, written a couple of years earlier. The first is to Marsh and Ralph Hodgson, who had sent Stephens a joint letter criticising the manuscript of his book *Songs from the Clay*, a title which in itself provides an interesting example of self-placing:

> My Dear Marsh and Hodgson,
>   That was a devil of a letter. Behold me ever since squatting with my chin on my knees in a cold silence, my hair plastering down and my eyes fixed. It was a good letter but I disagree with some of your accursed little crosses. (I will never like the Christian emblem again) & here's my trouble, that, even before

your letter arrived I had already signed my agreement to publish the poems and there's no getting out of it. It's up to me now to transmogrify that book within three more days, for even now the proofs are due. But all the same I vow to astonish you when it does appear. I will retrench certain of those poems, the Blakeish ones and I'm going to write a big, gorgeous, magnificent and truly inspired poem this almighty present minute. I will surround myself with lightning and fury, I will call on the gods and the devils, but that collection is going to have a big poem in it for which these other bubbles will be a pretty background. If I fail then I intend to allow the two of you to eat each others hats. Now (as the Americans say) watch me smoke!

There is something altogether too winsome about this which embarrasses in ways that the Ledwidge letter does not. One does not want to become too prim and righteous, but I do not think it unfair to read this as a case of Stephens changing his tune to what the forecast calls for. Here is the souped-up whimsicality, the permitted and expected 'innocence' of the neophyte from across the water. Obviously he was indeed a chirpy, swiftly adaptable and, as they say, puckish kind of a man; but equally obviously, like the children and country people he observed so accurately in his subsequent letter to Marsh, he was panoplied in the devices and disguises which the writer from the provinces is tempted to put on when he addresses the editors in the capital. Here he goes again, for example, writing to Harold Monro, editor of the *Poetry Review*:

Dear Sir,
    I return the two poems – I have made all the alterations you suggested. The word 'flighty' is to be read in the train of madness. I have got quit of the phrase 'Even when alive' and thank you for pointing it out. In the last verse of this poem I have removed the two lines with 'intent, sun and bent' and think that the new lines will meet that vacancy which you mentioned.... I have changed the title High Court of Justice with its humorous or grotesque implication to 'The Last Judgement'. It is in the tradition of artists to do this subject. If, however, you do not approve please change it. The golden book of poems are better as you have arranged them....

There is nothing shockingly culpable about being discovered in this posture of concession; editors have always exercised a not improper influence upon their contributors, and Stephen's craven obedience is, after all, exactly the sort which is nowadays required by the pert, post-doctoral, second-in-line editorial assistants at some New York publishing houses. The point is that his malleability is a symptom of the overall cultural situation in which the centre is privileged and the province is debilitated.

That debility stands out all the more clearly when we contrast Stephens's symptomatic letters to his editors with Joyce's epoch-making exchanges with his London publisher, Grant Richards. Grant Richards, as we know, would eventually publish *Dubliners* in 1914, but in 1906 he had broken his original contract and thereby gave George Roberts of Maunsel and Co. in Dublin the opportunity to do the same again in 1912. In each case the trouble was with the printer. Acting as litmus and censor for the plain peoples of Ireland and Britain, he objected on the grounds of decency to certain details and expressions in the submitted text. Joyce refused to see how publication of his book could be considered an 'outrage on public morality' and he maintained that if he removed the offending phrases his book would be like an egg without the salt. I realise that the following quotation is lengthy and not unfamiliar but it is a cogent illustration of the point I wish to make:

> I have written it for the most part in a style of scrupulous meanness and with the conviction that he is a very bold man who dares to alter in the presentment, still more to deform, whatever he has seen and heard. I cannot do any more than this. I cannot alter what I have written. All these objections of which the printer is now the mouthpiece arose in my mind when I was writing the book, both as to the themes of the stories and their manner of treatment. Had I listened to them I would not have written the book. I have come to the conclusion that I cannot write without offending people. The printer denounces *Two Gallants* and *Counterparts*. A Dubliner would denounce *Ivy Day in the Committee-Room*. The more subtle inquisitor will denounce *An Encounter*, the enormity of which the printer cannot see because he is, as I said, a plain blunt man. The Irish priest will denounce *The Sisters*. The Irish boarding-house keeper will denounce *The Boarding-House*. Do not let the printer

imagine, for goodness sake, that he is going to have all the barking to himself.

I can see plainly that there are two sides to the matter but unfortunately I can occupy only one of them. I will not fall into the error of suggesting to you which side you should occupy but it seems to me that you credit the printer with too infallible a knowledge of the future. I know very little of the state of English literature at present nor do I know whether it deserves or not the eminence which it occupies as the laughing stock of Europe. But I suspect that it will follow the other countries of Europe as it did in Chaucer's time.... And if a change is to take place I do not see why it should not begin now.

Joyce may be out in the cold but that gives him the opportunity to ice his blade; if he is displaced, it gives him the vantage from which to replace the emphasis. Obviously, the frigid beauty of this put-down derives from Joyce's unique atonal control and anger, and the whole thing is in one way accidental and private, part of an inevitable correspondence between the conventional publisher and the wounded author. But in the realm of art nothing is absolutely private or without significant potential. This passage offers Joyce's heirs in whatever country or tradition an example of resolution and presumption of a salutary kind. For it is not the truth or otherwise of Joyce's estimate of English literature that matters; what does matter is the tone of certitude, the appeal to a court beyond the jurisdiction which protects Grant Richards and the printer. This court is not yet in existence, however, since it resides in a realm which will come into being only when Joyce's imagined profile of himself becomes actual, on the publication of his work and the establishment of his authority in the minds of a judicious readership.

Joyce's appeal is finally made to an authority which is envisaged, a bench which sits over and beyond the given literary arbiters of any nation at any time. His appeal ignores, for example, the insular, humanist, Protestant line of English civilisation and directs itself instead towards a source that is Aristotelean, Thomistic and European. His appeal, interestingly enough, refuses to posit itself upon any specifically Irish grounds: he disdains political whinge and avoids any petulant nationalist snap-reaction. What Joyce is most needily supplying for himself is not the sop of ethnic self-respect but an alternative literary tradition which, with good luck, may some day become for others an indigenous one.

No matter how different their talents and temperaments, Joyce and James Stephens shared the plight which Joyce had once diagnosed in his favourite nineteenth-century Irish poet, James Clarence Mangan; Mangan wrote, according to Joyce, 'with no native literary tradition to guide him'. Granted that Joyce express-ed this notion more savagely and more characteristically when he said in *The Day of the Rabblement* that 'a nation which never advanced so far as the miracle play affords no model to the artist and he must look elsewhere'; and granted also his fastidious shrinking from the roused solidarity of Irish nationalist groups angling for his political support, it is nevertheless possible to recognise that he felt the pull of national gravity in a shared memory of conquest and defeat, a language lost and a native culture obliterated, and to see how he was subject like the rest of Irish people to the twin afflictions of resentment and nostalgia.

It was Stephen Dedalus, after all, who compared Irish art to the 'cracked looking-glass of a servant', a looking-glass which hung at certain weak moments above the desk of the letter-writing James Stephens. And it was also Stephen Dedalus who betrayed by the intensity of his reaction to the statue of Thomas Moore a certain identification with him. In the following short passage from *A Portrait of the Artist*, the severity of the sentence on Moore prompts the thought that the ghost of Moore's offence may have haunted the soul of his accuser. During the nineteenth century and much of the twentieth, Moore was a kind of Irish Burns, a song-writer of wonderful grace and sentiment, a national bard scorned by the more ardent patriots because of his success in the drawing-rooms of the British aristocracy where he notoriously 'dearly loved a lord'. To Stephen, the statue is at first merely 'droll', but then:

> He looked at it without anger: for, though sloth of the body and of the soul crept over it like unseen vermin, over the shuffling feet and up the folds of the cloak and around the servile head, it seemed humbly conscious of its indignity. It was a Firbolg in the borrowed cloak of a Milesian.

Without going into the niceties of social and genetic distinction implied by the terms Firbolg and Milesian, suffice it to say that Moore's statue shows a native Irish Catholic (who registered his religion as Protestant when he entered Trinity College in the late eighteenth century) dressed in the toga of an ancient Roman – upwardly mobile, as if a piece of the regional forecast got transposed upwards into the headlines of the general forecast itself.

By the mercilessness of his exposure of a fundamental unsureness within the Irish psyche, Joyce bestowed upon it a new legacy of assurance. But his legacy and example are obviously not confined to the Irish situation: anywhere where the English language and an imposed anglicised culture have radically altered the original social and linguistic conditions, there is likely to be a literary task which requires Joyce's sponsorship, a task of subversion and redefinition. For the writers in these situations this will involve – as I have suggested earlier – not just a simple programme of cultural nationalism but something more detached and vigilant. The writer's task will ultimately be visionary rather than social; the human rather than the national dream is his or her responsibility, a care for the logic and possibility of the medium rather than its utility and applicability; and it will be a personal task, not in the sense that its import will be private but in the sense that it will begin in a deeply felt inner need not to be appeased in any way other than by the achievement of a right form of expression.

I am talking here about poetry and it seems to me that in this particular art, every tradition has begun to feel exposed in a relativistic world and has grown self-conscious in a regional sort of way. This does not make poetry any easier to achieve and may even make it more difficult since the huge domestic prestige of masters in a monoglot situation has been dispersed by the very polyglot nature of our reading. For the poet beginning to write in Ireland or Scotland, there is of course an establishment scene to be discerned in the literary citadels of London and New York, but there is no singularly persuasive voice broadcasting. We turn on our radios and wait. All around there is good writing but where is the great carrying voice of the definitive centre? English poetry is still recognisably, even defensively, English, but its centrality is now in question and that question has come to constitute one of its abiding subjects. All the same, there is hardly an imaginative impetus commensurate with the control which London still exercises over publishing, distribution and promotion. Imposing figures are at work but it seems to me that what I said of Larkin, Hill and Hughes ten years ago remains true in a more general way:

All three treat England as a region – or rather treat their region as England – in different and complementary ways. I believe they are afflicted with a sense of history that was once the peculiar affliction of the poets of other nations who were not themselves natives of England but who spoke the English language. The poets of the mother culture ... are now possessed of that defensive love of their territory which was once shared by those poets whom we might call colonial – Yeats, MacDiarmid, Carlos Williams. They are aware of their Englishness as deposits in the descending storeys of the literary and historical past.

Obviously, Milton and Wordsworth and Auden were equally aware of their Englishness but it was not experienced as a condition to be either reckoned or reckoned with. These previous generations took their Englishness for granted; it was a contributing factor to their psychic robustness and if it was a burden, it was so in the musical sense of a recurrent and familiar and sustaining mental tunefulness – not in the sense of something that weighed them with self-consciousness. In the past, in other words, Englishness counted as an entitlement to what Osip Mandelstam once called 'world culture'; at present, the London publishers' outlets into Canada and Australia and Africa and Ireland and United States still keep the channels of world distribution open but I wonder if the indigenous English imagination has not very much drawn its horns in – not just the horns of the imperial war-helmet but those snail-horns of perception which wakened the far-ranging imaginations of Keats and Shakespeare.

It would seem that we are now witnessing the results of a process which began to speed up in the 1920s, 1930s and 1940s – and I do not mean just the loss of empire. During that period, official Anglo-Saxon culture withdrew many of its deposits from what T. S. Eliot called 'the mind of Europe'. Its metaphysical and classical-humanist agenda contracted, it gradually killed many of its support systems from biblical tradition and religious faith. A trivial symptom of this was the embargo by Kingsley Amis on poems about foreign cities; but a more reliable and relevant witness was to be found in the figure of Eliot himself. In 1943 he spoke to what must then have seemed, from the perspective of Russell Square, a regional group. In his lecture on 'The Social Function of Poetry', first delivered to the British–Norwegian Institute, Eliot concluded:

If finally, I am right in believing that poetry has a 'social function' for the whole of the people of the poet's language, whether they are aware of his existence or not, it follows that it matters to each people of Europe that the others should continue to have poetry. I cannot read Norwegian poetry, but if I were told that no more poetry was being written in the Norwegian language I should feel an alarm which would be much more than generous sympathy. I should regard it as a spot of malady which was likely to spread over the whole Continent; the beginning of a decline which would mean that people everywhere would cease to be able to express, and consequently be able to feel, the emotions of civilized beings. This of course might happen. Much has been said everywhere about the decline of religious belief; not so much notice has been taken of the decline of religious sensibility. The trouble of the modern age is not merely the inability to believe certain things about God and man which our forefathers believed, but the inability to *feel* towards God and man as they did. A belief in which you no longer believe is something which to some extent you can still understand; but when religious feeling disappears, the words in which men struggled to express it become meaningless. It is true that religious feeling varies naturally from country to country, and from age to age, just as poetic feeling does; the feeling varies even when the belief, the doctrine, remains the same. But this is a condition of human life, and what I am apprehensive of is death. It is equally possible that the feeling for poetry, and the feelings which are the material of poetry, may disappear everywhere: which might perhaps help to facilitate that unification of the world which some people consider undesirable for its own sake.

Even when we take into account that this was written in 1943 when the unification of the world was synonymous with the evil of Nazism, and also take into account Eliot's sedateness about religious matters, it still stands as a sombre warning. It represents an acknowledgement by the master who evoked the spectral London Bridge of *The Waste Land* that the unreal infernal city which his imagination had brought forth might come forth further into the domain of historical reality. Against this emptying of the world's meaning and significance, the last ditch of defence which Eliot can envisage is the fidelity of a region or a nation to its indigenous language, its poetry, and its particular religious sensibility.

We may think that Eliot sounds a bit too churchy until we recollect for a second the refusal of writers like Nadezdha Mandelstam or Czeslaw Milosz to lose their cultural memory or concede to the despiritualisation of the world; then we can divine behind the Anglican plangency of Eliot's peroration an equal faith and steadfastness which happily would never have to be equally tested by the fires of history. Yet four decades later, his fears that Europe might lose touch with its original beliefs and feelings seem less portentous. The odd fact of the matter is that it is in the officially secularised countries of Soviet Europe that the continuity and nurturing power of classical and Christian culture can best be witnessed. From Mandelstam's personal mythology of Hellenism right through to the poetry of Marin Sorescu in Romania, Miroslav Holub in Czechoslovakia, Zbigniew Herbert in Poland and Janos Pilinsky in Hungary, the old granaries have continued to supply the literal soul food.

I am reminded of the stirring faith of Joseph Brodsky in a civilisation's capacity for survival at the extremes, in the provinces and regions. The transfusions of energy which a language is capable of giving to itself and the renewals and sallies which can occur through the action of poetry have rarely been as exultantly affirmed as in Brodsky's essay on the poetry of Derek Walcott, which begins:

> Because civilizations are finite, in the life of each of them comes a moment when centers cease to hold. What keeps them at such times from disintegration is not legions but languages. Such was the case with Rome, and before that, with Hellenic Greece. The job of holding at such times is done by men from the provinces, from the outskirts. Contrary to popular belief, the outskirts are not where the world ends . . . .

I have a sense that nowadays the writers on the outskirts know more about one another than ever before and have begun to take cognisance of each other in ways that are fortifying and illuminating. My regional forecast is that in the new awareness created by translations and communications, all of us can find co-ordinates to establish (if necessary) a second literary home-from-home. The satellite picture can make Scotland look as sea-girt as Greece, and we might just get a fresh sense of what is happening in Scottish poetry if we thought of the work of, say, Norman MacCaig in relation to the work of somebody like Yannos Ritsos. Unlike Ritsos, MacCaig has never been in prison or political peril – things which are anyhow accidents in the life of a poet rather than the essentials; but the urgency and severity of mind which those things instil in a poet are possessed by MacCaig already in the clear air of his imagined Scotland. His deceptively simple late poems are testing the echo of the universe as authentically as even a persecuted poet could manage to. Phenomenological, metaphoric, metaphysical – whatever adjective we use and whatever European parallel we draw would be personally embarrassing to the decorous and sceptical MacCaig. But his skill in pretending – even to himself – to be a modest inscriber of glosses should not blind his native audience or any other audience to the modernity of his achievement in these lyrics which sing with the constancy and high nervousness of barbed wire on a moorland.

I mention MacCaig. I could adduce, too, the break into unsettling contemporaneity and phantasmagoria which Iain Crichton Smith has achieved without ever averting his gaze from the crystal of an origin both Hebridean and presbyterian. I could adduce the visionary universality of the most haughtily located of poets, Sorley MacLean. I could adduce the light in the desert which my countryman and contemporary Derek Mahon has seen without moving from the bleak cliffs of North Antrim. I could talk about Paul Muldoon and Les Murray and Derek Walcott. Instead I will conclude by maintaining that poets in these various regional, post-colonial or off-centre situations have long ago been freed to throw away the cracked looking-glass of the servant and to scan the world instead through the cunningly arranged and easily manoeuvreable periscope of their submerged sensibility.

2
Wordsworth, Regional or Provincial? The Epistolary Context

J. H. ALEXANDER

Towards the end of his life Wordsworth singled out Byron for special mention from among all those who, following Francis Jeffrey in the *Edinburgh Review*, had attacked him between 1807 and 1820. Byron's assault, he said, had been 'perhaps the worst, because the most enduring of all'.[1] In *Don Juan*, it will be recalled, the narrator had wished that Wordsworth would change his lakes for ocean (Dedication, 5); and a little later in the same poem, in the course of a brilliant digression directed against bluestockings, he exclaims:

> What, must I go to the oblivious cooks,
> Those Cornish plunderers of Parnassian wrecks?
> Ah, must I then the only minstrel be
> Proscribed from tasting your Castalian tea?
>
> (IV, 108)

Byron didn't quite accuse Wordsworth of being a bluestocking, but he would have had his distaste for the Lake poet confirmed by the revelation that he appears in his own and Dorothy's letters not so much as the 'simple water-drinking Bard' of *The Waggoner*, but as a notable tea-drinker. For 1808 the Wordsworth household paid Twining £13.14s for tea, and for 1809 they shared with Thomas Cookson a tea-bill amounting to £31.16s.[2] One can sense in Byron's attack on the Lake poets and the bluestockings a revulsion of feeling against the provincial: 'Oh! ye shades/Of Pope and Dryden, are we come to this?'[3] Provincialism is abhorrent, producing an almost physical antipathy (hints of Blake's famous bowel com-

24

plaint, and less spectacularly Arnold and Aldous Huxley) against the dated, the faded, the petty, the cosy, the complacent and the life-denying.

As one reads Wordsworth's letters a picture emerges of a poet skirting dangerously such a provinciality, but doing so deliberately during his principal creative period and winning through to a profound regionalism which breaks free of spatial and temporal restrictions to offer a radical challenge to *metropolitan* complacencies, snobberies, and denials of true life.

There is no sign in the letters of any sense of provincial inferiority. The Wordsworths relied on London for their supplies of tea, the variety available locally being 'very bad and very dear',[4] and for publishing – though in 1815 Ballantyne at Edinburgh was quicker than the southern printers.[5] That seems to have been almost the sum of their metropolitan dependencies, if one excludes Wordsworth's official salary for a very regional form of civil service from 1813. The tea, of course, was essential; but as for the publishing, the letters make it evident that Wordsworth was reluctant to publish his work,[6] probably in part because, being painfully aware of the opportunities for misreading, he valued oral communication to a close circle or (with a revealing natural simile) circulation in a local community along with 'half-penny Ballads, and penny and two-penny histories':

> I have so much felt the influence of these straggling papers, that I have many a time wished that I had talents to produce songs, poems, and little histories, that might circulate among other good things in this way, supplanting partly the bad; flowers and useful herbs to take place of weeds. Indeed some of the Poems which I have published were composed not without a hope that at some time or other they might answer this purpose.[7]

There is no sense in the letters that Cumbria, with its organic community, is in any way an obscure backwater. In 1792 Blois had been a 'petty provincial town',[8] but in 1801 Wordsworth described the Vale of Grasmere as 'a very beautiful spot of which almost every body has heard'.[9] Hawkshead Grammar School, though not one of the 'great schools' (the public schools),[10] had a long-standing connection with Cambridge and a reputation for mathematics beyond anything that the 'great schools' could muster at that period.[11] One does not sense that Wordsworth wished, as Burns had done, to render a neglected region classic. The list of earlier English Border authors is not obviously a distinguished one – Langhorne, Thomas Tickell, John Brown, and by a considerable stretch of the imagination Skelton and Addison – but in 1825 he offered it to Allan Cunningham without excessive apology. None of these is a dialect poet: Wordsworth acknowledged kinship with Burns, the ballads, and the Scottish Border poets, but he placed himself firmly in the *English* classical tradition of Chaucer, Spenser, Shakespeare and Milton as his natural heritage, writing in and of Cumbria in standard English (the occasional northern rhyme excepted) without the need for apology of any sort to Londoners or locals.[12]

There are in the letters many reminders to correspondents of the difficulty of obtaining books in the Lake District, but very little indication that Wordsworth regrets this. He does complain about the lack of newspapers, not surprisingly in view of his intense interest in political matters: in 1804 he claims to read only the *Morning Post*, and the following year to be receiving no papers at all.[13] But one senses a positive satisfaction in his isolation from new books and reviews. He is not unhappy to announce to Francis Wrangham in February 1801: 'We live quite out of the way of new books; I have not seen a single book since I came here now 13 Months ago',[14] and probably in the spring of 1812 he wrote to the same friend:

> You inquire after old Books. You might almost as well have asked for my teeth as for any of mine. The only *modern* Books that I read are those of travels, or such as relate to Matters of fact; and the only modern books that I care for; but as to old ones, I am like yourself; scarcely any thing comes amiss to me. The little money I have to spare the very little I may say, all goes that way.[15]

In 1822 he envied Landor's isolation from British literary life, in Florence:

> I am surprized, and rather sorry, when I hear you say you read little, because you are removed from the pressure of the trash which hourly issuing from the Press in England, tends to make the very name of writing and books disgusting. I am so situated as to see little of it, but one cannot stop one's ears, and I

sometimes envy you that distance which separates you altogether from this intrusion.[16]

A few months before the first of those two letters to Wrangham, Dorothy wrote to Mrs John Marshall: 'William writes verses, John goes a fishing, and we read the books we have and such as we procure.'[17] This must mean that they mostly read the books they had, and the overwhelming impression given by the letters is of a man who enjoys re-reading tried classics. Wordsworth's knowledge of old poets was encyclopaedic. After 1800 he particularly benefited from Robert Anderson's *A Complete Edition of the Poets of Great Britain*, and in 1804 he furnished Anderson with a list of numerous, and often very obscure, poets for inclusion in possible additional volumes.[18] When he asks for books to be sent, from the Racedown period on, they are either travel books (for *The Recluse*) or they are old favourites – Beattie's *Minstrel* in 1795, the Jacobean dramatists in 1804.[19] He habitually recommended 'the best old writers', the 'elder Writers', to enquirers,[20] and towards the end of his life he believed that 'Wherever I have written better than others, as far as style is concerned, it has been mainly owing to my early familiarity with the Works of the truly great Authors of past times.'[21]

One may link this literary self-limitation and preference for re-reading with the self-revision which obsessed Wordsworth from *An Evening Walk* and *Descriptive Sketches* to the end of his life, with the intensely retrospective nature of much of his work, and with the preference for a limited number of trusty words which he uses again and again in his poetry, viewing them from every angle. The same cast of mind can also be observed throughout the letters in the loving care of (rented) houses and of gardens furnished with local plants, in a concern for regional aesthetics and environmentalism anticipating the Friends of the Lake District, and in the careful observation of the effects of the changing seasons on the unchanging rocks and hills.

Two minor, though accidental, dependencies on London involved brother Richard's hand-me-down coats and complimentary legal writing paper,[22] reminders that for over a decade the Wordsworths were decidedly poorly off: tea was almost their only luxury, and at Windy Brow they had (appalling deprivation) forgone even that.[23] The consequent habits of frugality stayed with them all their lives: they had at first no opportunity, and later no

desire, to indulge in 'whimsy of the purse',[24] and one can trace
their parsimony from Dorothy's newspapering the walls of Dove
Cottage (Richard also sent down his cast-off newspapers at one
stage),[25] through a refusal to allow Lord Lonsdale to spend more
on a gift of land than it was worth,[26] to the notorious inability of
the Wordsworths to be smart.[27] It is no accident that in 1790
Wordsworth already finds himself (anticipating 'Tintern Abbey')
impelled to treasure up natural images from his continental tour
for future use:

> Ten thousand times in the course of this tour have I regretted
> the inability of my memory to retain a more strong impression of
> the beautiful forms before me, and again and again in quitting a
> fortunate station have I returned to it with the most eager
> avidity, with the hope of bearing away a more lively picture. At
> this moment when many of these landscapes are floating before
> my mind, I feel a high [enjoyment] in reflecting that perhaps
> scarce a day of my life will pass [in] which I shall not derive
> some happiness from these images.[28]

Nor is it accidental that in 1798 he thinks of his completed poetry
as a 'store' to which he is adding daily.[29]

The epistolary context that has emerged thus far for a study of
Wordsworth as universal regional poet involves the impression of
a man lacking any provincial inferiority complex, avoiding modern
metropolitan distractions in order to concentrate on re-reading a
limited range of reliable literary classics, and frugally husbanding
all his necessarily or deliberately limited resources.

The letters also provide a more positive sort of evidence of what
Wordsworth sought in his regional retirement. It might be
summed up as an active repose. Although he was drawn to
London on several occasions and did not quite share Dorothy's
entire satisfaction in the Lake District, he was liable to experience
nervous illness when he left the region,[30] and he wrote to his wife
from London on 9 May 1812: 'The life which is led by the
fashionable world in this great city is miserable; there is neither
dignity nor content nor love nor quiet to be found in it.'[31] In
Cumbria he could explore the slow, insensible, organic growth of

his own opinions, of friendship, and of people's affection for his poetry.[32] David Simpson has suggested that the complexity of multiple conflicting 'figurings of the real' worried him,[33] and this is borne out by an important letter of 21 May 1807 to Lady Beaumont with its commentary on the sonnet 'With Ships the Sea':

> who is there that has not felt that the mind can have no rest among a multitude of objects, of which it either cannot make one whole, or from which it cannot single out one individual, whereupon may be concentrated the attention divided among or distracted by a multitude?[34]

Throughout his residence in the Lake District Wordsworth found neighbours living a 'peaceable', ordered life, on which he could concentrate without fragmentation. To the outsider such lives might appear empty, but they are

> much more intellectual than a careless observer would suppose. One of our Neighbours, who lives as I have described, was yesterday walking with me, and as we were pacing on, talking about indifferent matters, by the side of a Brook, he suddenly said to me with great spirit and a lively smile: 'I like to walk where I can hear the sound of a Beck' (the word as you know in our dialect for a Brook) – I cannot but think that this Man, without being conscious of it, has had many devout feelings connected with the appearances which have presented themselves to him in his employment as a Shepherd, and the pleasure of his heart at the moment was an acceptable offering to the divine Being.[35]

That was in 1808. And in 1840 the gardener at Rydal Mount, James Dixon, was 'a little of a Poet. While he was working in the garden the other evening and we were admiring together the things [?] he said – "And look at Wansfell what a *heat* that is", pointing to the deep copper reflection of the light from the western clouds, in which the mountain was steeped, "each had his *glowing* Mountain", as you remember in the Excursion.'[36] Wordsworth appreciated the imaginative coherence of this life (the life of 'Michael') the more because he had himself worn a 'lordly dressing-gown' at Cambridge[37] and had now 'descended lower' to outward poverty but inner riches. This passage from the letter to the barely seventeen-year-old John Wilson is well known, but the last phrases are usually overlooked (my italics):

> where are we to find the best measure of this [that is, human nature]? I answer, [from with]in; by stripping our own hearts naked, and by looking out of ourselves to[wards me]n who lead the simplest lives most according to nature men who [ha]ve never known false refinements, wayward and artificial desires, false criti[ci]sms, effeminate habits of thinking and feeling, *or who, having known these [t]hings, have outgrown them. This latter class is the most to be depended upon, but it is very small in number.*[38]

By living such an apparently provincial life, the humbled and therefore most perceptive Wordsworth hopes to explore in his particular region the permanent qualities of human nature at its best, the task above all appropriate for a man of genius who (unlike Sir Joshua Reynolds) would recognise his full potential: 'The industry and love of truth which distinguish Sir Joshua's mind are most admirable, but he appears to me to have lived too much for the age in which he lived and the people among whom he lived'; it is to be regretted that 'he did not live more to himself', since the man of genius should fix 'his attention solely upon what is intrinsically interesting and permanent'.[39]

Most of the evidence adduced in this paper has been drawn from Wordsworth's youth, which ended around 1804. After the brief transition of a middle age which ended around 1812, the letters of the last forty years make depressing reading, as he declines into provincialism: local partisan politics, valetudinarian worries, the endless tinkering with technically assured but largely attenuated, lifeless verses, and (perhaps worst of all) the lack of any acknowledgement that he was, in Hartley Coleridge's sad words, 'yearly less of the Poet, and more of the respectable, talented, hospitable Country gentleman'.[40] But suddenly from all the drabness of the later volumes one short letter jumps out at the reader:

> My dearest Dora
>   They say I must write a letter – and what shall it be? News – news I must seek for news. My own thoughts are a wilderness –

'not pierceable by power of any star' – News then is my resting-place – news! news!

Poor Peggy Benson lies in Grasmere Church-yard beside her once beautiful Mother. Fanny Haigh is gone to a better world. My friend Mrs Rawson has ended her ninety and two years pilgrimage – and *I* have fought and fretted and striven – and am here beside the fire. The Doves behind me at the small window – the laburnum with its naked seed-pods shivers before my window and the pine-trees rock from their base. – More I cannot write so farewell!...[41]

That is, of course, not William, but a rare utterance by the prematurely doited Dorothy. Its sudden intensity leaps from that provincial drawing-room at Rydal Mount, with the never-extinguished fire in the grate, into the universal tragic world of the Border ballads or the Lucy poems, making startlingly clear the essential difference between the provincial and the regional-universal. Ultimately, as Cockneys Hazlitt and Keats knew well, it is a matter of intensity, of gusto, imaginative and linguistic. Or as Shelley (product of the greatest of the 'great schools') imaged it, of delaying the fading of the coal. Or as D. H. Lawrence – mighty regionalist turned globe-trotter – has it, reversing Wordsworth's spiritual movement but preserving his relaxed intensity (somewhat noisily) to the end:

The individual can but depart from the mass, and try to cleanse himself. Try to hold fast to the living thing, which destroys as it goes, but remains sweet. And in his soul fight, fight, fight to preserve that which is life in him from the ghastly kisses and poison-bites of the myriad evil ones. Retreat to the desert, and fight. But in his soul adhere to that which is life itself, creatively destroying as it goes: destroying the stiff old thing to let the new bud come through. The one passionate principle of creative being, which recognizes the natural good, and has a sword for the swarms of evil. Fights, fights, fights to protect itself. But with itself, is strong and at peace.[42]

NOTES

Unless otherwise stated, a roman numeral followed by an arabic refers to the volume and page number in the revised version, still in progress, of the standard edition of *The Letters of William and Dorothy Wordsworth* by E. de Selincourt, 6 vols (Oxford, 1967–), the revisers being Mary Moorman, Chester Shaver and Alan G. Hill. *LY* refers to *The Letters of William and Dorothy Wordsworth: The Last Years*, ed. E. de Selincourt, 3 vols (Oxford, 1939).

1. *LY*, III, 1306: 27 March 1847, to an unknown correspondent.
2. II, 367: 20 August [1809], DW to Richard W; II, 385: 9 January [1810], DW to Richard W. The tea-bill was thus at least £400 in contemporary terms.
3. *Don Juan*, III, 100. In this paper 'provincial' is used (for convenience only) as a pejorative term, and 'regional' as the corresponding neutral or commendatory word.
4. II, 361: ?22 June [1809], DW to De Quincey.
5. III, 226: 8 April 1815, DW to Sara Hutchinson.
6. I, 211: 6 March [1798], to J. W. Tobin; I, 636: 4 November [1805], DW to Lady Beaumont; II, 96: 10 November 1806, to Walter Scott; III, 273: 13 January [1816], to B.R. Haydon.
7. II, 248: 5 June 1808, to Francis Wrangham.
8. I, 77: 19 May 1792, to William Mathews.
9. I, 327: 9 April 1801, to Anna Taylor.
10. I, 165: [7 March 1796], DW to Mrs John Marshall.
11. Mary Moorman, *William Wordsworth: The Early Years* (Oxford, 1957) p. 89.
12. IV, 402–3: 23 November [1825].
13. I, 319: late February–early March 1801, DW to Sara Hutchinson; I, 433: mid-January 1804, to John Thelwall; I, 534: 7 February 1805, to Walter Scott.
14. I, 318.
15. III, 9.
16. IV, 124: 20 April 1822.
17. I, 300: [12 September 1800].
18. III, 151–5: 17 September 1814.
19. I, 212: 6 March [1798], to J. W. Tobin; I, 154: [20] October [1795], to William Mathews; I, 513: 27 December [1804], to John Wordsworth.
20. I, 662: 25 December 1805, DW (citing WW) to Thomas Clarkson; VI, 491: 15 December [1837], to Elizabeth Fisher. Cf. I, 400: 29 July 1803, to De Quincey.
21. VI, 491–2: 15 December [1837], to Elizabeth Fisher; cf. *LY*, III, 1159: 1 April 1843, to an unknown correspondent.
22. I, 341: *c*.21 November 1801, to Richard W.
23. I, 115: 21 April 1794, DW to Jane Pollard.
24. I, 518: 25 December 1804, to Sir George Beaumont.
25. I, 523: 27 December [1804], DW to Richard W.
26. II, 68: 5 August [1806], to Sir George Beaumont.

27. Mary Moorman, *William Wordsworth: The Later Years* (Oxford, 1965) p. 134n: 'Diary of James Losh'.
28. I, 35–6: 6 September [1790], to DW.
29. I, 215: 12 April 1798, to Joseph Cottle.
30. I, 516: 25 December 1804, to Sir George Beaumont.
31. *The Love Letters of William and Mary Wordsworth*, ed. Beth Darlington (London, 1982) p. 142.
32. I, 400: 29 July 1803, to De Quincey; II, 471: 27 March [1811], to John Edwards.
33. David Simpson, *Wordsworth and the Figurings of the Real* (London, 1982).
34. II, 148.
35. II, 247–8: 5 June 1808, to Francis Wrangham.
36. *LY*, II, 1018: [Spring 1840], to Dora Wordsworth.
37. *Prelude* III, 38 (1805).
38. I, 355: 7 June 1802.
39. I, 491, 517: 29 July and 25 December 1804, to Sir George Beaumont; I, 251: 27 February 1799, to Coleridge.
40. *The Letters of Hartley Coleridge*, ed. G. E. and E. L. Griggs (London, 1936) p. 111: to Derwent Coleridge. The observation is made with regret but (rightly) without recrimination.
41. VI, 528: *c*.March 1838, DW to Dora W.
42. D. H. Lawrence, *'St Mawr' and 'The Virgin and the Gypsy'* (Harmondsworth, 1950), p. 79.

3

Stations and Shadows: from Skiddaw to Duddon

J. R. WATSON

The aim of the present essay is to ask some questions about the way in which the literature of region functions. I have chosen to discuss regional rather than national literature because the latter has problems attached to it, problems of identity, of politics and of language; I intend to concentrate more on a different set of concerns, most notably those of perception, of selection, of the creation of a text, above all the problem of the text itself.

How closely, for example, can we relate the text to the place about which it is ostensibly written? *Is* it about the place, or is it, as some modern critical movements would suggest, a system of signs? Clearly, we cannot say that a work of art is simply *about* a place, because that would be over-simplifying: in what sense is it 'about' somewhere? Is it purely descriptive? In which case, whose description is it? We may say that it is the author's, but who is this author? or, as some theorists, such as Michel Foucault, would put it, what is this author? Is he or she an ordinary person, an exceptional one, a politician, a grinder of axes, a crank? Is he or she only, in the end, what we deduce from the text itself?

The author poses a problem. So does the region, or the landscape. We sometimes speak of an author 'creating' or 'discovering' a region (I live, for example, on the edge of the 'Catherine Cookson country'). How much is creation, and how much is discovery? Can we ever tell? In other words, is there any way in which we can describe the regions or landscapes that are found in literature as 'real'? Authors themselves create, discover, select, make myths, rewrite history: how are we to do justice to this? Regions and landscapes contain innumerable features, and are indeed made up (like a literary text) of the interaction of those features. Writing about landscape is in some ways a commentary

34

on a text which is already there (written by the hand of God, or the processes of geology, or human alteration, whichever you care to stress), so that regional writing is often equivalent to metalanguage, Roland Barthes's word for the language that is written about language.

Yet when we say that the text is already 'there', what do we mean? It is there, and yet it isn't. It is quite possible to find Hardy's Wessex, or Wordsworth's Lake District, on a map, and yet what is on the map, and on the ground, is not the same thing as the literary landscape. There appear to be two kinds of phenomenon: the region itself, as a geographical fact, an entity, and the literary work, as a system of signs. How can we relate the two?

In addition to the problems of the author and the region, there is the further problem of the reader. The reader may have experienced the landscape himself, in which case the business of reading literature about it will involve the pleasure of recognition. He may know nothing about it, in which case there will be a good deal of attempted imaginative picturing going on in his mind. On a number of occasions, for example, writers have complained that a landscape which is finally seen was disappointing afer the hopes they had entertained about it. When he first saw Mont Blanc, for example, Wordsworth grieved

> To have a soulless image on the eye
> That had usurped upon a living thought
> That never more could be.
> (*The Prelude* (1850) VI.526–8)

All environmental perception is affected by such subjective, accidental, and historical factors, so that there is a further indeterminacy at work. If it is taken in conjunction with the uncertain author and the real/unreal landscape, it can be seen that there is a triple, almost cubic indeterminacy, in that each can be multiplied by the others. So we are driven back to the text itself.

In the literature of region we are usually presented with (say) the Hardy country, or the D.H. Lawrence country; what is involved here is a regional literature which is individual-author-region-literature, and in what follows I hope to disentangle some of the hyphens and their significance in that compound. I do so in a very arbitrary manner, selecting two elements of the Lake District landscape, and selecting also two ways of looking at landscape. By Skiddaw, I refer to the well known, the grand, the sublime, and the central; by Duddon, I refer to the obscure, the moving, the marginal. By 'stations' I refer to the fixed, limited and prescribed point of view which is found in the writings of eighteenth-century visitors to the Lake District; by 'shadows' I refer to the movement of light and shade across the mountainside, which was noticed by one of those visitors, William Gilpin, as one of the great pleasures of Lake District scenery (*Observations, ... particularly the Mountains, and Lakes of Cumberland, and Westmorland* (1786) I.90). Here it is used, again quite arbitrarily, to represent a perception of landscape which is fluctuating, changeable and indeterminate.

I used to think that regional literature was a simple matter, a study of the interaction between a writer and his place. Had I read Wordsworth more carefully, I might have noticed that he, too, directs our attention to the text, or (as he calls it) the 'creation':

> How exquisitely the individual Mind
> (And the progressive powers perhaps no less
> Of the whole species) to the external World
> Is fitted: – and how exquisitely, too –
> Theme this but little heard of among men –
> The external World is fitted to the Mind;
> And the creation (by no lower name
> Can it be called) which they with blended might
> Accomplish: – this is our high argument.
> (Preface to The Excursion, 63–71)

There is a three-fold arrangement here, not a two-fold one; and as literary critics we begin with the only stable element which we have. The pattern of interaction is no longer

writer ⟸⟹ landscape

but

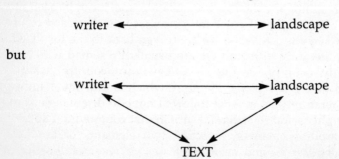

and if we introduce the reader, we have a further line:

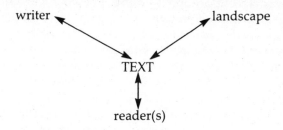

This is then complicated by the addition of three more lines:

1. Although continuing to insist on the centrality and primacy of the text, the relationship between the writer and the landscape (as Wordsworth suggests) has to be acknowledged as pre-existing.

2. The reader may have a relationship with the landscape: he may compare what he reads with what he knows, or what he has heard others say, or photographs, or other books on the subject. He may himself have experienced the landscape, or been born in the region, and have the same kind of affinities with it as the author.

3. From the text, and from other texts, the reader can deduce something about the author. This is a complex and difficult business: it requires a knowledge of the author's work that is reasonably complete and unselective. In the case of an author as profound and difficult as Wordsworth, for example, few university teachers would want to deduce much about the author from 'I wandered lonely as a cloud'; yet for many who visit the Lake District every year, this is Wordsworth's best-known poem. The unpredictability of the relationship between the reader and the author is clear, but the line between them has to be drawn.

So the final pattern is like this:

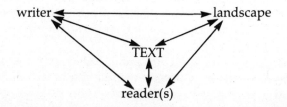

In practice, I think that this diagram means that there is a kind of swirling movement around the text and impinging upon it, a series of interconnections which makes it very difficult to be precise about the literature of region, especially during the Romantic period. One only has to think of the flexible, shifting perceptions of Wordsworth's poetry to be aware of an extremely complex process; and, indeed, part of Wordsworth's greatness is owing to his portrayal of complex perceptions and states of mind.

As we look back to the eighteenth century, past the Romantic period, we may well wonder at the degree of selection and simplifying that went on. I take as an example a representative and popular guide book, *A Guide to the Lakes, in Cumberland, Westmorland, and Lancashire, By the Author of the Antiquities of Furness*. I have used the seventh edition of 1799, published in London and Kendal, which has a quotation from *Paradise Lost* on the title page:

> For Nature here
> Wanton'd as in her prime, and play'd at will
> Her virgin fancies.
> Wild above rule or art (and beauteous form'd)
> A happy rural seat of various view.

We may notice several things here. The author is given no name, although we know him now as Thomas West. He is, however, given a persona: as the Author of the Antiquities of Furness he is a learned man, an antiquarian, and he has some local knowledge. He has some sensitivity to poetry, too, and his quotation from Milton is highly appropriate. It suggests that one of the reasons for admiring the Lake District is that it is unspoiled, unaffected by modern taste ('rule or art'), 'happy' and possessing various views. All these may be deduced by a reader from the title page: they give a strong impression that the text which will follow is to be governed by certain specific conditions, personal and historical. The text will be by a man of a certain learning, and no doubt of a certain class: the appreciation of landscape will be governed by certain late eighteenth-century habits of perception – the preference for the wild and natural over the tame and improved, the love of views and prospects.

The publisher, Pennington of Kendal, added an 'Advertisement' to the seventh edition, which drew attention to two illustrations which had been engraved for the work:

The view of Grasmere is in the placid rural stile, with its magnificent accompaniments, and that of Lowdore exhibits a specimen of the rude grandeur of the environs of Keswick.

This suggests, as do the engravings themselves, that Pennington is still thinking in terms of the eighteenth-century antithesis between the beautiful and the sublime, as indeed Wordsworth did in the opening paragraph of *An Evening Walk*:

> Far from my dearest friend, 'tis mine to rove
> Thro' bare grey dell, high wood, and pastoral cove;
> His wizard course where hoary Derwent takes
> Thro' craggs, and forest glooms, and opening lakes,
> Staying his silent waves, to hear the roar
> That stuns the tremulous cliffs of high Lodore:
> Where silver rocks the savage prospect chear
> Of giant yews that frown on Rydale's mere;
> Where peace to Grasmere's lonely island leads,
> To willowy hedgerows, and to emerald meads;
> Leads to her bridge, rude church, and cottag'd grounds,
> Her rocky sheepwalks, and her woodland bounds;
> Where, bosom'd deep, the shy Winander peeps
> 'Mid clust'ring isles, and holly-sprinkl'd steeps;
> Where twilight glens endear my Esthwaite's shore,
> And memory of departed pleasures, more.
>
> (lines 1–16, 1793 text)

Similarly, West's views are chosen with reference to the antithesis between peace on the one hand, often associated with Grasmere, and unpeaceful chaos on the other. West describes Grasmere:

> This vale of peace is about four miles in circumference, and guarded at the upper end by Helm-crag, a broken pyramidal mountain, that exhibits an immense mass of antediluvian ruins.

West quotes Thomas Gray's description of Grasmere, which was by way of becoming a classic for eighteenth-century visitors to the Lake District. The difference between them is in West's interest in 'stations', places where the view has a specific composition, often complete with side-screens, and where the viewer is instructed on where to stand, what light gives the best effect, and what to notice.

As an example, I take 'Station IV' in Borrowdale:

> From the top of Castle-crag in Borrowdale there is a most
> astonishing view of the lake and vale of Keswick, spread out to
> the north in the most picturesque manner. Every bend of the
> river is distinctly seen, from the pass of Borrowdale, till it joins
> the lake; the lake itself, spotted with islands; the most extraor-
> dinary line of shore, varied with all the surprising accompani-
> ments of rock and wood; the village of Grange at the foot of the
> Crag, and the white houses of Keswick, with Crosthwaite
> church at the lower end of the lake; behind these, much
> cultivation, with a beautiful mixture of villages, houses, cots,
> and farms, standing round the skirts of Skiddaw, which rises in
> the grandest manner, from a verdant base, and closes this
> prospect in the noblest stile of nature's true sublime.

Here there is a mixture of language between the descriptive – the
view 'spread out', the lake 'spotted with islands', the 'line of
shore', the mountain which 'closes this prospect' – and the
affective: the view is 'astonishing', the shore line is 'extraordinary',
the accompaniments of rock and wood are 'surprising'. But there is
no indeterminacy of language: the viewer is told what to see and
what to feel. The control which is exercised over the view is
remarkable, and limiting. It extends on some occasions to the time
of day, and always includes instructions on where and how to
look:

> STATION V.   This view is seen to much greater advantage from
> the side of Swinside, a little before sun-set, where the vale and
> both the lakes are in full view, with the whole extent of rocky
> shore of the upper, and the flexures of the lower lake. And when
> the last beams of the sun rest on the purple summit of Skiddaw,
> and the deep shade of Wythop's wooded brows is stretched over
> the lake, the effect is amazingly great.

Not only do these descriptions of stations control the responses of
the viewers: there are other suggestions of control and limitation.
The first is the sense of orderly progress, by which the tourist
proceeds. At one point, West quotes Gray, viewing Keswick from
near the Druid circle at Castlerigg, when

the sun breaking out, discovered the most enchanting view I have yet seen, of the whole valley behind me; the two lakes, the river, the mountains in all their glory; so that I had almost a mind to have gone back again.

Almost a mind, we observe: not sufficient of a mind to compel a return, but enough to wish for one. To compel a return would be to upset the progression, the movement through the landscape from station to station.

Other controls are found throughout. Pictorial ones are provided by the way in which the landscape is edged or *bounded* by recognisable enclosing features, such as side-screens of rock or tree. Occasionally the most detailed instructions are given, as they are for viewing Windermere from the west side of the ferry point:

STATION I. Near the isthmus of the ferry point, observe two small oak trees that inclose the road, these will guide you to this celebrated station. Behind the tree, on the western side ascend to the top of the nearest rock, and from thence, in two views, command all the beauties of this magnificent lake. But it will be more convenient to stop short of the two trees, and ascend the west side of the rock, for here the ascent is easier, and you open on the view at once. – To do this, just when you cross the road, observe on the left a sharp-edged procumbent rock; turn from that a little to the right, and gain the summit of the crag. The trees are of singular use in answering the purposes of fore-ground, and of intersecting the lake. The rock rises perpendicu-larly from the lake, and forms a pretty bay. In front, Ramps-Holme, or Berkshire-island, presents itself in all its length, clothed in wood. To the left, the ferry point, closing with Crow-Holme, a wooded island, forms an agreeable promontory.... Above it, the mountain rises in an agreeable wildness, variega-ted with scattered trees, and silver-grey rocks. / (pp. 55–6)

Such descriptions are found everywhere in West's book. They differ from other texts in that they tell the viewer not only what to see, but how to see it. Many guide-books tell travellers where to go to see the view, and many, like West, name the features: but not many presuppose such a shared taste, or think it worthwhile to draw attention to such pictorial features as shape, colour and texture.

The problem for West is that such precise and detailed descriptions were impossible in the space and with the method he employs. He admits this at one point, saying that he prefers 'to point out the station' and then leave the viewer to 'the enjoyment of reflection, and the pleasures of the imagination'. When West does this, he appears to be preparing the way for something more open-ended and romantic; but in fact, this is no more than an illusory freedom, for two reasons. One is that West is still choosing the stations, and (as in the placing of a camera in a documentary film) the choice of viewpoint is the most important single factor in the determination of landscape vision. The second is that in the descriptions which are provided, the text is governed by some extremely powerful assumptions. At one point, West describes the view from a boat on Derwentwater:

> Skiddaw shows its vast base, and, bounding all that part of the vale, rises gently to a height that sinks the neighbouring hills; opens a pleasing front, smooth and verdant, smiling over the country like a gentle generous lord, while the fells of Borrowdale frown on it like a hardened tyrant.   (p. 111)

Here the language intends to control and govern the reader's and the viewer's response. It is a language which relates to the landscape in one way (by simple contrast between Skiddaw and Borrowdale); to the author in another (by its implied value-judgements contrasting the gentle generous lord with the hardened tyrant); and to the reader in a third, assuming his agreement.

One of the limiting features of all guide books of this period was the absence of any suggestion that mountains could be climbed (by the time of Wordsworth's *Guide to the Lakes*, originally written in 1810, he was recommending the ascent of Scawfell and Helvellyn, and Keats climbed Skiddaw). West made the journey, with a guide, over the Stake Pass from Borrowdale to Langdale, passing beneath the Langdale Pikes: 'Langdale Pike', he wrote, 'called Pike-a-Stickle, and Steel Pike, is an inaccessible pyramidal rock, and commands the whole.' This clearly sets limits to the traveller's adventures just as the side-screens set limits to the views: indeed, one reason for not climbing the Langdale Pikes may have been that the view was too limitless. It was unpicturesque because at that height it was too wide to be composed into any pictorial composition. For someone like West, in fact, it was of no significance, and he saw it as useless, a piece of confusion left over from the creation of the world. All the elements of nature that could not be used in ordering the universe had been collected here, like some rubbish-dump of the creating hand: 'Here nature seems to have discharged all her useless load of matter and rock, when form was first impressed on chaos.' Clearly for West there was sensible, ordered nature, and this kind of chaotic and inexplicable phenomenon. It suggests a creation which has as its principle a fundamental good sense, an explicable landscape in terms of a sensible Creator behind it; a peak such as Pike-a-Stickle was inexplicable, which suggests a very limited view of the Creator and his power.

What is found in West's *Guide*, therefore, is a regionalism of a certain kind, a perception of the Lake District that was limited by the needs of his age: it was circumscribed by presuppositions of a political and religious kind, and by particular habits of viewing. I propose now to contrast this with one or two examples from Wordsworth's Duddon sonnets. I have chosen to use these sonnets because other comparisons would have been too easy: Wordsworth's greatest regional poetry is so obviously inspired by concerns that are outside West's range that to compare the two would be like comparing chalk and cheese. The Duddon sonnets, however, are primarily descriptive. Together with the *Guide to the Lakes* (with which they were first published) they record impressions, and reactions to a regional landscape.

The Duddon flows westward out of Lakeland to the sea. It rises, Wordsworth tells us in his introductory note, 'Upon Wrynose Fell, on the confines of Westmoreland, Cumberland, and Lancashire; and, having served as a boundary to the last two Counties for the space of about twenty-five miles, enters the Irish Sea, between the Isle of Walney and the Lordship of Millom.' Clearly it was not a well-known river, or this would not have been necessary.

The sonnets form a descriptive sequence of 33 sonnets, with an 'After-thought' sonnet following the conclusion. They follow the course of the stream from source to mouth, and, according to Mary Wordsworth during their composition, 'they all together compose one poem' (*PW*, 3.506).* The same thing was said by Wordsworth himself in a long note (*PW*, 3.508 ff) appended to

---

*The Poetical Works of William Wordsworth, ed. E. de Selincourt and Helen Darbishire (Oxford: Clarendon Press, 1946; 2nd edn 1954).

sonnets XVII and XVIII, which quotes Green's *Guide to the Lakes*, recommends a walk, and describes the grave of the curate of Seathwaite in the churchyard there. This is followed by a long account of the life of the curate, the Revd Robert Walker, who was curate of Seathwaite for 66 years and who is described by Wordsworth as 'a worthy compeer of the country parson of Chaucer' (*PW*, 3.510). The note on his life extends to several pages, and makes a considerable detour from the main purpose of the sonnet sequence. It forms a complete diversion from the main sequence of sonnets, a kind of interruption: the churchyard at Seathwaite features as a different mode of discourse and a different subject-matter. I mention this, because one of the most interesting things about the sonnets is the way in which the perspective is continually shifting: and we have there what I believe to be a characteristic of Wordsworth's landscape poetry, and indeed of much subsequent landscape writing.

What happens, I think, is a kind of subtle modification of the stations of the eighteenth-century landscape viewers. Each sonnet of the 33 is an individual sonnet of observation and reflection, yet each is a part of a whole. And in that whole there is an endless shifting of the viewpoint, a total inconsistency in the use of 'I'. We have become accustomed to the idea that there is no particular stable self at the centre of the literary expression, and the Duddon Sonnets might have been made to be an example of that. Sonnet I, for example, presents an 'I', setting out to disregard classical rivers in order to introduce a remote and unspectacular stream in the north-west of England.

> Not envying Latian shades – if yet they throw
> A grateful coolness round that crystal Spring,
> Blandusia, prattling as when long ago
> The Sabine Bard was moved her praise to sing;

Here the reference to Horace and *O fons Blandusiae* (*Odes*, Bk III.13) is a piece of obvious and deliberate intertextuality which immediately indicates the dependence of the author on a tradition, and begins a complex process of signification and placing. In a note Wordsworth refers to the sonnet sequence in relation to John Dyer's *The Ruins of Rome* (1740) and William Crowe's *Lewesdon Hill* (1780), and to Coleridge's projected poem 'The Brook': he goes on to quote from the Psalms, from Virgil and from Burns, and to mention Armstrong's 'sublime apostrophe to the great rivers of the earth' in his poem *The Art of Preserving Health*. All this is exceptionally sophisticated, and designed, I think, to create a contrary impression in the reader's mind. On the one hand we are invited to see the River Duddon as a river like all the others, a fit subject for a poetic endeavour; on the other hand, we are meant to see it as a small, humble, dear stream. The result is a curious double sense of the 'I' of the sonnet, as an author who belongs to the great European tradition, and as one who does not, who turns his back on it: so, after the octave of the sonnet gestures towards the Horatian vision, Persian fountains, and Alpine torrents, the syntax simplifies as the sestet begins:

I seek the birthplace of a native Stream. –

Now who – or, as Foucault would have us put it, *What* – is this author? He is described, is he not, in the language of the sonnet's octave as 'Not envying', 'Careless' and 'Heedless' of the European culture which he describes with such intricacy. The syntax is valuable here because it provides a thicket of subordinate and sub-subordinate clauses, from which the clarity of line 9 emerges with an increased impact. That line, 'I seek the birthplace of a native Stream', is also extremely interesting in its structure and expression. The poet seeks 'the birthplace' of the stream, as though the stream *had* a birthplace as a human being does; the stream itself is a 'native stream' as though the poet had been born beside it. He seeks, in a sense, the birthplace of his birthplace. The contrast which I wish to attend to is between the first author, with his complex syntax, his present participles and his conditional clauses: this author sees the River Duddon as separate from and different from all the other places, so that we have, as it were, an intertextuality of rivers. The second author is a seeker, who looks to discover the beginning or centre of his place of origins. As he does so, he gives vent to his feelings in simple shouts:

All hail ye mountains! hail, thou morning light!

The celebration of light (here echoing Milton) is a recognition of the first great miracle of Creation; beside it Wordsworth puts the mountains, as another part of the primal creation. So here there is a third 'poet' at work, the poet as celebrant and worshipper. He has his own belief:

> Better to breathe at large on this clear height
> Than toil in needless sleep from dream to dream:

which is a very unusual transformation of the usual antithesis between toil and rest. Now freedom is the opposed quality to 'needless sleep': to be out on the mountainside (vaguely stated as 'this clear height') is superior to sleeping and dreaming. Since these last two are usually seen as sources of life and of spiritual energy, the poet has here played something of an unexpected trick on the reader. Dreams now seem a succession of events through which one toils: in their place is the studied vagueness, the unspecified 'clear height'. Only in the final couplet is the experience localised:

> Pure flow the verse, pure, vigorous, free, and bright,
> For Duddon, long-loved Duddon, is my theme!

At last, the procedure of the sonnet becomes clear: it is a holding back, a final line which justifies all the previous ones (we may compare the opposite structure in 'Dear native regions'). But this is not the most remarkable feature of the final couplet. What is totally unexpected is the first phrase – 'Pure flow the verse'. In the context of the native stream, one would expect the verb 'flow' to govern 'water': Wordsworth has defamiliarised the tired metaphor about flowing verse by placing it on the banks of the river.

What I have been trying to point out about this first sonnet is the unusual way in which the poet shifts from position to position, varying his methods, constantly surprising the reader with unexpected ideas and proposals, not to mention unexpected images and unfamiliar stances. Indeed, it seems to be too insistently defamiliarising, allowing no place of rest until the last line; and this is what happens throughout the 33 sonnets. The reader is presented with a great number of 'poets', an endlessly varied landscape, and constant challenges to his own consistency as a reader. There is a pattern of surprise and change throughout, a confounding of expectations, as in Sonnet 3, which begins 'How shall I paint thee?' and proceeds to give no answer at all.

Expectations of sonnet form and sonnet sequence are continually being deflected. The unifying principle is curiously detached from the poetry, because the unifying principle is the course of the river itself and not the systems of signs. A final teasing example of Wordsworth's freedom is the title of Sonnet 33, 'Conclusion', followed by Sonnet 34, 'After-thought'. The very numbering is a contribution to the indeterminacy that is found everywhere: is it an afterthought, or is it the final sonnet?

In the 33 preceding sonnets, the stream has been described from source to mouth, though not 'described' in the sense of 'painted', rather meditated upon. Sonnet 33, 'Conclusion', describes the stream, going into the sea, where it loses itself and so dies – where (sonnet 32)

> mightiest rivers into powerless sleep
> Sink, and forget their nature –

The concluding sonnet contrasts the northern sea with the Thames and Kent: this is a place of lowly ships, of humble sails – but then it is also a place where

> less disturbed than in the narrow Vale
> Through which with strange vicissitudes he passed,
> The Wanderer seeks that receptacle vast
> Where all his unambitious functions fail.

The Wanderer could be anyone: the poet, a nameless wanderer, or the wandering stream itself. In the sea he, or it, is lost – human beings, or streams, are prepared

> in calm of mind
> And soul, to mingle with Eternity!

So far so good, for a conclusion. The 'After-thought' alters all that in a sonnet which is bewildering in its speedy changes of position and idea.

> I thought of Thee, my partner and my guide,
> As being past away. – Vain sympathies!
> For backward, Duddon! as I cast my eyes,
> I see what was, and is, and will abide.

There is a sudden shift here. The first images are those of partner and guide: the stream going alongside the poet as he walks from source to mouth, accompanying him and showing him the way. This is clearly a stream in the sense of a moving piece of water, the piece of water whose progress parallels the progress of human life. When it gets to the sea it disappears, into death and freedom, which (in sonnet 33) is an appropriate image for Eternity. Now the point of view is suddenly different. The poet casts his eyes backwards, and the whole river is still there. So, we are confronted with the word 'Duddon': what *is* the river Duddon? Is it that which has passed from source to mouth, or is it that which 'was, and is, and will abide'?

Wordsworth's answer is the sublime one:

> Still glides the Stream, and shall for ever glide;
> The form remains, the Function never dies;

as opposed to human mortality, the stream continues. The perception is gained, however, by the great moment of looking *backward*, which suddenly reverses all the procedure of the 33 earlier sonnets. By their disposition as a sequence, by their orderly progression from landmark to landmark, they imply firmly the process of change and the supremacy of time.

The verse has flowed, pure, vigorous, free and bright, and it, too, proclaims the passage of time by coming to an end. Now the poet presents us with a sudden about-face: he appears to turn round, to look backwards and to find something which totally contradicts the progression of the stream and the progression of the sonnet-sequence: we are suddenly presented with a totally contrary image, that of a stream that was, and is and is to be. Beside it is another transformation, as the poet recognises the limitations of human mortality, the fact that

> We, the brave, the mighty, and the wise,
> We men, who in our morn of youth defied
> The elements, must vanish; be it so!

This is part of the insight gained by looking backwards at the stream, an insight of humility and of acceptance. Gray, we may remember, had 'almost a mind to have gone back again': Wordsworth goes back, looks back. The Lake District becomes not so much a series of views as a series of spots of time, able to be visited and revisited in the memory.

Yet this final sonnet seems to suggest that one of the things which all human beings have to come to terms with is that the process of perception and re-perception, of visiting and revisiting, of vision and revision, has to cease with death. Wordsworth looks towards death, as the final end of all sight and insight, 'as toward the silent tomb we go'. Yet, at that moment of anticipating death there is the human resonance of feeling: we have enough –

> if, as toward the silent tomb we go,
> Through love, through hope, and faith's transcendent dower,
> We feel that we are greater than we know.

There is an endless process in which we are born, grow old and die, and yet we *feel*. The silent tomb brings to an end not only the sounds of life but also the endless variability of it. That variability is beautifully emphasised at the end (after the unfortunate overblown-ness of 'faith's transcendent dower') by the two verbs 'feel' and 'know', so close and yet so different. And in relationship to these variables of the internal mind there is the river, with its multiple and continually changing appearances and impressions. It can be viewed forwards, sideways and backwards: writing about it can involve complexities of intertextuality and also simplicities of directly expressed feeling.

The processes which I have tried to contrast, therefore, are those of the station and those of the shadow, those of the still mountain and those of the moving river, the clouds over the hillside. In the former, the firm visual relationship is established and held from a fixed position; in the second, there are shifting viewpoints, changing viewers and unexpected moments. What is involved is as indeterminate as life itself, and D. H. Lawrence came nearer to describing it than anyone else when (in 'Morality and the Novel') he wrote about 'subtle interrelatedness', and 'the relation between man and his circumambient universe, at the living moment'. Lawrence was right; but Wordsworth had been there before him.

And in the literature of region and nation, I wish to suggest, the significant literature is that which most effectively remains open to indeterminacy, variety, vision and revision. Its authenticity comes not from description, nor even the celebration of feeling, but from the sense of an open text, with all its possibilities of reflecting the fields of force that surround it. It is only in the text that we can say what happens in the local writing of Hardy, or Lawrence, or Wordsworth, because what is involved elsewhere is as indeterminate as life itself. Of all literary forms, the writing about local landscape is perhaps the most elusive; and perhaps because of this, it is one of the most affecting and absorbing. At its best it becomes not a study of views, nor a study of an author's landscape, but (in Lawrence's words) 'the subtle, perfected relation between me and my whole circumambient universe'.

4

Regional and Provincial in Victorian Literature

ROBIN GILMOUR

A conference like this provides an opportunity to reflect on the differing fortunes and status of the words 'regional' and 'provincial' in literary criticism. Although they are used often interchangeably, there is a distinction between them in modern usage. 'Provincial' and 'provincialism' are now, I take it, pejorative terms: they imply narrowness, dilution, a smug satisfaction with the local and the loss of due proportion that goes with it. 'Regional' and 'regionalism', on the other hand, are at the least neutral, and more usually positive terms, suggesting valid and vigorous differences from metropolitan norms – attractive alternative modes of speech, custom, landscape, culture. Good regional art, we acknowledge, is in touch with universals, with the paradigms of myth or tragedy, with the forces of history, with the submerged kingdoms of race and nation.

The negative connotations of 'provincial' date from the eighteenth century. When Dr Johnson gave as one of his definitions 'rude' and 'unpolished' in his *Dictionary* (1755), he was reflecting the self-consciously metropolitan bias of high Augustan culture. But in the following century, after Scott and Wordsworth had done their work in opening up new regions to the imagination, the metropolitan standard loses for a time some of its dominance. George Eliot can subtitle *Middlemarch* 'A Study of Provincial Life' without the word carrying suggestions of marginality. On the contrary, the title in its entirety suggests centrality – a town in the centre of England geographically, its inhabitants involved in the ferment of the First Reform Bill, which in turn is a provisional stage (a 'middle march') in the progress of reform towards the Second Reform Bill settlement through which the novel's first readers had lived. George Eliot's attitude to her provincial world is uncondescending, because it rests upon an understanding of the manifold

51

links between the centre and the periphery which is partly the product of the historical distance at which she stands from that world. When one moves on to Hardy, however, the tone is noticeably less secure. Take the often-quoted passage from the opening chapter of *The Woodlanders* (1887), describing Little Hintock:

> It was one of those sequestered spots outside the gates of the world where may usually be found more meditation than action, and more listlessness than meditation; where reasoning proceeds on narrow premises, and results in inferences wildly imaginative; yet where, from time to time, dramas of a grandeur and unity truly Sophoclean are enacted in the real, by virtue of the concentrated passions and closely-knit interdependence of the lives therein.

The voice here is characteristic of Hardy, at first conceding the metropolitan view of such 'sequestered spots outside the gates of the world', and then trumping it with the reference to Sophocles. And yet the voice seems to protest too much. When George Eliot says of Mr Tulliver in *The Mill on the Floss* (1860) that he 'had a destiny as well as Oedipus' (I, 13), the irony tells against the classically trained reader who has not yet learned to associate the idea of destiny with the lives of provincial millers, but it leaves the relative positions of Oedipus and Mr Tulliver unchanged. Hardy raises the stakes. The word 'truly' in 'dramas of a grandeur and unity truly Sophoclean' reveals the degree of assertiveness at work, and also its corollary: a defensive awareness of the possible marginality, the provincialism, of Little Hintock to a metropolitan eye.

This difference between George Eliot and Hardy may mean little more than that Wessex was further from London than Warwickshire, and could never be conceived as central to English national life in the way that Middlemarch was. I believe there is more to it than this, however, and I want to suggest that Hardy's uncertainties of tone reflect a more widespread problematics of the provincial in late Victorian culture, a separation of the provincial from the national which is absent from the work of the great mid-Victorian regional novelists like George Eliot, the Brontës and Elizabeth Gaskell. To understand this development, it is necessary to look briefly at the Victorian regional novel and its origins.

A sense of region in literature, unlike the sense of nation, is the product of social change: it comes with the awareness of disruption and dislocation. Just as the historical novel was born when Scott realised, in the words of the 'Postscript' to *Waverley*, that there was 'no European nation which, within the course of half a century or little more, has undergone so complete a change as this kingdom of Scotland', so the English regional novel was born in the 1840s out of a comparable recognition of change, in this case an unprecedented change in communications. 'Railways have set all the towns of Britain a-dancing', Carlyle wrote in his *Latter-Day Pamphlet* on 'Hudson's Statue' (1850), 'Reading is coming up to London, Basingstoke is going down to Gosport or Southampton, Dumfries to Liverpool and Glasgow'. Railway travel made the metropolitan passenger aware of living in a land of regions, but it also accelerated the process by which those regions were in time standardised to a national norm. The process can be seen in miniature in the imposition of a standard 'railway time' (which meant London time) upon regional differences, and more gradually in the loss or decline of regional customs and individuality. For, as James Hannay observed in his 1865 essay on 'Provincialism' in the *Cornhill Magazine*, 'if the railways bring the country into London, they also carry London into the country. The Londoner sees more of his own county and other counties than he used to do, and cockneyism diminishes from the same cause which diminish the rusticity of the provincial'.[1]

In *Le Roman régionalistique dans les Iles Britanniques, 1800–1950* (1954), Lucien Leclaire distinguishes three phases in the development of the regional novel: (1) 1800–30, the era of the 'national' novel of Ireland and Scotland pioneered by Maria Edgeworth and Scott; (2) 1830–70, a time of unselfconscious expansion in the fictional treatment of regional life; and (3) 1870–1950, a period of diversification and sophistication. If we can accept these broad divisions, then it is possible to see a certain continuity of purpose between the 'national' novels of Edgeworth and Scott and the regional novels of the Brontës, Elizabeth Gaskell and George Eliot. Scott speaks in the 'Postscript' to *Waverley* of the rapid changes which have made 'the present people of Scotland a class of beings as different from their grandfathers as the existing English are from those of Queen Elizabeth's time', and in similar vein Elizabeth Gaskell writes in 'The Last Generation in England' (1849), the essay from which *Cranford* grew, of her wish to put upon record some of the details of country town life, either observed by myself, or handed down to me by older relations; for even in small towns, scarcely removed from villages, the phases of society are rapidly changing; and much will appear strange, which yet occurred only in the generation immediately preceding ours.[2]

Of course *Cranford* is not *Waverley*, nor vice versa, but the impulse is similar – to record and interpret change, and by doing so to achieve that imaginative interpretation of changing ways which makes the title of Newman's novel, *Loss and Gain*, such an apt summation of much Victorian fiction. To recognise this continuity is perhaps to see afresh just how confident and unapologetic the early Victorian regional novel is, how uncondescending to its regional subject-matter. I think we still tend to take this for granted in reading (say) the Brontës, forgetting how daring it was in the 1840s to shift the centre of the action away from the dominant London focus of Dickens, Thackeray and the silver-fork or fashionable novelists. One contemporary French reviewer of *Jane Eyre* was sufficiently struck by this fact to comment, almost with surprise, that it was 'quite simply a novel of country life. This book contains not a hint of a description of a London season, a stay at a watering-place, or a point-to-point race; no social lions appear, nor even the briefest sketch of the Beau Brummell or the Count d'Orsay of the day.'[3] In *Wuthering Heights* Emily Brontë shows herself well aware of the conventional expectations she was challenging, by making her initial narrator, Lockwood, just the sort of character who would read, and see his fantasy-life reflected in, the fashionable novel. A bridge is built between the world her readers were used to and regional Yorkshire, and then blown up when Lockwood has his violent dream in the oak closet. 'Provincial' in these novels is not the inevitably lesser and pejorative term it is in the novels of Stendhal and Flaubert, and this is surely a sign of strength in the English tradition.

And yet by the 1860s the climate was changing. In his *Cornhill* essay on 'Provincialism' James Hannay detected 'the increasing frequency of the use of the words "provincial" and "provincialism" in our popular literature' (p. 673), and cites a disparaging reference to 'provincial rhetoric' in one of Disraeli's novels. He might also have mentioned, and may indeed have had in mind, a much more influential article published in the *Cornhill* the previous year, Matthew Arnold's 'The Literary Influence of Academies' (1864). The essay is a *locus classicus* in the discussion of provincialism and regionalism in the nineteenth century. Arnold allows the English nation the qualities of 'energy and honesty', but argues that the lack of an authoritative central institution like the French Academy makes for a discernible *'note of provinciality'* in contemporary literature. And he goes on to define 'the provincial spirit' as follows:

> The provincial spirit ... exaggerates the value of its ideas for want of a high standard at hand by which to try them. Or rather, for want of such a standard, it gives one idea too much prominence at the expense of others; it orders its ideas amiss; it is hurried away by fancies; it likes and dislikes too passionately, too exclusively. Its admiration weeps hysterical tears, and its disapprobation foams at the mouth. So we get the *eruptive* and the *aggressive* manner in literature; the former prevails most in our criticism, the latter in our newspapers. For, not having the lucidity of a large and centrally placed intelligence, the provincial spirit has not its graciousness; it does not persuade, it makes war; it has not urbanity, the tone of the city, of the centre, the tone which always aims at a spiritual and intellectual effect, and not excluding the use of banter, never disjoins banter itself from politeness, from felicity. But the provincial tone is more violent, and seems to aim rather at an effect upon the blood and senses than upon the spirit and intellect; it loves hard-hitting rather than persuading.... [4]

Arnold's target here is the critical spirit shown in contemporary newspapers and periodicals rather than imaginative literature as such, but his argument was capable of a wider application and was so applied by the later generation of writers he influenced. What gives this essay its historical importance is the firmness – one might almost say the polite ruthlessness – with which 'the provincial spirit' is separated from 'the tone of the centre'. There is no feeling here for the kind of provincial culture that, for example, George Eliot found in Coventry, where the Brays and Hennells could play such an essential part in her intellectual liberation. The centre for Arnold can only be the metropolis, and the provincial spirit is allowed only the crude energy (*'eruptive'* and *'aggressive'*) which is the slight praise Arnold usually gives to those he wants to damn.

Moreover, the argument against provincialism is reinforced by – indeed is inseparable from – the exclusivity of Arnold's tone. His notion of aesthetic decorum leans upon the vocabulary of social decorum, of a kind of transcendental good form. The much-promoted 'urbanity' of Arnold's criticism implies the social confidence of the Victorian gentleman. You can invoke 'the tone of the city, of the centre' with this confidence only if you are sure you live there; and if you do even your 'banter' will be seen as a mark of social grace, so different from the tone of the rude provincials erupting outside the gates. 'Where there is no centre like an academy', Arnold writes, 'if you have genius and powerful ideas, you are apt not to have the best style going' (pp. 248–9), and the phrase is revealing: to have 'the best style going' sounds perilously close to having 'the best claret going' or 'the best tailor going'.

'The Literary Influence of Academies' was published in the greatly influential first series of *Essays in Criticism* (1865), where its recommendation of 'urbanity' and 'the tone of the centre' would have been reinforced – for the provincial reader – by the embarrassingly effusive hymn to Oxford in the Preface. The 'Adorable dreamer', the 'home of lost causes, and forsaken beliefs, and unpopular names, and impossible loyalties', is in Arnold's prose the ally of urbanity and Culture, and its doors are firmly shut on the provincial spirit. The collection, and the work which is in many ways its sequel, *Culture and Anarchy* (1869), could not but have an influence on the later generation of regional novelists to which Hardy belonged. The *Literary Notebooks* reveal how closely Hardy read Arnold's critical writings, including 'The Literary Influence of Academies', but in his wife's biogaphy, which we now know to be largely the work of Hardy himself, he took care also to register his dissent, by including this entry from 1880:

> Arnold is wrong about provincialism, if he means anything more than a provincialism of style and manner in exposition. A certain provincialism of feeling is invaluable. It is of the essence of individuality, and is largely made up of that crude enthusiasm without which no great thoughts are thought, no great deeds done.[5]

Here Hardy takes his side with the 'crude' energy Arnold tended to disdain. It is a defiant note, and necessarily so, for the influence of Arnold was an intensely problematic one for a writer of Hardy's background.

Arnold's legacy was contradictory. On the one hand he was the author of *Essays in Criticism*, with its expressed disdain for provinciality and its famous Preface evoking the enchantment of a serene and classical Oxford. On the other he was the poet of 'The Scholar Gipsy' (a figure who is almost the patron saint of autodidacts), and the prophet of Culture. And *Culture and Anarchy* was, I would suggest, a tantalising, provocative document for a writer like Hardy, for it offered a transcendent idea of culture as a timeless pantheon of greater writers, available to all classes and conditions of men, and perhaps especially to those marginal figures Arnold called the 'aliens':

> Therefore, when we speak of ourselves as divided into Barba-
> rians, Philistines, and Populace, we must be understood always
> to imply that within each of these classes there are a certain
> number of *aliens*, if we may so call them, – persons who are
> mainly led, not by their class spirit, but by a general *humane*
> spirit, by the love of human perfection; and that this number is
> capable of being diminished or augmented.[6]

These 'aliens' form the central characters in several of Hardy's novels, as well as in the novels of contemporaries like Gissing and 'Mark Rutherford' (William Hale White), and the attractiveness of this category for the provincial intellectual of humble origins is easy to see. It promised an escape from class into a republic of Culture. Yet at the same time it required, or seemed to require, a severing of local links, for the Preface to *Culture and Anarchy* continues the campaign initiated in 'The Literary Influence of Academies' against provincialism. Arnold's formulation of Cul-ture as a transcendent value is a crucial development, because it drove a wedge between regionalism and culture, stigmatising the one as an enfeebled provincialism, and raising the other above the claims of time and place.

Hardy's response to Arnold's writings on these matters has a representative force, not simply because he is the greatest of the English regional novelists after George Eliot, but also because his situation – that of the lower-middle-class intellectual from the provinces drawn to Arnold's ideal republic of Culture – looks forward to the next generation of novelists, the generation of H. G. Wells and D. H. Lawrence. These were the writers, liberated and yet left intellectually hungry by the partial reforms of the 1870 Education Act, for whom *Jude the Obscure* was a seminal work. The question of Arnold's influence on Hardy has, of course, been widely discussed, if in a rather piecemeal way – notably by David De Laura in a well-known essay on ' "The Ache of Modernism" in Hardy's Later Novels', where De Laura explores Hardy's troubled response to Arnold's idea of the 'modern' in the ethical and religious spheres.[7] What is not so often considered is the problem which Arnold's *tone* created for the regional writer.

I want to suggest – necessarily briefly – that in his last two novels, *Tess* and *Jude*, we can see Hardy confronting the paradox at the heart of Arnold's formulation of Culture in its relation to provinciality. The paradox is that while Arnold's message was the availability of Culture to all, regardless of class or region, his medium was a prose style imbued with the tone and idiom of the urbane Victorian gentleman, classical by training and Anglican in religious disposition. The key terms of praise in Arnold's critical vocabulary are words like 'tact', 'amenity', 'poise', 'urbanity'; the terms of dispraise words like 'vulgar', 'crude' and, as we have seen, 'provincial'. The argument in favour of Culture in *Culture and Anarchy* is less a chain of reasoning (as, in fairness to him, Arnold was the first to admit) than a kind of implicit recommendation of a delicate and tactful good form. Thus the Pilgrim Fathers are put in their place by an invitation to the reader to imagine Shakespeare and Virgil 'accompanying them on their voyage, and think what intolerable company Shakespeare and Virgil would have found them!' (p. 102). It is in the name of an implicit standard of good form, and perhaps good company, that Arnold attacks the 'provinciality' of those outside the circle provided by the Anglican Establishment, and mounts his criticism of the measures proposed by 'Our Liberal Practitioners' to disestablish the Irish Church or allow a man to marry his deceased wife's sister. (The latter is one of his stranger crotchets, and seems to be motivated by a strong distaste for what he senses is the covert lubricity of the Philistine middle classes.)

Although Clym Yeobright in *The Return of the Native* (1878) attempts to initiate a 'culture scheme' (Book IV, ch. 2) for the locals, this is never really developed in the novel, and it is in *Tess*, and more especially in *Jude*, that Hardy's engagement with the

Arnoldian legacy is keenest. Professor De Laura has argued that Angel Clare should be seen as a disciple of Arnold and Mill, whose sin, like that of the later Arnold, is precisely his imperfect modernism, his slavery in the ethical sphere to "custom and conventionality" ' (p. 382). It might be added that he is also a character imbued with an Arnoldian 'Hellenic Paganism' (ch. 49), whose cultivated detachment undergoes a heuristic exposure to the flesh-and-blood realities of provincial Wessex until he reaches the point, in his Brazilian exile, of becoming ashamed of what is called the 'parochialism' (ch. 49) of his attitude to Tess. When he and Liza-Lu 'ben[d] themselves down to the earth' (ch. 59) at the end, he is acknowledging a tragedy on Wessex soil for which his reading in Greek literature had not prepared him. (The fact that their hands are joined indicates that Angel will in due course marry his deceased wife's sister, which may be seen as an additional riposte to Arnold.) And *Jude* is a bitter anatomy of the failed promise of Oxford, a specifically Arnoldian Oxford where 'the last enchantments of the Middle Age' celebrated in the Preface to *Essays in Criticism* turn into the forbidding, windowless walls of Sarcophagus College, and where 'mediaevalism' is described as being 'as dead as a fern-leaf in a lump of coal' (Part II, ch. 2). The eager provincial who comes looking for Culture finds its guardians, in this bastion of Arnold's Church Establishment, sunk in intellectual and social convention; the 'tone of the centre' speaks here in the words of the Master of Biblioll College, advising Jude that ' "you will have a much better chance of success in life by remaining in your own sphere and sticking to your trade than by adopting any other course" ' (Part II, ch. 6).

It is customary now to see Hardy as a writer caught between two worlds, the region and the metropolis, and in his attitude to Wessex being, as Raymond Williams says, 'both the educated observer and the passionate participant'.[8] The uncertainty of tone which can be detected at times in his prose style, and which I noted at the start, comes from the strain of holding these perspectives together in an era of continuing change in the relations between the two worlds. The purpose of this paper has been to suggest that the task was made much harder for him than it was for George Eliot by the Victorian debate about provincialism, and in particular by Arnold's influential separation of 'Culture' from 'provinciality'. Even allowing for the detachment from native roots which is necessary for the creation of any literary region, it is possible to feel that a certain innocence was lost after Arnold. Hardy's attempt to portray 'dramas of a grandeur and unity truly Sophoclean' in 'those sequestered spots' was a heroic effort to yoke together worlds which were even then drifting rapidly apart.

NOTES

All references to Hardy's novels are to the New Wessex Edition, ed. P. N. Furbank (London: Macmillan, 1974–).

1. James Hannay, 'Provincialism', *Cornhill Magazine*, XI (1865) p. 674.
2. Quoted in Elizabeth Gaskell, *Cranford*, ed. E. P. Watson (London: Oxford University Press, 1972) p. 161.
3. Eugène Forçade, *Revue des Deux Mondes*, 31 October 1848; quoted in *The Brontës: The Critical Heritage*, ed. Miriam Allott (London: Routledge & Kegan Paul, 1974) p. 102.
4. Matthew Arnold, 'The Literary Influence of Academies', *Essays in Criticism*, ed. R. H. Super (Ann Arbor, Mich.: University of Michigan Press, 1962) p. 249.
5. F. E. Hardy, *The Life of Thomas Hardy* (London: Macmillan, 1962) pp. 146–7. For Hardy's reading in Arnold see *The Literary Notebooks of Thomas Hardy*, ed. Lennart Björk, 2 vols (London: Macmillan, 1985).
6. Matthew Arnold, *Culture and Anarchy*, ed. R. H. Super (Ann Arbor, Mich.: University of Michigan Press, 1965) p. 146.
7. David De Laura, '"The Ache of Modernism" in Hardy's Later Novels', *ELH*, 34 (1967) pp. 380–99. See also Ward Hellstrom, 'Hardy's Scholar-Gipsy', in *The English Novel in the Nineteenth Century*, ed. G. Goodin (Urbana, Ill. and London: University of Illinois Press, 1972) pp. 196–213.
8. Raymond Williams, *The Country and the City* (St Albans: Paladin, 1975) p. 247.

5

Unreal Estate: Reflections on Wessex and Yoknapatawpha

MICHAEL MILLGATE

Most people, confronted by the juxtaposition of the names of Thomas Hardy and William Faulkner, are likely to be struck by the obvious contrasts between them – the differences of nation, region, period, technique and so on. But before turning to the major reasons why I believe it may be instructive to consider them together, it may be worth pausing for a moment to review some of the curious points of similarity in their lives and careers. Although Faulkner was so much younger than Hardy – having been born in 1897, the year in which Hardy published the book version of his last novel, *The Well-Beloved* – they were for a brief moment literary contemporaries, Faulkner's first novel appearing in 1926, two years before Hardy's death. They were both small men, well below the average in height; both largely self-educated; both unhappy in marriage; both intensely private men, always fighting off the intrusions of interviewers and tourists and would-be biographers. It was Hardy who achieved the ultimate in evasive tactics by ghost-writing his own posthumous official biography but Faulkner gained at least temporary respite by the simple device of permitting the circulation of the wildest kinds of misinformation about himself and his work.

But these are not the topics I intend to pursue today. Nor is it my purpose to attempt to establish specific links between the two authors – to argue, that is, that Faulkner's work was significantly affected by an awareness of Hardy's. That might at some point be an appropriate subject for speculation, but there is precious little direct evidence to go on. Faulkner did have in his library a copy of the 1917 Modern Library edition of *The Mayor of Casterbridge*, complete with a truly terrible introduction by Joyce Kilmer – who might have done better, perhaps, had he been asked to introduce *The Woodlanders*. And since Faulkner wrote his name in the book in two separate places there is a strong presumption that he read it, probably quite early in his career. He also owned and signed a copy of *Jude the Obscure*, but what seem to be of most interest are the similarities between the town and community of Casterbridge as presented in the *Mayor* and the town and community of Faulkner's Jefferson, especially as presented in *Light in August*. Both novels, interestingly enough, involve the deaths of what might in critical shorthand be called 'scapegoat' figures who arrive from elsewhere and eventually suffer communal rejection – although it is perhaps obvious enough that any novelist given to the creation of closed communities, whether regional or otherwise, is likely to deal largely in intruders and intruder plots. I also bring somewhat hesitantly to your attention the irrefutable though not readily manageable fact that 2 June 1910, the date of the second section of *The Sound and the Fury*, hence of Quentin Compson's death, was also the date of Hardy's seventieth birthday. Was Faulkner engaged in the operation of killing off a literary father? I don't think so, though I suppose it might strengthen or at any rate enliven my case if I did and you are all very welcome to think it if you wish.

To come, then, to that case, which is, in truth, not so much a pleading of a cause as a series of reflections, as advertised in my sub-title, upon the similarities and differences between Hardy and Faulkner as practitioners of regionalism and creators of fictional worlds.

It is, of course, a distressing characteristic, perhaps a basic problem, of regionalism that those who live what are thought of as the most truly regional lives – living and working close to the land, rooted for generations in one dear or dreadful but at any rate perpetual spot – are unlikely to be those who will write about it. They may, however, talk about it, and it is clear that for both Hardy and Faulkner the tradition of local storytelling and the experience of hearing such stories in childhood and early youth was fundamental to the formation of a sense of regional identity. As Ezra Pound so succinctly put it, 'The life of a village is narrative' – by which he, of course, meant comprised of well-worn stories about the past and new-minted gossip about the present: '[Y]ou have not been there three weeks before you know that in the revolution et cetera, and when M le Comte et cetera, and so forth.'[1]

One thinks in this context of that densely evocative passage in *The Woodlanders* which enumerates the elements of 'old association' essential to anyone who hopes to escape boredom in a rural spot as lonely as Little Hintock. They must include, the narrator declares,

> an almost exhaustive biographical or historical acquaintance with every object, animate and inanimate, within the observer's horizon. He must know all about those invisible ones of the days gone by, whose feet have traversed the fields which look so grey from his windows; recall whose hands planted the trees that form a crest to the opposite hill; whose horses and hounds have torn through that underwood; what birds affect that particular brake; what bygone domestic dramas of love, jealousy, revenge, or disappointment have been enacted in the cottages, the mansion, the street or on the green.[2]

Landscape itself, this seems to suggest, is significant and apprehensible only to those capable of approaching it as a document in which the skilled reader may discern, faded perhaps but legible still, the records of the local past.

The men and women thus visibly or associatively memorialised are by definition obscure, isolated from the acknowledged main currents and power structures of their time, insignificant in the eyes of the great world, and it is, of course, a part of Hardy's distinction as a novelist that he gives substance and meaning to such lives through the recognition and recreation of their inherent dramatic patterns. As one who was later to demonstrate that no subject is too trivial for a poem, Hardy had no difficulty in accepting, even embracing, the Wordsworthian proposition that the human passions are no less human or less passionate when experienced by the humble and inarticulate – that they may then appear, indeed, in their sharpest outline. He does not, it is true, treat at length of what he clearly saw as the total economic entrapment and hopeless drudgery of the agricultural labourer, but he returns again and again to the situation of those, male and female, who are of the class of minimally independent tradesmen to which his own father belonged and into which he himself was born – the class of such as Giles Winterborne, Gabriel Oak and the Dewy family in *Under the Greenwood Tree*, possessed of the potential for at least minor class transitions in either an upward or a downward direction.

Such shifts, apparently so trivial to external view (including that of Hardy's likely readers in his own time), obviously demanded sustained and detailed treatment in order to establish their importance, their treatability, their potential inclusion among those 'dramas of a grandeur and unity truly Sophoclean'[3] that Hardy claimed could occur in the recesses of Wessex. His general procedure as a novelist was therefore one of incremental enlargement, the deployment of the full dramatic and even melodramatic resources of post-romantic fiction in the interests of bringing such sequestered spots and unconsidered events sharply and unignorably before the reader's attention. The central Wessex texts, it seems fair to say, are characteristically centred upon small and isolated communities and upon the intensity of social and personal interaction within those communities. Individually, in fact, the novels tend to be geographically restricted, narrowly focused and worked out in terms of some combination of a wheel-of-fortune pattern and an intruder plot. Remember, the director Ann Jellicoe is said to have told the author of last autumn's Dorchester community play: community plays are consensus plays, so the villains should always be from out of town.[4] Although in a Hardy novel the intruder may already be physically entrenched in the community's midst, but separated from it and from its values by differences in wealth, morality, education or social class – often, indeed, by a combination of these.

Hardy, of course, spent his childhood and youth within just such a community. In fact, he acquired as a child an almost impeccable set of regional credentials – growing up as he did in a splendidly vernacular and romantically, not to say inconveniently, isolated thatched cottage (recently given top billing by being featured on the dust-jacket of *The Oxford Literary Guide*) and as the child of singing, dancing, storytelling and musical parents – make that folksinging, folkdancing, folkstorytelling and folkmusical parents – who, while not themselves of the labouring class, were in social and economic terms only marginally superior to it. That they felt themselves hugely superior I don't doubt – that was the difference which made it possible for Hardy's mother to propel him in the direction of a professional education and the middle class – but the modest heyday of Thomas Hardy senior's prosperity as a builder came at a later date and not during the years of Hardy's own childhood.

Hardy soon lost his regional innocence, however. And what

corrupted him was not that reputed snobbery upon which, as upon his father's status as a small employer, his recent critics have all too eagerly seized,[5] but the closeness of Bockhampton to a Dorchester which by the late 1840s had advanced, as he says in that ghosted biography, 'to railways and telegraphs and daily London papers',[6] and his own embarkation upon that process of educational, professional and social advancement which in his early twenties took him out of Dorset altogether and into London itself.

And yet it was, of course, London that made him a regionalist, as perhaps all regional artists must leave their regions – or come to them from elsewhere – before becoming conscious of their calling. Even William Barnes had been out of Dorset before he became its poet, and the choric figures in *The Mayor of Casterbridge* offer some particularly disenchanted remarks on Farfrae's hard-headed abandonment of a Scotland of which he sings with such soft-hearted longing. It was, at all events, London that first turned Hardy toward the novel, by exposing him to the urban market for fiction and to the possibility of pursuing his own literary ambitions in that direction. It was London, too, that provided him with the perspective from which he would in due course recognise the advantages not only of an essentially rural subject-matter but also of a specific fictional area, geographically defined and distinctively named, that could be explored and exploited in a series of stories over a period of time. That recognition came slowly, even so, and what we know of Hardy's vanished first novel, *The Poor Man and the Lady*, should remind us that there was nothing inevitable about his selection of rural characters in regional settings as the subject-matter of his fiction. And even the examples of Scott, Blackmore and Trollope and the realisation that people liked to read about unfamiliar places and little-known social groups – as he put it in his essay on 'The Profitable Reading of Fiction', 'The town man finds what he seeks in novels of the country'[7] – even these pragmatic marketplace considerations may have been less influential in leading him to Wessex than such essentially accidental factors as his association of London with personal ill-health and the fact that the professional readers of *The Poor Man* were especially impressed by the scenes which later provided the starting-point for *Under the Greenwood Tree*.

'The series of novels I projected being mainly of the kind called local, they seemed to require a territorial definition of some sort to

lend unity to their scene.'[8] So Hardy recalled in the preface to the
1895 edition of *Far from the Madding Crowd*, though with what
degree of accuracy it is difficult to estimate. What does seem worth
noticing is the element of arbitrariness involved. Whether or not
Hardy did, in fact, envisage a whole series of specific novels as
early as 1874, it does not sound from this account as though he
had at that time any clear conception of the elaborated structure
that Wessex would eventually become. He speaks of 'local' novels
– presumably novels set, like *The Return of the Native*, *Under the
Greenwood Tree*, *The Woodlanders* and *Far from the Madding Crowd*
itself, within sharply individualised and narrowly restricted areas
– and it seems significant that he should concern himself only
secondarily, as a kind of afterthought, with the possibility of
lending unity to their settings by the superimposition of some sort
of 'territorial definition'. Wessex, that is to say, was not in itself the
point of imaginative growth but came into being as a kind of
geographical umbrella organisation to which the separate novels
could be as tightly or loosely related as circumstances seemed to
dictate. What was crucial, clearly, if not as early as 1874 then not
long afterwards, was the assertion of an overall name – like the
Waverley Novels, or the Barsetshire Novels, or 'La Comédie
humaine' – which would be distinctive in itself and provide an
invitation, perhaps even an incentive, to the reader to move from
one text on to another.

That this was a deliberate strategy on Hardy's part is made clear
by the fact that he persisted in it – persisted in the invocation of
Wessex names and settings – even during those years between *Far
from the Madding Crowd* and *The Mayor of Casterbridge* when he
seemed for extended periods to have abandoned altogether any
perspective compatible with the regional stance as customarily
understood. It was, nevertheless, a strategy of which he to some
extent lost control as a consequence of its very success, of the
enthusiasm with which it was seized upon by his readers, so that
there is a real sense in which it can be said that the concept of
Wessex at which he had arrived by the end of his novel-writing
career was not only very different from the one he had held in 1874
but was almost as much a creation of his audience and of the
contemporary media as it was of the author himself.

My colleague W. J. Keith wrote several years ago about Hardy's
responsiveness to the 'literary pilgrims' who descended upon
Dorchester and its surroundings from the later years of the

nineteenth century onwards,[9] and it is clear from Hardy's own retrospective comments that he and his work were deeply affected by the extraordinarily rapid acceptance of Wessex as a name for the south-western English portion of the world commonly called real. It was in that 1895 preface to *Far from the Madding Crowd* in particular that he spoke of the way in which the name Wessex, which he had 'thought to reserve to the horizons and landscapes of a merely realistic dream-country' had in fact 'become more and more popular as a practical provincial definition', with the consequence that

> the dream-country [had], by degrees, solidified into a utilitarian region which people can go to, take a house in, and write to the papers from. But [he went on] I ask all good and gentle readers to be so kind as to forget this, and to refuse steadfastly to believe that there are any inhabitants of a Victorian Wessex outside the pages of this and the companion volumes in which they were first discovered.[10]

Though humorously phrased, this appeal does show that in 1895, at least, Hardy was perfectly clear as to the necessity of maintaining a sharp distinction between his own created world and those actual locations into which his admirers persisted in pursuing the figments of his imagination.

But the pressures from his audience were very much in the opposite direction. Books and articles about Wessex appeared in profusion, almost all of them offering paintings, sketches or photographs illustrative of 'scenes from the Wessex novels' and confident identifications of the 'real places' underlying Hardy's often complex fictions. Photographers and interviewers and newspaper paragraphists, as their subject scathingly called them, hunted eagerly for usable material, often infuriating Hardy by their biographical impertinences and their disturbance of his own peace at Max Gate and that of his family still living in the Bockhampton cottage. The pilgrims manifested themselves in the streets of a Dorchester they confusingly insisted on referring to as Casterbridge, and it was not long before the indigenous inhabitants began to reconceive of themselves, individually and even corporately, under such now familiar names as Wessex Motors, the Wessex Water Board, the Wessex Saddleback Pig Society, the Casterbridge Hotel, the Mellstock Tea Rooms, and so on. I've yet to encounter a Jude the Obscure Pork Butchers or a Withered Arm Pharmacy, but they too may be out there somewhere.

A distinction needs to be drawn here between the specifically Hardyan names and the general acceptance of Wessex as a name for a region roughly corresponding to the area defined by Hardy's maps but excluding those counties of Devon and Cornwall whose inclusion was enforced for Hardy himself by the autobiographical importunities of *A Pair of Blue Eyes*. The late nineteenth century was a period when regionalism as an historical, cultural, economic and political concept was very much in the contemporary air, and in asserting such a concept within and through his fiction Hardy was closely aligned with the broader movements of history. (Even in the provision of a name for the region, he has to share some of the credit with William Barnes, King Alfred and a large number of anonymous West Saxons.)

Given all these pressures from his audience, from the press and from the times themselves – given, too, his own shrewd sense of what was most likely to enhance the continuing sales of his books – it is not surprisng that Hardy, who had originally paid little systematic attention to the topographical details of his fictional places, should have begun increasingly to accept, or at any rate entertain, propositions advanced as to the correspondences between scenes in his fiction and towns, villages, buildings and natural features discoverable on maps and visitable in person. And there seems every reason to suspect that he came in the end to develop a kind of genial Scott-like antiquarian interest in his own accomplished work, considered both as a series of interrelated narratives and as a quasi-historical, quasi-topographical reflection of the world into which he had been born.

It was in the course of the extensive revisions that Hardy made to the Osgood, McIlvaine collected edition of 1895–7 and the Macmillan Wessex Edition of 1912–13 that Wessex eventually evolved into a systematic conceptual unit: not only did all the texts appear in the same format but they were made consistent one with another in such matters as the naming of places and the specification of distances. A Wessex map, based on one drawn by Hardy himself, appeared at the back of each volume, and in 1913 Hardy even went so far as to collaborate with his photographer friend Hermann Lea in the production of *Thomas Hardy's Wessex*, a book entirely dedicated to the 'identification' of the 'originals' of scenes invoked in the stories. As such, it stood as the 'official' answer to all such queries and so contributed to the deflection of impertinent inquiries into his own life and upbringing and especially into that childhood world so defensively cherished in his memory as the source not only of his deepest personal relationships – those with his father, his mother and his sister Mary – but also of so much of the material from which his novels had been built up.

Hardy's fiction – including, and perhaps even especially, his shorter fiction – is full of references to local customs, traditions, folklore, and so on, and it is characteristic that when questioned as to their source he would often cite the authority of old people he had known. In several instances it is obvious that the information had in fact come from his own father or mother, and I have argued in *Thomas Hardy: A Biography* and perhaps don't need to repeat here the proposition that his parents, both in themselves and as the embodiment of memories going back to a time before his own birth, always constituted for him one of the most powerful – perhaps *the* most powerful – of his imaginative resources. Wessex had always been for Hardy a device for transposing selected elements of the real into a mode of existence formally declared unreal – fictional, imaginative, a country of dreams. But in its later phases Wessex became increasingly a technique for keeping reality at bay – a means of arresting time, of preserving the treasured past of his parents and of his own childhood and projecting it forward into a future beyond the moment of his own death. Because it thus constituted a kind of temporal suspension, with only a minimum of chronological specificity or perspective, it was inevitably and, I suspect, deliberately elusive of historical definition. Though it might indeed chart an historical process, that is to say, it did not claim or even seek to correlate that process at all precisely with the chronologies of public, of actual history. It was also vague in terms of spatial definition. '[T]hings were like that in Wessex,' Hardy once declared,[11] but Wessex, as defined by him and represented in the maps he drew, was perhaps too big to be a region, too extensive and various to be conceptually grasped by anyone other than a geographer – especially in a country such as Britain in which differences of just a few miles could (and sometimes still can) make an enormous difference to customs, speech and local loyalties. But the fact that the Wessex fiction remained as a body somewhat lacking in definition did not run counter to Hardy's larger purposes as a regionalist, in so far as it allowed him to comprehend a wide range of essentially local novels within the boundaries of a nominal Wessex and thus project a generalised sense of a rural area with the geographical expansiveness, human density, temporal depth and sociological distinctiveness sufficient to enable it to be set over against the dominant urban culture of the day – of his day and, even more overwhelmingly, of our own.

William Faulkner, who died in 1962, almost a quarter of a century ago now, stands in a sense between Hardy's day and ours, and many things that in Hardy the late Victorian remain tentative and uncertain are in Faulkner the modernist deliberate and unmistakably clear. Where Hardy, for instance, found his way very gradually to the evolution of a fictional world that remained, even in its evolved condition, quite loosely organised and only partially integrated, Faulkner seems to have recognised immediately upon becoming a novelist the advantages not only of anchoring his stories in a particular region but also of linking them one to another by specific repetitions and continuities of location, character and event. That first novel, *Soldiers' Pay* (1926), was set almost exclusively in a small Southern town supposed to be situated in the state of Georgia, while his second, *Mosquitoes* (1927), was in a sense even more intensively local, in that the characters he placed on board his contemporary ship of fools constituted a microcosm of the New Orleans literary world he was seeking to satirise. By the time he came to begin his third novel, *Flags in the Dust* – a book that appeared in his lifetime only in the shortened version entitled *Sartoris* (1929) – Faulkner was already seized with the ambition, and with the strategic conception, of devoting himself to the composition of an entire sequence of novels and stories that would severally and jointly explore the history, topography and social texture – exploit the narrative possibilities, in short – of the area of northern Mississippi in which he had himself been born and raised.

This may, of course, have been a coolly practical decision, based on the examples of such novelists as Scott, Balzac and James Fenimore Cooper, with all of whom he seems to have been thoroughly familiar. As I suggested earlier, it may even have been inspired in part by familiarity with Hardy's work. It remains in any case true that whereas Hardy had almost to be shown by others what he had in fact achieved in and through his creation of Wessex, Faulkner's creation of Yoknapatawpha County was a matter from the first of profound emotional and almost visionary

investment. He spoke in 1957 of the moment in the middle 1920s
when he 'thought of the whole story at once like a bolt of lightning
lights up a landscape and you see everything',[12] and although it is
possible that he meant by 'the whole story' only the narrative
sequences that eventually emerged as the novels and short stories
dealing with the Snopeses, it seems more likely that a great deal of
additional material was already present in his mind. It is not quite
certain when he actually named Yoknapatawpha County, but
there is no doubt that well before the end of the 1920s he had
already conceived of himself as devoting his life to the creation and
elaboration of a regionally defined, narratively incremental and
fundamentally symbolic fictional world. After *Soldiers' Pay*, Faulkner once said, he found out 'that not only each book had to have a
design but the whole output or sum of an artist's work had to have
a design'.[13]

The word 'artist' is important there. Whatever extraordinary
blend of profound modesty and sublime vanity Hardy may be
imagined as arriving at in old age, when he was beyond question
the most famous writer not only in Britain but throughout the
world, his literary ambitions in his earlier years seem not to have
gone much higher than becoming a parson in a retired rural spot
and writing in his spare time (obviously projected as considerable)
some verses that might or might not be published. Years later he
confessed that his greatest hope had been to write one poem good
enough to be included in an anthology such as *The Golden Treasury*.
Faulkner, on the other hand, was determined to become an artist
even before he had any firm ideas as to what kind of art he might
best be cut out for, and nobody who knows anything of his
biography can doubt for a moment that he formed very early on a
high conception both of the artist's role and of his personal
capacity to fulfil it. 'An artist is a creature driven by demons',
Faulkner once said. 'He don't know why they choose him and he's
usually too busy to wonder why. He is completely amoral in that
he will rob, borrow, beg, or steal from anybody and everybody to
get the work done.' And he added: 'If a writer has to rob his
mother, he will not hesitate; the *Ode on a Grecian Urn* is worth any
number of old ladies.'[14] Nor was this a merely rhetorical statement. I don't mean that he robbed his mother – much of his
energy, indeed, was taken up with providing economic support for
a whole series of relatives, connections and family retainers
('parasites', as he said, who did not 'even have the grace to be

sycophants').[15] But the most unforgettable moment in the television film made about Faulkner a few years ago was his daughter's recollection of his responding to some inconvenient request of hers with the words, 'No one remembers Shakespeare's children.'

If I emphasise this point, it is not because I do not realise that Hardy, closeted in his study all those years of days, was as ruthless in his way as Faulkner in his. (Is it appropriate at this point to imagine the two Mrs Hardys nodding their heads in melancholy agreement?) Faulkner's tough-mindedness is important simply because his earlier and greater self-assurance, his sheer determination to match himself against the world's best from Shakspeare on down, had major consequences for his subsequent career and for the character of his created world. Like Hardy, Faulkner started out as a poet, and throughout his career he continued to speak of himself as a failed poet. It was, I may say, an excellent description, for his verse is for the most part gauche, derivative and oddly incoherent, interesting chiefly for its demonstration of the self-consciously literary attitudes that Faulkner from the first took towards his work, towards the subject-matter of that work and even towards himself. The sequence of rhyming octosyllabic pastorals that went into that very first volume, *The Marble Faun*, is set in a Pan- and nymph-haunted, relentlessly 'sylvan' landscape, half-classical and more than half-Keatsian, that is impossible to locate outside the book's own pages. And yet the Preface, written by Phil Stone but presumably approved by Faulkner himself, implicitly invites a regionalist reading:

> The author of these poems is a man steeped in the soil of his native land, a Southerner by every instinct, and, more than that, a Mississippian. George Moore said that all universal art became great by first being provincial, and the sunlight and mocking-birds and blue hills of North Mississippi are a part of this young man's very being.[16]

It is well to recall, before dismissing such flourishes out of hand, that Faulkner did subsequently prove himself to be among the greatest nature-writers of the present century: one thinks, for example, of the opening chapter of *Light in August*, of the wilderness sections of *Go Down, Moses*, and of the ecstatic evocation – at once perceptually primitive and verbally complex – of Ike Snopes's idyll with his beloved cow in *The Hamlet*. (It is, by the way, well worth setting Hardy's description in *Tess of the d'Urbervilles* of the difference in the quality of light at dawn and at dusk alongside Faulkner's densely specific and richly poetic elaboration of a similar perception in that same section of *The Hamlet*.[17]) Having said that, however, it still seems most appropriate to think of the *Marble Faun* preface as constituting an anticipation of the various literary poses that Faulkner self-consciously adopted during his apprenticeship and even of the deliberate and often profoundly innovative literary strategies that he formulated and prosecuted during the major phases of his subsequent career. In the volume itself – published (you will recall) by a vanity press at someone else's expense – Faulkner seems less concerned with taking a regional stand than with committing a literary act, publicly identifying himself as an artist.

Literary strategies often have biographical implications, of course. Hardy has sometimes been criticised for trying always to keep one foot in the door of London even while the other remained firmly planted on the soil of Dorset. But, tricky as such a manoeuvre might seem, it is at least equalled in complexity by the consequences of Faulkner's decision to combine his careers as a novelist and Hollywood screenwriter with the ownership and restoration of a pre-Civil War house, the subsequent purchase and management of a small farm a few miles out of town, the riding and jumping of horses, and, especially in his later years, the pose of being just a simple farmer rather than a man of letters. Visiting the United States Military Academy at West Point only a few weeks before his death – West Point of all places, you may well interject, but I should remind you that Faulkner was as susceptible as Hardy to the romance of the military and that the West Point computer facilities have for many years been happily employed in the production of concordances of Faulkner's novels – visiting West Point Faulkner found himself being portentously asked what he despaired of most in contemporary life, 'in moving about the market place?' He didn't despair of any of it, he said. What, then, delighted him most? To which he had a simple and unequivocal answer: 'What I like best is fox hunting.'[18] Clearly, however, Faulkner felt it creatively useful as well as personally rewarding to live such a life: at the very least it helped to give him a sense of connection with both the past and the present of northern Mississippi; at best, it can perhaps be said to have contributed to that sympathy with which he treated both the deprivations of the rural poor and the peculiar exasperations of farm management in an area such as north Mississippi where the soil was so eroded and the prevailing sharecropping system so devoid of incentives.

As with Hardy, temporary exile from the region seems to have been for Faulkner a prerequisite of the development of full regionalist self-consciousness, but in Faulkner's case the processes of developing awareness and consequent action were greatly speeded up. His visits to New York, New Orleans and Paris in the middle 1920s look, at least in retrospect, like a series of testings of the waters of the literary centres currently most favoured by American writers, and the decisions he then made to avoid the talking-shops and marketplaces of literature, to devote himself absolutely to the art which would thus become his trade, to stay permanently in Mississippi and to live a certain kind of regionally authenticated life in a certain kind of historically authenticated house were absolutely crucial to the character, quality and sheer quantity of his subsequent work.

Faulkner, unlike Hardy, had no need to break free of an initial profession, for he had refused to adopt one, or of his family background, for the Falkners had long been comfortably established in northern Mississippi, and although he had to endure (as do most writers) some local scorn and distrust of his apparent lack of occupation, he was able in his early thirties to adopt, with unstrenuous deliberation, a mode of life comparable at least in its externals to that of his locally famous great-grandfather, Colonel William Clark Falkner, the 'original' of Colonel Sartoris. The straightforwardness of that act of self-determination seems far removed from the angularity of Hardy's class-conscious return to Dorchester in his middle forties as the architect and owner-occupier of a house whose middle-class solidity and red-bricked modernity asserted not perhaps its rejection of but cetainly its difference from the traditional simplicities of the Bockhampton cottage. Whatever other problems Faulkner may have had to contend with, a sense of class or indeed of any other inferiority was not among them – except in so far as he may have shared in the general Southern sense of exclusion from the national mainstream.

Those early and subsequently unswerving decisions of Faulkner's about his art and his life and the relationship between them gave his career almost from the first a coherence of shape and consistency of direction that Hardy's tended to lack. Faulkner discovered early and never forgot the truth embodied in André Gide's observation as to the artist's need of 'a special world of which he alone has the key'.[19] Faulkner himself once spoke of Balzac's having created 'an intact world of his own. His people don't just move from page one to page 320 of one book. There is a continuity between them all like a blood-stream which flows from page one through to page 20,000 of one book.'[20] And for all the extraordinary variety of Faulkner's own novels – each one of which is distinct in technique and indeed in most other respects from all of the others – they do establish, in whatever sequence they are read, something of that sense of imaginative coherence that he himself so much admired in Balzac.

Partly, of course, this is an effect established, as in Balzac, by an extensive use of recurrent characters and recurrent settings. In Hardy there are no recurrent characters proper: a name and even a personality may sometimes be reinvoked – that of William Dewy, for example – but I think I am right in saying that no character is actually on stage, so to speak, in more than one novel. Nor is there much reuse of specific settings, despite the attention paid to topographical detail during the later revisions: *The Mayor of Casterbridge* established, once and for all, the centrality of Caster-bridge itself, and Budmouth turns up a few times, sometimes as a setting, sometimes merely as a point of romantic reference, but for the most part topography tends to be invoked in Hardy as a way of establishing the *particularity* of locations and their separateness one from another. In Faulkner, however, the same settings frequently reappear, so that we become aware of them – of the square in Jefferson, the gaol and the courthouse, the Old Frenchman place, and so on – as locations where a series of significant actions have occurred over time, each at least potential-ly relevant to all of the others.

I think this difference may have something to do with Faulkner's awareness of addressing an urban and predominantly northern audience for whom Mississippi was not merely a backward rural world (as Wessex was for Hardy's first readers) but primitive and downright hostile, unvisited and certainly unvisit-able – an audience, therefore, for whom the significance and potential symbolism of particular settings had to be established virtually from scratch. Hardy, on the other hand, seemed to be recreating for city dwellers the kind of world to which they or their ancestors had once belonged, and for which they had already been taught nostalgically to yearn. He also had a wealth of associative allusion on which to draw. His settings often came front-end-loaded, with readily recognisable significances already built in: Casterbridge speaks of Rome in every street and Budmouth can cite King George III as a character reference. Faulkner was dealing with a region whose human history, apart from that of the rapidly displaced and almost recordless Indians, was at one and the same time remarkably short, remarkably violent and remarkably destructive of the natural environment. The violence occurred chiefly during that Civil War period to which Faulkner's fiction so often returns – though his great-grandfather's three trials for murder and final assassination all occurred outside the war years – but the erosion of the environment was continuous, and the melancholy rhythm of Ike McCaslin's successive returns to the steadily retreating wilderness in *Go Down, Moses* is only one of several features in that novel that make it discussible as a paradigmatic Faulknerian work.

God Down, Moses is especially typical in its central concern with the elusiveness of 'truth', the inscrutability of the past, the problem of history itself. Faulkner is often inaccurate in referring to historical events – the battles of the Civil War, for example – and he declared on more than one occasion that he wasn't much interested in facts. He was also strongly criticised during the civil rights battles of the 1950s for what was generally referrred to as his 'misrepresentin' Mississippi', and in more recent years he has been taken to task for his portrayals of black characters. (As with criticisms of Hardy's representation of the agricultural labourer, such attacks often seem primarily theoretical, grounded in the assumption that Faulkner as a white man could not, by definition, comprehend let alone recreate the consciousness of a black man or woman.) Faulkner has even so escaped for the most part the kind of negative socio-historical criticism recently directed at Hardy, perhaps precisely because when dealing with the past he tends to do so specifically as an historical novelist, writing of times beyond his own memory and first-hand knowledge, and because, as I have said, the whole structure of a novel such as *Go Down, Moses* or *Absalom, Absalom!* is directed towards the problematisation of history, hence contains within itself its own demurrals.

Such inbuilt antitheses are entirely characteristic of Faulkner's work, and there is, I think, a sense in which the specifically historical elements in that work – always allusive, part of the novel's frame rather than central to its action – function largely as a counterweight to or restraint upon an inherent tendency towards romance. It was in some such terms that Faulkner himself once spoke of the role of the outsider, the unimplicated Canadian Shreve McCannon, in relation to the narrative development of *Absalom, Absalom!*:

> Shreve was the commentator that held the thing to something of reality. If Quentin had been let alone to tell it, it would have become completely unreal. It had to have a solvent to keep it real, keep it believable, creditable, otherwise it would have vanished into smoke and fury.[21]

Not all readers of the novel would see Shreve in quite those terms, of course, and it is equally possible, I think, to see the historical reference or the presence of the outsider as tending rather to *authenticate* the intrinsically extravagant and implausible, the narrative surrendered to sound and fury from the start. Perhaps – to turn back to Hardy again for a moment – perhaps it is in some such terms that one should regard those shadowy, anonymous scene-setting observers who appear in the early pages of the Wessex novels but promptly and permanently vanish once the narrative is under way: the unspecified furzecutter invoked in the second paragraph of *The Return of the Native*, the putative 'casual observer' who witnesses the arrival of Henchard and his family at Weydon Priors, the anonymous ramblers who first view the landscapes of *The Woodlanders* and *Tess of the d'Urbervilles*. It is as if by introducing such unidentified and uninvolved observers Hardy sought to give the regional landscapes and settings of his novels an importance and standing that was independent not only of the characters within the narration but also, to some degree, of the otherwise authoritative voice of the narrator himself.

I have already suggested that public avidity for the reassurances of the actual was soon sufficient to turn Wessex into what might prhaps be called an apparent reality. The case of Blackmore's *Lorna Doone* is perhaps even more remarkable, and even in Mississippi now the process of actualising Yoknapatawpha County is well under way. At one level, of course, that is all good clean fun: the Hardy Conference in Dorchester (27 July–2 August 1986) exactly coincided with a Faulkner Conference in Oxford, Mississippi, and

Hardy at least seems in some of his novels to have taken satisfaction in his enhancement of the local tourist industry. But there is also a sense – an altogether more serious sense – in which regionalism is forever trying to free itself from the trivialisation of 'local colour' and from the widespread view that regionalism itself is a limiting term: one of the reasons why Faulkner is so little appreciated in Britain, I suspect, is that he is perceived as writing about a region about which the great British reading public knows almost nothing except that it doesn't want to know anything. When in fact (the point seems almost too obvious to make to a group such as this) Faulkner writes of a region which is fundamentally of the mind, non-existent outside the world – the extraordinarily expansive and multi-dimensional world – of the collective Yoknapatawpha sequence.

Although his work never achieved, and never sought, the intensive and adhesive intertextuality of Faulkner's, Hardy seems nevertheless to have been – at least to have become – fully conscious of the literary implications of his acts of world–creation. He liked to think that Egdon Heath might have been the scene of King Lear's madness (and who is to say that it was not?), and he once declared, apropos of *Under the Greenwood Tree*, that Mellstock, based on his native Stinsford, *was* Stoke Poges, the scene of Gray's meditation in a country churchyard. He seems also to have projected an essentially pastoral function – implicit in their very titles – for novels such as *Under the Greenwood Tree*, *Far from the Madding Crowd* and *The Woodlanders* from the very beginning of his career.

As for Faulkner, I have argued elsewhere[22] that in finally choosing *The Hamlet* as the title of one of the finest and most distinctively pastoral of his novels he was in effect asserting its kinship not only with Gray's hamlet with the rude forefathers, not only with Hardy's Mellstock, but with all the hamlets of literature – with Goldsmith's 'Sweet Auburn', Washington Irving's Sleepy Hollow, Sherwood Anderson's Winesburg, and the one that must have been tucked away somewhere in the Forest of Arden. The history of Lake Wobegone had not yet been made a matter of public record.

Regional literature is always didactic – that is perhaps what most clearly distinguishes it from 'local colour' – and Yoknapataw-pha County is at one with Wessex, and with the 'Elegy in a Country Churchyard', in enforcing a characteristically pastoralist reconsideration of the reader's society and its values in the light of implicit comparisons with other and simpler places and times. But Yoknapatawpha goes much further than Wessex in exploiting its own fictiveness, in asserting those narrative and symbolic freedoms special-worldliness ideally bestows. Where Hardy thought of himself as creating a 'partly-real, partly-dream' kingdom, only to find the dream portion progressively overbuilt by speculators of the real, Faulkner invested from the start in solid unreal estate, doubtless suspecting that, as Ishmael in *Moby-Dick* says of Queequeg's native country, 'It is not down on any map; true places never are.'

NOTES

1. Ezra Pound, review of Jean Cocteau, *Poesies, 1917–1920*, in *The Dial*, 70 (January 1921) p. 110.
2. Thomas Hardy, *The Woodlanders* (London: Macmillan, 1912) p. 146.
3. Ibid., p. 4.
4. *The Sunday Times*, 24 November 1985, p. 41.
5. See, for example, K. D. M. Snell, *Annals of the Labouring Poor: Social Change and Agrarian England, 1660–1900* (Cambridge: Cambridge University Press, 1985) p. 396.
6. Michael Millgate (ed.), *The Life and Work of Thomas Hardy* (London, Macmillan, 1984) p. 36.
7. Harold Orel (ed.), *Thomas Hardy's Personal Writings* (Lawrence, Kan.: University Press of Kansas, 1969) p. 111.
8. Thomas Hardy, *Far from the Madding Crowd* (London: Osgood, McIlvaine, 1895) p. v.
9. W. J. Keith, 'Thomas Hardy and the Literary Pilgrims', *Nineteenth-Century Fiction*, 24 (1969) pp. 80–92.
10. Hardy, *Far from the Madding Crowd*, p. vi.
11. Orel (ed.), *Thomas Hardy's Personal Writings*, p. 46.
12. Frederick L. Gwynn and Joseph L. Blotner (eds), *Faulkner in the University: Class Conferences at the University of Virginia, 1957–58* (Charlottesville, Va.: University of Virginia Press, 1959) p. 90.
13. James B. Meriwether and Michael Millgate (eds), *Lion in the Garden: Interviews with William Faulkner, 1926–1962* (New York: Random House, 1968) p. 255.
14. Ibid., p. 239.
15. Joseph Blotner (ed.), *Selected Letters of William Faulkner* (New York: Random House, 1977) p. 339.
16. William Faulkner, *The Marble Faun and A Green Bough* (New York: Random House, 1965) p. 7. In *Hail and Farewell* (1911) Moore wrote: '[A]rt must be parochial in the beginning to become cosmopolitan in the end.'

17. Thomas Hardy, *Tess of the d'Urbervilles* (London: Macmillan, 1912) p. 166; William Faulkner, *The Hamlet* (New York: Random House, 1940) p. 207.

18. Joseph L. Fant III and Robert Ashley (eds), *Faulkner at West Point* (New York: Random House, 1964) p. 64.

19. André Gide, *Journals, 1889–1949*, ed. Justin O'Brien (Harmondsworth: Penguin, 1967) p. 54.

20. Meriwether and Millgate (eds), *Lion in the Garden*, p. 217.

21. Gwynn and Blotner (eds), *Faulkner in the University*, p. 75.

22. See my 'Faulkner and the South: some Reflections', in Evans Harrington and Ann J. Abadie (eds), *The South and Faulkner's Yoknapatawpha* (Jackson, Miss.: University Press of Mississippi, 1977) pp. 195–210.

6

Philip Larkin: Provincial Poet

R. P. DRAPER

The special Philip Larkin issue of *Phoenix* (Nos 11/12, Autumn and Winter 1973–4) has a picture on the front cover of Larkin sitting beside the sign that says 'England' on the border between England and Scotland (at, I believe, Coldstream on the River Tweed). As Larkin must have been asked to pose for this photograph I presume it means that he gave his approval to such an association between himself and his native country. Certainly critics seem to be in general agreement that he is very much an English poet. In 1963 Donald Davie wrote: 'I think everyone knows, really, that Philip Larkin is the effective Laureate of our England.'[1] Andrew Motion has placed him centrally in the distinctively English line of poetry which includes Cowper, Clare, Wordsworth and Edward Thomas; and Seamus Heaney has compared him with Joyce, remarking that '*Dubliners* is a book very close to the spirit of Larkin, whose collected work would fit happily under the title *Englanders*'.[2]

He was well known to have loathed what he called 'Abroad' and very rarely ever set foot outside of Britain – though he was happy enough with Northern Ireland, where he worked as Librarian at Queen's University, Belfast, and the Scottish islands, where he took occasional holidays, even if he did deplore the gastronomy of the Isle of Skye.[3] As Robert Conquest says, 'This insularity is one of the strengths of Larkin's poetry, signifying a resolve to base himself firmly upon the experience, the language, the culture which have formed him, in which he is rooted.'[4] But that slightly aggressive-defensive Englishness is provincial rather than nationalist. It has a strong Midlands-cum-North-of-England flavour, as befits a man who was born in Coventry and worked as a librarian in Wellington, Shropshire, in Leicester and in Hull. Larkin is not a regional poet in the sense that Clare, or Barnes, or even Hardy, is;

and it may well seem at times – as in the much-quoted last line of 'I Remember, I Remember' ('Nothing, like something, happens anywhere') – that particular locality has no significance for him. Nevertheless, he is, in a number of poems, distinctly a poet of place (the outstanding example is 'Here'; and 'Dublinesque' is perhaps a less usual example in which the place in question is actually named), and in a poem like 'Show Saturday' he celebrates local activities as Hardy might celebrate a sheep-shearing supper or a harvest-home.

More importantly, however, he is a poet of provincial, as against metropolitan, life, and the provincial is not only his subject-matter, but also his cultural anchorage. It may overstate the case to say, as Betjeman did, that 'He is the John Clare of the building-estates, and as true to them as was Clare to the fields and trees of Northamptonshire';[5] nor is he a democratic poet in the manner of Wordsworth, or in the very different manner of Walt Whitman. But one could take his words on the novelist Barbara Pym and apply them to his own poetry:

> I like to read about people who have done nothing spectacular, who try to behave well in the limited field of activity they command, but who can see, in little autumnal moments of vision, that the so called 'big' experiences of life are going to miss them; and I like to read about such things presented not with self pity or despair or romanticism, but with realistic firmness and even humour.[6]

Not only does Larkin like to read about 'people who have done nothing spectacular', but he also chooses to write about such people – and in a manner which is likewise neither self-pitying nor romantic, but shows 'realistic firmness' and 'humour'. These chosen people usually live in the provinces, and, not unsurprisingly, exhibit the mediocrity and unadventurousness which we associate with the pejorative use of the word 'provincial'. It is part of Larkin's 'realistic firmness' that he neither glosses over nor disguises that. On the other hand, unlike the satirical metropolitan, he does not remain scornfully outside such characters. Like Flaubert he can both mock his bourgeois and lower-middle-class characters and identify with them: he could well say, 'Mr Bleaney, c'est moi'. Though he goes further than Flaubert, and – more like his admired predecessor, Hardy – also finds a virtue in the provincial which is missing from the more 'with-it' critic.

Awareness of the regional and provincial is stimulated by the migratory habits of nineteenth- and twentieth-century man. It is modern man, 'on the move', who becomes consciously concerned with a way of life which is at once more limited and more stable than his, and which derives from steady contact with people and places of a particular region. Great regionalists like Hardy and D.H. Lawrence are those who have known both conditions of living. Hardy's experience, as Raymond Williams has expressed it, is that of the 'educated observer and the passionate participant' – he was brought up in Dorset, saw it changed by contact with the outer world, himself lived and worked in the metropolis, and returned to Dorset with a dual sensibility which caused him to be both involved with its traditional pattern of life and detached from it. D.H. Lawrence was steeped in his provincial environment of Nottinghamshire and Derbyshire, became an exile from it, and married a liberated continental woman with the entrée to 'advanced' and sophisticated opinions. As a result he acquired a very ambiguous attitude towards that very environment, loving and hating it simultaneously.

There is no simple direct parallel between these two and Larkin, but there is something of the same paradox of *odi et amo*, detachment and involvement, in his poetry of the provinces. He, too, is 'on the move' in these poems – in 'The Whitsun Weddings' between Hull and London; in 'Dockery and Son' between Oxford and, presumably, Hull; and in 'Here' between a point of departure somewhere south and west, probably London, and, once again, Hull. The setting of 'Mr Bleaney' is not specified, but the reference to 'the Bodies' (meaning, of course, car bodies) makes it probably somewhere like Cowley, Birmingham or Coventry, and the 'I' of that poem is clearly only a temporary occupier of Bleaney's room. The 'I' of 'Naturally the Foundation Will Bear Your Expenses', a more ironically treated persona, is also on the move, perpetually and restlessly so, it seems, being whisked by jet-propelled Comet, rather than slow, lumbering British Rail, from Berkeley to Heathrow, and from Heathrow to Bombay – a trendy, peripatetic academic who despises the 'solemn-sinister / Wreath-rubbish' going on at Whitehall on Armistice Day.

In the latter poem it is a national, not a provincial, occasion that the ironic 'I' despises, and yet the observance of Armistice Day takes on the colouring of a piece of outdated provincialism in the mind of the trendy jet-setter who voices the sentiments of the poem. His view of the commemorative ceremony which holds up his taxi on its way to the airport, and particularly his dismissive reference to the people involved in it ('Crowds, colourless and careworn'), shows him to be deplorably indifferent to the ordinary man's serious emotions and shared respect for the dead; while the jaunty trochaic rhythms of the verse point up, from within the dramatic monologue, his own shallowness, thinly covered by a slick self-confidence:

> It used to make me throw up,
>   These mawkish nursery games:
> O when will England grow up?

And the line which immediately follows, '– But I outsoar the Thames', reveals his egregiousness in congratulating himself on transcending all that local time and place stand for.

What is missing from this itinerant scholar's psychological make-up is precisely that duality of attitude which, in the more profoundly provincial poem 'Here', deepens jauntiness into sympathy, and sympathy into imaginative resonance. The, as so often, cunning, but unobtrusive, craftsmanship of Larkin's opening puts a frame round the city to which it leads:

> Swerving east, from rich industrial shadows
> And traffic all night north; swerving through fields
> Too thin and thistled to be called meadows,
> And now and then a harsh-named halt, that shields
> Workmen at dawn; swerving to solitude
> Of skies and scarecrows, haystacks, hares and pheasants,
> And the widening river's slow presence,
> The piled gold clouds, the shining gull-marked mud,
>
> Gathers to the surprise of a large town:

The sense of direction conveyed by 'Swerving' is exact with regard to the geographical relationship of Hull to London and the industrial areas of the Midlands (as is the 'slow and stopping curve', though going the opposite way, of 'The Whitsun Weddings'); but it is also a participle which builds up a telling syntactical suspension. The reader is taken through a countryside which might seem drearily nondescript, but in fact acquires a novel beauty and serenity not unlike that which Hardy in *The Return of the Native* attributes to Egdon heath as more appropriately modern than the traditional, classical beauty of the Mediterranean. And when, at the beginning of the second stanza, the awaited main clause and its verb, 'Gathers', at last arrives (seemingly without a subject, though one could construe 'swerving' as a nominative gerund), it is itself a surprise, acting out its own statement: 'Gathers to the surprise of a large town'. The dull, yet transformed countryside which leads up to this town projects something of its newly-seen quality on to the otherwise drab, featureless place. Suddenly, in this second stanza, the casual collocation – 'domes and statues, spires and cranes', 'grain-scattered streets, barge-crowded water', the 'raw estates', the 'flat-faced trolleys' and the 'plate-glass swing doors' of the big stores – brings life, even originality, to what might easily be dismissed as humdrum. Of course, Larkin's double vision also recognises it as humdrum; the shoddy glamour of early 1960s affluence is accurately caught in the catalogue of

Cheap suits, red kitchen-ware, sharp shoes, iced lollies,
Electric mixers, toasters, washers, driers.

And when the people whose desires are focused on such things are designated, in stanza 3, as 'A cut-price crowd', the transferred epithet seems to put them on the same level as the 'bargains' they are hunting. Yet it is wrong to isolate that phrase from the rest of the line: 'A cut-price crowd, urban yet simple, dwelling'. 'Urban yet simple' dignifies what 'cut-price' apparently demeans; it looks forward to the collage of surprising juxtapositions which constitutes the rest of that stanza, and, in particular, it leads to an oddly pleasing vista (bringing a shock of recognition to those of us who live in the sea-port of Aberdeen) of 'a terminate and fishy-smelling / Pastoral of ships up streets'. As John Gay produced in *The Beggar's Opera* a 'Newgate pastoral', adjusting and redeeming, a fading literary mode to the urban realities of eighteenth-century London, so Larkin produces in 'Here' a Hull pastoral, bringing the poetic imagination right into the heart of the twentieth-century provincial city.

Taken as a whole, however, 'Here' is a still more complex poem than I have so far represented it. The 'solitude' towards which the journey swerves in the first stanza is renewed in the fourth, and last, as the mental journey continues beyond the town to 'isolate villages' and reaches, finally, the 'unfenced existence' of the sea. Like the mysterious 'sun-comprehending glass' of 'High Windows', which concludes that poem by showing 'Nothing, and is nowhere, and is endless', this non-human freedom comes as an ambiguous blessing: 'Facing the sun, untalkative, out of reach'. In other words, 'Here' is not just a well-balanced portrait of a provincial society. Beyond this human world there is another world and another experience, characterised by a 'loneliness' which 'clarifies', a silence that 'stands / Like heat' and air which is 'luminously-peopled'; above all, it is ultimately, and quite simply, 'untalkative'. Larkin carefully refrains from any definition of this other world, probably because it is something which transcends consciousness – something which can only be gestured towards, not stated; but whatever it is, it seems necessary as a means of keeping the more immediately recognisable human world in perspective. If provincial Hull in this poem functions as a kind of ambivalently critical pastoral in relation to the metropolitan, this silence is also ambivalently and critically pastoral in relation to the whole human world, provincial included.

Larkin was, of course, a notoriously lonely, though by no means unsociable man. I do not, at this point, want to make a biographical connection – apart from anything else, I am not qualified to do so. But the fact of loneliness, and to some extent the desire to be alone, is a recurrent theme in his poetry. Yet this loneliness is qualified by a recognition of the need for company. 'Vers de Société' is the classic example. The whole of this poem is an enactment of the process whereby an initially off-the-cuff dismissal of an invitation to take part in a social gathering is converted into a more thoughtful acceptance. A truculent defence of treasured loneliness is none the less exchanged, if somewhat reluctantly, for a wiser sociability.

The primary cause for the change in 'Vers de Société' is, of course, the ever-present fear of death, which Larkin has, if not exorcised, at least faced more honestly – and (as I have tried to show elsewhere[7]) to that extent more valuably – than any other poet of his generation. But this is not the sole motivating force. The change is also part of a process, highly characteristic of Larkin, in which separation gives way to involvement and a deeper awareness which can at least verge on the communal in the sense that it reveals an underlying community value. This is the deepening process which gradually makes itself felt in 'Church Going', bringing a change of heart which issues in a reaffirmation of traditional values:

> A serious house on serious earth it is,
> In whose blent air all our compulsions meet,
> Are recognised, and robed as destinies.

The attitude is a conservative one – 'conservative' with a small 'c' (though I admit that 'Conservative' with a capital 'C' may also be applicable to occasional poems such as 'Naturally the Foundation' and 'Homage to a Government'). I bother to say this because it seems to me that it is not in the main a political attitude, but the result of an imaginative act combined with that very Larkinian process of dis-illusionment which causes him to start in a very contemporary fashion of ironic dismissiveness, but end with a recognition that the society he looks at embodies something human which is worth conserving, if at all possible. Furthermore, the loneliness previously discussed in connection with 'Here' is a necessary means by which all this is precipitated. It is the Hardyesque paradox of involved onlooker that provides the feeling of isolation which makes this conservative discovery possible.

What I am trying to argue is that there is, so to speak, a buried social self in this seemingly aloof and isolated poet, and that the characteristically deepening process in his poems draws him not only towards the recognition of mortality, but also – and with increasing frequency in his last complete volume, *High Windows*, though it is in evidence earlier as well – towards a rediscovery, perhaps even a revaluation, of traditionally provincial values.

Two poems offer themselves as fairly straightforward illustrations of this process, namely: 'The Whitsun Weddings' and 'Show Saturday'. I shall say something about each of these. But I would also like to give brief consideration to three others – 'Dublines-que', 'Livings' and 'The Card-Players' – which, though they are rather less obvious examples, also seem to imply a basically similar process of recognition.

'The Whitsun Weddings' and 'Show Saturday' are both poems which remind one that Larkin began his writing career as a novelist. They are full of documentary brilliance, recording

provincial society, urban and rural respectively, with the cool eye
of a traveller who is not quite a fellow-traveller. Fellowship
develops, however; though not through chummy participation,
but a kind of imaginative warming up to what is observed until, in
the case of 'The Whitsun Weddings', 'this frail / Travelling coincidence' becomes a potentially creative event:

> and what it held
> Stood ready to be loosed with all the power
> That being changed can give.

Perhaps the ending of this particular poem is more rhetorically
appropriate than poetically inevitable. The chucking forward
motion as the train brakes on the approach to King's Cross is
beautifully caught, and the image of an arrow at the apex of its
upward curve now beginning to drop is marvellous; but its fusion
with the further image of a shower of rain falling on unknown,
and presumably parched, ground – despite the fact that it has to
some extent been prepared for by the references to 'a religious
wounding', 'squares of wheat', and so on – pushes the analogy
with fertility rites a little too hard. But setting that slight
reservation aside, what I find deeply convincing is the recognition
that weddings may be vulgar without being trite. The lonely
persona of the poem is not an expenses-paid Foundation man, but
rather an ironic observer who discovers, and is able to conserve,
the profound emotional truth which still survives beneath the all-
too-easily-mocked banality.

Similarly with 'Show Saturday', except that here the 1960s irony
has abated, giving place to a more neutral willingness to let things
stand plainly for themselves:

> four brown eggs, four white eggs,
> Four plain scones, four dropped scones, pure
> excellences that enclose
> A recession of skills.

'A recession of skills' also quietly, unobtrusively, implies long-
standing rural tradition. This is not to deny that the dis-illusioned
witty Larkin is still present ('Children all saddle-swank' is a nice
example of what he can do, as is 'car-tuning curt-haired sons'). The
Show is not sentimentalised. When it all packs up, the 'loud

occasions' of everyday life are going to take over again; but the sense of communal event rhythmically recurring survives precisely because it has been recognised as the substance of art, not merely the occasion for wit. Consequently, the final lifting of the verbal register seems to have been earned:

> something they share
> That breaks ancestrally each year into
> Regenerate union. Let it always be there.

I must be brief with my other examples. 'Dublinesque' and 'Livings' are states-of-being rather than process poems; but they imply that some such deepening process as I have been commenting on has already taken place. They are different, however, in that they are more distanced, either in place or in time. 'Dublinesque' is Dublin seen by the tourist (if I can use that word without derogatory implications). Its tripping dactyls and trochees echo the jauntiness of the dancing and singing accompanying an Irish wake, while the superimposed colloquial rhythms sober it all down to a more involved seriousness, the result being 'an air of great friendliness ... And of great sadness also'. It is an exercise in identification with a provincial culture and customs which are not the poet's own (if the Irish won't protest against their capital city, Dublin, being called 'provincial'), but one that still constitutes a valid extension of imaginative sympathy and a discovery of something worth conserving.

'Livings' is a kind of triptych: faithful studies of a 1929 agricultural merchant, and of a group of Fellows of an eighteenth-century Oxford college, compose its two outer wings, and a 1930s (or possibly 1940s – but not wartime) lighthouse keeper provides the centre-piece. All three are humanly orientated, but the centre-piece has more of the raw presence of nature, and this serves to hold the outer wings in a steadying perspective not unlike that which is provided by the natural framing of the sea-port town in 'Here'. And as with 'Dublinesque', each picture of this triptych is a more posed and deliberate study than we find in 'The Whitsun Weddings' or 'Show Saturday'. The first picture is obviously a scene from past provincial life. The third is also clearly provincial, even though the culture is supposedly metropolitan. The second, however, presents an isolated lighthouse keeper dwarfed by images of elemental timelessness, which he 'rejoices' in and 'cherishes', and welcoming the isolation of the sea. (As a rare example of deliberate allusion Larkin transforms the Arnoldian 'unplumb'd, salt, estranging sea' into the much more positive 'salt/ Unsown stirring fields'.) Humanity is put in its place. And yet none of the human beings is without the support of a respectable (in the strict sense of 'capable of being respected') way of life. Only the international, transatlantic 'Lit shelved liners' seem to have lost their human validity and 'Grope like mad worlds westward'.

My last example, 'The Card-Players', follows on conveniently from what I have called the 'triptych' structure of 'Livings'. It is an imaginative reconstruction of crude provincial life as recorded in the realistic painting of the seventeenth-century Dutch masters, with specific visual allusions to paintings by Brouwer and Brueghel (though, as far as I know, there is no one individual painting of which it is a faithful imitation). This, too, is seen from a distance, that is, it is a portrait of a past, perhaps vanished, society, not the provincial world of which Larkin has immediate, intimate knowledge. Nevertheless, it is an astonishing effort of imaginative projection. The old witty mockery is there, not least in the joke names, 'Jan van Hogspeuw', 'Dirk Dogstoerd' and 'Old Prijck'; and the coarse humour for which Larkin is famous, or notorious, in poems like 'Sunny Prestatyn' and the opening of 'High Windows', recurs in the pissing, snoring, farting and gobbing which fill this poem. At the same time it is a poem of immense vitality. The natural forces of the centre-piece of 'Livings' are here interfused with the raw energies of Jan, Dirk and Old Prijck: the elements of rain, wind and fire which are apostrophised in the last line are frantically, and yet compellingly, echoed in, for example, Jan's pissing (which anticipates the rain), Prijck's snoring (he 'snores with the gale'), Jan's farting (his 'wind'), and the clay-pipe which Dirk lights with a cinder (from the fire). In addition, the whole interior of the inn is a 'lamplit cave', emphasising its man-made, yet natural, quality, and in the final exclamation: 'The secret, bestial peace!' the vulgarity of this provincial scene combines with its animal vigour to create a beastliness which is a composite paradox of the comic and the serious, the disgusting and the marvellously primitive.

The structure of this remarkable poem is not to be overlooked either. It is an example of that most artificial and traditional form, the sonnet, but one which is divided into thirteen lines and one, instead of the usual octave and sestet. As a result, the last line gets unusual prominence. In a strikingly compact manner 'Rain, wind and fire! The secret, bestial peace!' does for this poem what the closing stanzas of 'Church Going', 'The Whitsun Weddings' and 'Show Saturday' do more extensively for their respective poems. It reveals that a process of deepening awareness and sympathy has taken place; and the fact that the whole poem is a sonnet exemplifies the conserving and reaffirmation of tradition which has been effected. This, too, is a provincial poem, and, though not about either English or contemporary provincialism, one that finds strength and value, even if ambiguously, in an image of the provincial.

In the volume, *High Windows*, 'The Card Players' is placed immediately after the poem, 'Going, Going', in which old-fashioned Englishness is seen as threatened with extinction:

> And that will be England gone,
> The shadows, the meadows, the lanes,
> The guildhalls, the carved choirs.

Coming after this, 'The Card Players' might, therefore, seem to be something of a deliberately archaic, nostalgic study – a comment on something that is irrevocably lost. Taken, however, in conjunction with some of the other poems I have discussed, it may be that it can be seen as giving a hint of something which is still capable of being conserved by the right conservatively provincial approach – a 'secret, bestial peace' worth the imaginative effort of rediscovery. And however conditioned and qualified it may be, by irony and archaic distancing, it adds confirmation to the impression created elsewhere that Larkin is a 'provincial' poet in no derogatory sense of that word.

NOTES

1. Donald Davie, 'Poetry and Landscape in Present England', *Granta*, 19 October 1963, p. 2; quoted by Ernst Zillekens, *The Themes of Philip Larkin's Poetry* (Bonn, 1983) p. 27.
2. Contributions by Andrew Motion and Seamus Heaney to *Larkin at Sixty*, ed. Anthony Thwaite (London, 1982) pp. 66 and 135.
3. See the limerick quoted by Robert Conquest, ibid., p. 32.
4. Ibid.

5.   John Betjeman, 'Common Experiences', *The Listener*, vol. LXXI, no. 1825 (19 March 1964) p. 483.

6.   Letter to Charles Monteith, quoted in Thwaite (ed.), *Larkin at Sixty*, p. 42.

7.   In my chapter on Larkin, 'Philip Larkin: "the bone's truth"', *Lyric Tragedy* (London, 1985) pp. 201–14.

7

Region and Nation: R. S. Thomas and Dylan Thomas

BARBARA HARDY

I

Regional poetry, I suggest, does not become a genre unless it also becomes nationalist poetry, as frequently happens in war, conquest or revolution. The discussion of nationalist poetry is bound to be ideologically biased, and this essay on two Welsh poets will reveal my preference for internationalism over nationalism and pacifism over militancy. Dylan Thomas and R. S. Thomas offer a poetic and ideological contrast, both being poets of region, and Welsh regions, but showing a different perception both of their own Welshness and of region as a subject for poetry. Dylan Thomas writes a regional poetry which is not only apolitical, but which always abstracts and often metonymises the regional subject, though retaining the sense of beloved place and time. R. S. Thomas has a larger range of subject, including a body of some of the most concentrated religious poetry in contemporary writing, but includes within that range a conspicuously didactic nationalist verse, ranging from clearly propagandist poetry, especially in the small volume, *What is a Welshman?*, to poetry using character and landscape in more indirect and implicit hortatory or persuasive ways.

R. S. Thomas continues to write and speak polemically, as an apparently committed Welsh nationalist, but only in prose. His last three volumes of poetry have more or less avoided the subject of nationalism, and his regional themes have become larger and more generalised in geographical and historical reference. Although the recent or recently published poems do not politicise region, they reveal some continuities of feeling. R. S. Thomas's regional poetry perfectly illustrates Gerard Manley Hopkins's opinion that the mainspring of poetry is feeling, but does not reveal what Hopkins called 'love in particular'. (Or if it does, does so in covert and indirect ways.) One of the interesting aspects of regional feeling in R. S. Thomas, whether shown through a place or a typified person, is its rootedness in forms of antipathy. Unlike political poetry written to propagandist formulae, it is powerfully expressive in form and language, but the emotions expressed are not those most commonly associated with patriotic verses. His poetry tends to be the poetry of hostile feeling. The hostility is not directed only against the foreign oppressor or intruder – English boss or English tourist – but often towards the Welsh themselves. Thomas writes a sour pastoral. He may invoke ideologically enlarged and stereotyped rural figures, almost in the manner of Wordsworth, but in an affective medium which is more often wry and scornful than compassionate or exalting. The typology of the Welsh peasant (oddly called peasant, in an archaic, perhaps Welsh-influenced but not currently idiomatic English) is shot through with glimpses of pity or admiration, but these are not the prevailing passions.

I begin at the end, with the latest volume, *Experimenting with an Amen*, because here some of the earlier prevailing hostilities are clearly seen, diverted to other subjects and contexts. The strength and danger of the politicised regional poetry in R. S. Thomas's *oeuvre* seem to me best approached in terms of dominant feelings.

The new volume contains a poem, 'Unposted', an address to a bad poet submitting work for advice and judgement. The title signals *occupatio* rather than sensitive reticence, since the poet (outside the poem) has allowed himself the luxury of writing such a reply. The fictitious nature of poetry in no way affects my argument: the prevailing feeling is unsympathetic, and whether or not the dismissive and retaliatory expression is a response to 'life-experience' does not matter. The poet in the poem calls the bad poet 'dear' and 'friend'; he admits brotherhood, but also a failure to understand why the poems have been sent to him. (A disingenuous question; reputation must bear its burdens.) He has harsher things to say, asking why the writer hasn't buried the poems, as a cat disposes of its faeces – a not too oblique way of calling the verses 'shit'. The poem goes on to imagine the recipient as disabled, perhaps writing with his foot, needing the poet's opinion as gold to pay a way past Giant Despair. It concludes with the admission that he wrote back to lie and call the poems great, to get a bland reception. The poem dares to use the word 'charity' but bears out its own comment that charity is in short supply. It is fuelled by contempt.

In the title-poem of 'Poetry for Supper' two old poets enjoy an argument about poetry, while sharply and uncompromisingly distinguished from their environment which is full of noisy talk, 'glib with prose'. One of the painting poems, in *Between Here and Now*, interprets the peasants in Cézanne's painting *The Cardplayers* as representatives of boredom and monotony. Interpretations differ, of course, but since it is certainly possible to read Cézanne's seized moment as a vision of intense concentration, this poem seems to be another instance of poetry desiring to shape the opposite of love and sympathy. This is in no way to dismiss such poetry, merely to observe that it often appears to find antipathy congenial.

Antipathy, then, is not confined to R. S. Thomas's nationalist poetry, and one might argue that the poetry of politicised regionalism taps, rather than creates, rejections. There are many instances of a region and a character-typology matched or joined by feelings of rejection. The much-discussed poems about the character Iago Prytherch, for instance, are at times like reversals of Wordsworth's exaltation of heroic people in appropriate landscapes, and the bleakness of Welsh hill country is compounded by, and compounds, harshness, vacancy and dirt. 'The Muck Farmer' in *Poetry for Supper* is another rustic stereotype, brilliantly incised. The farmer's language, 'his speech is a rank garden', his mind, 'crazed and alone', and his body, 'swaying dully before us', are matched with the farm-muck, with the weather, 'wan-moon' and 'thin cloud' and with his dwelling, a house with cracked window, 'sagging under its weight of moss'. Such examples can be multiplied, though some of the antipathetic verses reveal a wrung or wry acceptance. This is especially true of the many Iago Prytherch poems, whose continued permutations show ambivalence, change of heart and awareness of criticism, though many of them continue to demonstrate a taste for hostility.

How is such antipathy specialised and politicised? The poetic habitats of dilapidated farms and unreceptive earth – often reinforced by images of rain and bad weather – attack an agricultural decay and neglect, and sound their laments for a pre-industrial past, but disgust shows itself more often than pastoral nostalgias. English responsibilities are indicted, but frequently what is displayed is a history shared by Welsh and English alike, though with a poetic dominance of Welsh victims. At times the despoliation of agriculture, culture, and history is summed up, and condemned, in a distaste for the human products of civilisation's discontents. In the interesting long poem 'Border Blues' (*Poetry for Supper*) saints, heroes, singers and lovers have been replaced by the resented stereotypes, 'ladies from the council houses' and farmworkers whose tunes come from 'the world's dance-halls'. Snatches of poetry and hymns in Welsh make a polyglot counterpane of cultures, in which figures from the Mabinogion are as debased as T.S. Eliot's Rhine-Maidens, in a poem which owes much, in language, fragmented structure, allusiveness, myth and mood, to *The Waste Land*. Olwen still teases 'a smile / Of bright flowers out of the grass' but wears nylons, and her marriage is prevented by a Welsh matriarch whose cunning beats that of the old villain-giant, Ysbaddaden Penkawr. It isn't always clear what is being demythologised and degraded, but the dislike for remnants of a fast-fading heritage seems to compound an attack on the conqueror.

And much of the poetry deals with conquest and conqueror. 'A Welshman to any Tourist' (*Song at the Year's Turning*) is powerfully ironic, but also, I think, less than accurate, as it insists that 'We've nothing vast to offer you'. The dismissal of our ancient mountains is specious, worked through the invocation of a geography both vague and beside the point, 'No canyons / Where the pterodactyl's wing / Casts a cold shadow', and an insult facilitated – and cheapened – by metaphor, 'no deserts / Except the waste of thought / Forming from mind erosion'. In 'The Small Window' (*Not That He Brought Flowers*) exclusiveness is not even nationalist: it is crowds, of any race, who are the enemy. This is a poem which begins with some of the fine sensuous particularities which Thomas often achieves, fixing the shimmering spectrum of rainy lands:

> A hill lights up
> Suddenly; a field trembles
> With colour and goes out
> In its turn.

But the landscape's splendour is realised and then narrowed in order to use the metaphor 'rich', in 'rich with looking', then to exploit it for all it is worth, warning that the 'wealth is for the few / And chosen. Those who crowd / A small window dirty it / With their breathing'. Like 'A Welshman to any Tourist', this seems to be a way of using metaphor in order to tell lies. The jewelled landscape is more unlike the small window than the poem admits. This is a political distortion through imagery, its yearning for exclusive views candid but not ingratiating.

Poetic language and fiction are used to make more explicit and sustained attacks, some on the Welsh culture itself, as in the long (by Thomas's standards) dramatic poem, 'The Minister'. Included in the volume *Song at the Year's Turning*, 'The Minister' is a play for voices, originally broadcast on the Welsh Regional programme of the BBC in 1952. It tells an uncomfortably and uncompromisingly harsh story of religious hypocrisy and materialism, agricultural decay, harsh lands, bad weather, joyless sex and joyless celibacy, and cultural aridity. Almost every detail of scene and action is bitter. Buzzards riddle 'love's text' with their 'inhuman cry', the chapel vestry is 'sour with books and wet clothes', the cow is 'bored with its grass world' and 'an owl cried / Derision on a God of love'. The images of the natural world are violently pressed into the service of antipathy, though the narrative of the isolated and repressed minister, surrounded by grasping deacons and adulter-ous parishioners, could have been dramatised without such a total and unqualified symbolic support system. The occasional image of beauty is admitted, but its reluctant entry behaves as the exceptional exception which really does prove the rule, or, in this case, the ruling passion: the valleys below the hill country are praised in a fine metaphor, 'an open book, / Bound in sunlight', but the deceptive image of text is there to impute falsehood (not too clearly): 'the green tale / Told in its pages is not true'. When the bitter young minister admits to some good moments, 'But let me be fair, let me be fair. / It was not all like this', the three instances he gives – the moor's moods softened by bog cotton, a child's present of an egg, and a bland mellow moon – are few and frail in a context where nature, like typography and plot, is there to create bad images.

Sex is denigrated harshly, not only in the hypocrisy of the deacon, but through a collocation of sexuality and money:

> It was sex, sex, sex, and money, money,
> God's mistake and the devil's creation

says the Narrator, in hostile incantation which is at once borne out by the speech of Buddug, a character whose language lapses into banal echoes of *Cold Comfort Farm*. The portrait of a loose woman is crude, and crudely sexist:

> Your eyes
> Scare me, yet my bowels ache
> With a strange frenzy. This is what
> My mother and her mother felt
> For the men who took them under the hedge.

The Narrator and the male characters have a more vivid style, though this is poetic drama where characters are deliberately simplified, emblematically manipulated to attack a dying or dead culture, but whose generalised and didactic passages show no sense of imaginative limits. As the young minister is killed by the hard parish, blackness is unrelieved. Morgan speaks of having the *hwyl*, but his language is never rapturous. His repression even leads him to uproot a few flowers under his window and replace them with cinders. The only woman who fancies him is 'not right in the head'. Some of this is unbelievable, even in an allegory, and all of it is an over-reaching denigration of a community. It lacks the range, individualisation and violent humour of *A Tale of a Tub* but reminds us that Swift's allegorical representation of Anglicanism was denigrated by association, and found offensive, even blasphemous. 'The Minister' is such a concentrated drama of hatred, especially coming from a Welsh nationalist, that it strikes this Welsh reader as insulting. Some of its distaste is sectarian:

> Is there no passion in Wales? There is none
> Except in the racked hearts of men like Morgan,
> Condemned to wither and starve in the cramped cell
> Of thought their fathers made them.
> Protestantism – the adroit castrator
> Of art: the bitter negation
> Of song and dance and the heart's innocent joy ...

The poem is not without compassion, but anger rules. The poem, like that valley's text, can be accused of telling a tale which is less than true. The metonymy through which a parish drama is made to stand for a larger national culture is a structural falsification.

Inspirational hatred – sometimes politicised, sometimes not – is only one strand, though a strongly woven one, in the web of R. S. Thomas's poetry. Many of his religious poems do the things 'A Small Window', 'The Minister' and some of the peasant poems do not: tentatively imagine, and mix wryness or bitterness with hope, humour, praise and affection. The religious poetry successfully imagines a God, or scrupulously imagines the possibility of prayer and faith, under hard stress or against heavy odds. This kind of imaginative striving contrasts strikingly with the confident and uncharitable emotions in the poems with human or humane subjects (or objects). Thomas's poetry is much better at contemplating or approaching God than at contemplating or approaching human beings. Like Morgan admitting the soft bog-cotton bloom, one must be fair: there are many poems that seem to strive towards the sense that human beings, like Iago Prytherch, are more complex than the poet has made them in his characters. There is occasionally a poem, like the splendid lyric 'Song for Gwydion' (*Song at the Year's Turning*), which imagines and binds together extremities of love as well as pain.

Gwydion was a bard and a brilliant magician, and for his Gwydion the poet imagines the loss of innocence as an enlargement of simple or single vision, beautifully imaged as the blood sacrifice of a killed trout. Life and death are thoroughly imagined, appropriately in a song for a poet. (And for what seems to be a son's song and a father's song.) The child's growth is rendered with physical tact and love: 'the soft flesh was forming / Quietly as snow on the bare boughs of bone'. It is imagined as fed by its nourishing opposite, the killed fish. The animal's dying is imaged, with compassion and sensuous precision, as a dulling of eyes, a fading of the 'beautiful, blithe garland / Of stipples', and the poem imaginatively enters the act of death, as the fish leaves its element and 'light shocked the brain'. It is interesting that a poem which is about imagination should possess a sensuous richness not often found in this poet's work. Apt, too, is the fellow-feeling the bard in the poem has for the inhuman phenomenal world: 'From whose chill lips the water song had flown'. There are Christian as well as pagan undertones, but Christ the fish coexists with a wonderfully familiar and defamiliarised creaturely presence. One could suggest that certain experiences as a priest, as an English speaker acquiring Welsh, as a writer wounded by the English words and constructions he uses, have encouraged a political poetry whose didacticism and polemic have narrowed and darkened the poet's affective range, but since propagandist poetry needs and flourishes on such narrowing and darkening, such speculation would be circular and profitless. I would add, as a postscript, my sense that 'Song for Gwydion' has a sweetness, as well as a bittersweetness, which shows itself in a conspicuously stylised, structured, musical and rich texture, resembling traditional Welsh poetry more than the balder and more prosaic poems about rural Wales and the peasants. It has a marked balance and antithetical structure, and a delighted natural imagery, which link it with some of R. S. Thomas's beautiful translations from Welsh, like 'Night and Morning' and 'The Cry of Elisha after Elijah'. I do not want to sentimentalise this most unsentimental poet (though hate, as well as love, can have softness and excesses) but I suggest that he may be most Welsh when he is least nationalist. 'Song for Gwydion' is a regional poem – historically, culturally, even perhaps geographically – of a most subtle kind.

II

A cradle Welsh poet, not a convert, Dylan Thomas is at ease with his Welshness, relaxed in a deep sense of region. There are no traces in his poetry of national pride, nor of its familiar, national self-deprecation, nor of national defensiveness and defence. His feelings about being Welsh in England, and English in Wales, though true enough to his own experience and that of other frequent crossers of the border, and his jokes about being remote from the Welshness of the mining valleys, Welsh costume and Welsh language, also a fair response in time and place, are surface growths of observation and memory. They do not go deep enough for poetry. He is a poet of region, not nation. His regionalism is in no way obsessive, and praises a composite beloved landscape and seascape. The praise works reticently and impartially. His poetry is not, I think, Welsh, except in that radical and complex sense in which good poetry is rooted in all the times and places of sensuous and emotional experience. R. S. Thomas says that he cannot write poetry in Welsh, and he would like to, because he acquired the language too late, and feels the deprivation as a wound. Born outside Wales, and gradually moving further into its geographical, social and linguistic depth, he has come relatively late to region as well as language, and perhaps his poetry shows traces of regional deprivation. Of course, one can turn violently against the childhood country, but R. S. Thomas's distaste for Welsh weather, for instance, seems to me to be a visitor's grumbling; his ability to put down a Welsh natural sublime is very unWelsh; and his rejections of the landscape are usually polemic.

Dylan Thomas drinks from a deep well, and takes care to keep its waters pure. Jokes and caricatures and sociologies he keeps for prose and *Under Milk Wood*. The prose and the poetry have some common superficial features, which might be loosely called Welsh. In prose and poetry he tends to be fast, fluent, talkative, rich, musical, excited, even rapturous. But in poetry he moves behind or beyond Welsh surfaces. Although R. S. Thomas's minister Morgan tells us he had the *hwyl*, that roll, rise, carol and creation (as Hopkins put it) is not given utterance, but summarised in brief narration. Strong feeling is a norm in Dylan Thomas, who creates a hyperbolic language for praise, of which he is clearly conscious. The consciousness exercises control. 'The lovely gift of the gab' is both used and criticised in 'After the Funeral', which is specifically Welsh in style and subject. The subject of elegy, Ann Jones, died when Thomas was an adult, and the poem significantly splits the poet as mourner in two. One is a larger-than-life figure, the poet writing elegy and epitaph, the other a boy watching and crying. The desolate boy 'who slits his throat/In the dark of the coffin and sheds dry leaves' isn't essential to the poem's action, but acts as a bridge-figure to connect the poet with his childhood. The death is part of adult experience but the responses to front-parlour Welshness, and Welsh funeral rites, are specified in close-up detail. The hideous sacred objects, stuffed fox and stale potted fern, are doubly dead. The funeral blinds and mourning are imaged in jokes and exaggerations: 'blinds down the lids, the teeth in black'. These metaphors are common in *Under Milk Wood* but here they are modulated, assimilated into the elegy through grotesque transference, 'spittled eyes, the salt ponds in the sleeves', and other images of a childlike and bizarre melancholia:

> The spittled eyes, the salt ponds in the sleeves,
> Morning smack of the spade that wakes up sleep,
> Shakes a desolate boy who slits his throat
> In the dark of the coffin and sheds dry leaves ...

The gap between Thomas's first unsympathetic response to Ann Jones's death and this poem of laments and praise, was probably filled by that boy, whose half-jokey, half-miserable responses start a complex emotional trajectory, moving through an adult emotional exaggeration, to attempts at imagining the dead woman. The schoolboy humour was perhaps a way into a childhood scene, and thence to a mood of imaginative comprehension. Hyperbole is marked in the first mention of Wales:

> I stand, for this memorial's sake, alone
> In the snivelling hours with dead, humped Ann
> Whose hooded, fountain heart once fell in puddles
> Round the parched worlds of Wales ....

Here he makes Ann a kind of schoolboy version of the Fisher King, plainly enjoying that joke about the parched worlds – compare the rain always raining in R. S. Thomas's Wales. More important, he develops two strands of language: the conceit which starts as a wisecrack grows into exaggeration and conceit. But often language contains a criticism of its own loftiness, which is rejected as unthought-out or imprecise ('blindly magnified'), inept ('her death was a still drop'), and unwanted ('she would lie dumb and deep / And need no druid of her broken body'). The self-conscious critical insertion does not change the hyperbole by toning it down, but lets it continue, defiantly: 'But I, Ann's bard on a raised hearth, call all / The seas to service'. The poem promotes the exaltation of elegy, which is metonymised as a gigantic marble monument, but constantly keeps in mind the dimensions of the meek, hardlabouring, narrowly religious 'real' woman. There are two languages at the beginning, schoolboy-humorous and grave, and a divided style is elaborated. Each kind is metaphorical, but one announced as hyperbolic: 'Her flesh was meek as milk' is given its opposite and response, 'this skyward statue / With the wild breast and blessed and giant skull'. The closely observed and keenly recalled 'scrubbed and sour humble hands' meet 'these cloud-sopped, marble hands', gravely converting the clever joke into a tender appositeness as soap suds become cloud-lather, in the kind of conceit which allowed Donne to make a joke about lovers breathing each other's breath. This is not only a poem describing a particularly Welsh funeral, but one which mentions Wales, goes into some social or anthropological detail, and indicts in a brief bitter word that narrow and fanatical religion R. S. Thomas blames in 'The Minister'. Ann's scrubbed and sour humble hands 'Lie with religion in their cramp': the gesture of a working woman's arthritic hands is delineated realistically and at the same time acts as metaphor for a cramping religion. Welsh poverty and Welsh religion are causally linked through the witty interchange of vehicle and tenor – all in one stroke. The act of appraising and praising the dead is done in Welsh terms. Even the stylistic mannerism is Welsh: Thomas probably learnt whatever he knew about Welsh prosody from Gerard Manley Hopkins, whose poetry took on a new syntax and music when he started to learn Welsh at St Beuno's; and 'After the Funeral' has some fine effects of internal and linked assonance and alliteration, derivations from *cynganedd*. It is probably the poet's most Welsh poem, and in it he presents and dramatises himself, child, druid and bard, in a way which licenses, complicates and criticises a richly conceited and extravagant local style of mourning. It creates an elaborate, amusing and touching Welsh *occupatio*.

There are one or two mediocre poems with a Welsh subject-matter, published posthumously, like the comic epistle 'New Quay', which has fun with Jones the Cake, a 'hymning Gooseberry', who is first cousin to R. S. Thomas's randy deacon Davies, though more rudely sexual: 'His head's in a nest where no bird lays her egg' is one of the more polite lines. The randy Welsh are much in evidence, lurking and larking in 'the Welsh lechered / Caves'. This is *Under Milk Wood*'s style of fun and games, a regionalised seaside postcard, knickers and all. It has an ingenious dirty joke version of cramped religion as 'the Bethel-worm', generous at last, puts his penny in 'the moist collection plate'. Many of the things R. S. Thomas dislikes about the Welsh Dylan Thomas sees, but finds them funny, and keeps them out of his poetry.

The image-bank of childhood memory contained the sweep of Swansea Bay and Town Hill, 'blue distances' of Gower, some birdlife, and a few buildings. There is Cefn Coed, the psychiatric hospital on a hill, starkly visible and once commonly referred to in the town as 'the asylum', until the mere place-name became a sinister metonymy. There is the Grammar School, on Mount Pleasant Hill, and on at least one occasion allusively said to be on 'Heaven's Hill', in an ironic deflation of pastoral image only intelligible to natives. And there is the now famous Cwmdonkin Park, where Thomas played as a boy, and where, as a watcher from his house in Cwmdonkin Drive, he saw, and imagined, children at play. (One small image, 'Star-shaped', is a delighted rendering of cartwheeling playfulness.) These Swansea images were joined by the inland pastoral farm and farm animals of Fernhill, celebrated in many poems, directly and indirectly. Later were added the sea and estuarine shapes, birds and countryside of Laugharne, like Fernhill in what was once Carmarthenshire. These scenes and images slowly accumulated to compound memories and sensations. They become sublimed, impersonalised and generalised, but retain sensuousness. They are saturated in praise and delight, to form a map of the mind which is made out of Welsh things but never nationalistic, and not even precisely regional. Landscape and seascape are remade.

In 'The Hunchback in the Park', Thomas uses, distinctly and not compositely, images from Cwmdonkin – its gate, bell, drinking-fountain, hunchback, seats, games, groves, rockery, lake, willows, railings and grass. The real Swansea park, which has changed but keeps the fountain and groves, is of interest to topographically minded scholars and biographers, but the salient features of the park in the poem are not Welsh. Thomas is using a familiar peopled landscape, containing young and old, the children and down-and-outs of all parks, to create a poem about creativity. He collates the creativity of the playing boys, miming sailors in fun or the hunchback in malice, the creativity of the hunchback who builds his sublimated ideal form, a woman figure straight as an elm, and the creativity of a vision which makes and remakes the park itself. This is regional invention, not mimesis. Like 'After the Funeral', it is an artistically reflexive poem. Its subjects – creativity, loneliness and need, the collision and identity of young and old – are located in the archetypal park, but happen to be particularised in this one. Though the real park now contains a Dylan Thomas Memorial water-garden, with a memorial stone quoting 'Time held me green and dying / But I sang in my chains like the sea', the park poem is not even called Cwmdonkin. He loved the park as a place, in and beyond childhood, but when it was bombed in the blitz of Swansea, and at least one bomb fell on the reservoir, Thomas does not mention it, nor any Swansea bombings, in the war poems in *Deaths and Entrances*. Instead, he mourns a London casualty in 'A Refusal to Mourn the Death, By Fire, of a Child in London'. The lament is dignified by a sense of London's region, wonderfully sustained in the image of 'the unmourning water / Of the riding Thames'. Thomas refuses to nationalise war and its deaths. Like so much of his poetry the poem draws on biblical imagery, even specifying a chapel name, familiar in South Wales, as 'the round Zion', but this particular is generalised by the addition of 'synagogue of the ear of corn', and even the Swansea chapel has to take a place in an English region.

In the 'Author's Prologue', later called 'Prologue' prefaced to *Collected Poems*, Thomas uses the Welsh word for hill, 'Bryn' (which even non-Welsh speakers know because it is familiarised in place names, like Cefn Bryn, a hill in Gower), and a Welsh form, 'Dai mouse'. This poem uses the conceit of Noah's ark as its image of creativity, joining the funeral monument and carving, the park, games and mimicry, as metaphors for the poet's art and craft. The flood is located in Wales, streaming over the 'Sheep white hollow farms: to Wales in my arms', at the centre of the poems, where rhymes meet, to start branching apart until the last line rhymes with the first, in *rime riche* ('now'), flaunted but not always noticed, in this rhyming *tour de force*. It is a Laugharne poem, timed at summer's end, 'In my seashaken house', and with the castle in view. The poet summons a familiar bestiary to his ark – gulls, pipers, cockles, crows, geese, salmon, curlew, heron and others. The poet in the poem is a good Noah because Noah built, and drank too much. The animals are listed rather than specified but the rooks are 'dark Welsh and reverent'. There are several references to Wales, but though it is a local poem, its subject is a brilliant biblical and literary joke about the poet and poetry. It calls what he makes 'Hubbub and fiddled', imaging the poem as tune 'On a tongued puffball' and patch work. The fields are called holy, because the poem joins an affection for an abstracted, though affectionately hailed, fauna, to a delight in his favourite subject of poetry.

Another poem of generalised region is the ironic elegy, 'Sir John's Hill', which images and animates the Laugharne landscape, specifying 'the tear of the Towy' (ambiguous only to the eye) but uses the regional flora and fauna to create a self-conscious fable in which roles are assigned, and reassigned, sometimes aptly, sometimes arbitrarily and playfully. The hawk is victim and killer; the hill fulfils the role of judge the better for having a black cap of jackdaws at its summit. It is amusingly extravagant in celebratory apostrophe, reworking biblical languages and Christian rituals. It uses region to present cruel and triumphant nature and within its scene and story the poet places the character of 'young Aesop', a narrator who fables but also engraves and sings, as the poet is doing in this musical allegory. The poem is well aware that region is being displaced, enlarged and drawn on to demonstrate habits of affirmation, praise, and fondness. The Towy estuary is made strange.

In 'Fernhill', a romantic celebration of the holiness of the heart's affections, Thomas does not allegorise but playfully gilds the landscape of the farm with radiance. This poem, which always reminds me of Chagall's rainbow canvasses and creatures, creates images of making in musical instruments, games and singing. It contains a rare example of a favourite Welsh intensifier, 'Lovely and watery' (Welsh to the Welsh but not to the English reader), but the poem creates a region made sacred by childhood, surrealised and abstracted. It metamorphoses the objects of Thomas's known and familiar landscape, using the region for more than regional poetry. The 'autobiographical' imprinting of the sea and country images makes plain that the early habits of affection, created early, continue to warm and fire experience into poetry.

A poem that uses and also discusses this regional imprinting is 'Poem in October', where the primal landscape is the site for imagined travel in time and place:

It turned away from the blithe country
And down the other air and the blue altered sky
    Streamed again a wonder of summer
            With apples
        Pears and red currants
And I saw in the turning so clearly a child's
Forgotten mornings when he walked with his mother
        Through the parables
            Of sun light
    And the legends of the green chapels

    And the twice told fields of infancy
That his tears burned my cheeks and his heart moved in mine.
    These were the woods the river the sea
            Where a boy
        In the listening

Summertime of the dead whispered the truth of his joy
To the trees and the stones and the fish in the tide.
      And the mystery
        Sang alive
   Still in the water and singingbirds.

The fields of infancy are more than twice told. The poem says
simply and clearly that the imprint, deepened by accumulating
birthdays, was made by joy, an emotion compounded of rapture
and freedom and aroused by the phenomenal world, family
affections and religious pieties. This time a celebration of a past is
made explicit, as the poet speaks of joy's origins and continuities,
sensuously particularised in natural (and regional) images but also
generalised and abstracted. Sensations remembered join and blur,
layered in time. The religious images, for instance, are signifiers of
the natural phenomena, and natural images are used to symbolise
religion: 'parables of sun light / And the legends of the green
chapels'. We are explicitly told of the level below conscious recall
at which these continuities are created by a Wordsworthian
natural piety and recreation. The vital child in this poem is the
ecstatic mouthpiece for the origin of creativity, imaged as the
singer. The subjects of continuity and stability are brilliantly joined
in the oxymoron:

> And I saw in the turning so clearly a child's
> Forgotten mornings ...

Region must be remembered and forgotten.

8

The View from the North: Region and Nation in *The Silver Darlings* and *A Scots Quair*

THOMAS CRAWFORD

A NOTE ON THEORY

Any discussion of regional literature implies a mimetic theory of art – that there are, 'out there', objectively existing regions that can be plotted on a map, and that the writer's attempt to define his region involves him in some kind of mirroring or reflection. This holds good even when the region has an invented name: Yoknapatawpha County bears a recognisable relation to a particular area of the southern United States, Hardy's Wessex to the south-west of England, and Gibbon's Kinraddie, Segget and Duncairn to parts of the Mearns, to Aberdeen, and even – very slightly – to Dundee.

It is remotely possible that a writer might have an idealist concept of nationhood, but hardly, I feel sure, of region. 'What individuals feel in their hearts *is* the nation', wrote Achad Ha'am. Once it came into existence, national feeling was for him independent of external or objective actuality. 'If I feel the spirit of Jewish nationality in my heart so that it stamps all my inward life with its seal, then the spirit of Jewish nationality exists in me; and its existence is not at an end even if all my Jewish contemporaries should cease to feel it in their hearts.'[1] One can easily conceive of a poet, dramatist or novelist creating a character or a persona like Achad Ha'am, who would behave in accord with Renan's formulation that 'a nation is a soul, a spiritual principle',[2] particularly if the work were a psychological study of a person fixated on an entirely imaginary entity, or else an anti-nationalist satire written from a cosmopolite point of view. But it seems almost impossible to extend these definitions to the other term in our discussion – region.

'What individuals feel in their hearts is the region', 'a region is a soul, a spiritual principle': I do not think I am speaking in the spirit of Dr Johnson kicking the stone when I say these statements seem to me almost nonsensical. A person may feel an intense love for the region he was born in or to which he has migrated, but that region, whether upland country or capital city, is a geographical, cultural, and historical entity, and it is such features that first occur to us whenever we think of 'region'. Something like both these emotions was no doubt felt by countless Jews of the diaspora – an emotional attachment to Galicia or Yorkshire or Granada or wherever they happened to live, and an intense feeling for an ideal Jewish nation, transferred today to the real nation of Israel located in the historic homeland. And a third loyalty or commitment was often present, to the nation their region was part of – to Austria, or England, or Russia, or Spain.

The orthodox English treatment of the national question just before mid-century, H. M. Chadwick's,[3] seems unhelpful to the literary historian, and the most distinguished of recent academic accounts, Ernest Gellner's, still owes a lot to the idealism of Renan or Achad Ha'am. 'It is nationalism', Gellner writes, 'which engenders nations, and not the other way round.' Thus for him it is a set of doctrines and emotions that come first, not organised communities living in specific areas. True, he admits that 'nationalism uses the previously inherited proliferation of cultures or cultural wealth, though it uses them very selectively, and it most often transforms them radically' (*Nations and Nationalism* (1983) p. 55); and that nationalism is for him the creation of a particular era, 'the historical period from the French Revolution onwards'. Of all the accounts treated in Anthony D. Smith's *Theories of Nationalism* (2nd edn, 1983), the various Marxist ones seem the most useful and – irony of ironies, in view of his later career – none is more serviceable than Stalin's (*Marxism and the National Question*, 1913). It may well be, as the most recent study (Ronaldo Munck, *The Difficult Dialogue: Marxism and Nationalism*, 1986) maintains, that Stalin's famous definition of a nation is characterised by 'formalism and reductionism' and an 'undialectical and scholastic approach' (p. 77), but it nevertheless provides an admirable starting point for our discussion:

> A nation is a historically evolved, stable community of language, territory, economic life and psychological make-up manifested in a community of culture. (Joseph Stalin, *Marxism and the National Question* (1945) p. 11)

By 'historically evolved', Stalin meant that nations arose by a long process of evolution out of previous tribal and other ethnic groups, and we can surely accept this even if we do not agree with him that there were no true nations before capitalism began to develop – 'a nation is not merely a historical category, but a historical category belonging to a definite epoch, the epoch of rising capitalism'; 'the national movement ... is essentially a bourgeois movement' (p. 24). Certainly, all the features listed by Stalin are also present in regions. Almost every region has some kind of difference in language or dialect from neighbouring regions; its boundaries are geographically determined; it has its own subordinate economic and social structure centred in a provincial town or, as in Germany and the USA, a state capital; its people have their own psychological peculiarities (Sicilian vindictiveness, Cockney humour); its cultural variants include both material culture (building in brick or stone, scattered or nucleated villages, roofing in thatch, slate or tile), clothing (for example, in Scandinavia, variants of 'national costume'), and spiritual culture (predominance of certain religious groupings like the 'Wee Frees' in Lewis and the Catholics in Barra); particular folk dances, painted ikons, inn signs, sports and games, musical instruments and groupings (brass bands, massed choirs). Applying the Stalin definition, apparently so simple, to regions as well as to nations enables us to see that *all* its features necessarily apply to regions, whereas a nation can possibly get by without a territory (the Jews of the diaspora) and may even have fewer linguistic differentials (Australia, New Zealand, English-speaking Canada) than many a region (Buchan dialect as compared with south-west Scots). In certain circumstances religious differentials are important for nationality (Poland, southern Ireland, the Jews) – a fact which Stalin was reluctant to recognise.

W. B. Yeats was early aware that the creative writer may well have a series of loyalties extending from the smallest to the largest unit – indeed, he included the Deity in his series:

> To the greater poets everything they see has its relation to the national life, and through that to the universal and divine life:

nothing is an isolated artistic moment; there is a unity everywhere; everything fulfills a purpose that is not its own; the
hailstone is a journeyman of God; the grass blade carries the
universe upon its point. But to this universalism, this seeing of
unity everywhere, you can only attain through what is near you,
your nation, or, if you be no traveller, your village and the
cobwebs on your walls. You can no more have the greater poetry
without a nation than religion without symbols. One can only
reach out to the universe with a gloved hand – that glove is one's
nation, the only thing one knows even a little of.

(2 September 1888)

And today the writer may relate beyond the region and the nation
to larger human organisations, such as Europe; if he belongs to an
English-speaking country, to 'Anglo-Saxon' culture, broadly considered; and surely, in this age when human life itself is under
threat, to the species we all belong to and 'the great globe itself'.

NEIL GUNN, *THE SILVER DARLINGS*

One of the most important qualities that *A Scots Quair*[4] and *The
Silver Darlings*[5] have in common is that both are at least partly epic
in intention, both have an epic dimension. Both make use of
modes and structures that are older than the novel and will outlast
it: myth, allegory, folk narrative and folk speech, and poetically
organised patterns and symbols. Both, in terms of the quotation
from Yeats, reach out towards universalism through the gloved
hands of region and nation; both try to know a wider community
by first knowing the nation, the cobwebs on the walls, the
drudgery of ploughing and milking, the planks of the boats and
the salt drops from coiled nets. And both, like all true epics, are
concerned with history.

By the time *The Silver Darlings* came out in 1941 Gunn had eight
novels and one book of short stories behind him, not to speak of
articles, plays and a book on whisky. Two of the novels, *Morning
Tide* (1931) and *Highland River* (1937) were centred on a boy's first
awareness of nature, his family, and himself, which were also the
subject of that truly beautiful work published the year after *The
Silver Darlings* – *Young Art and Old Hector*. In these three novels,

and in varying degrees in all the others, there occur moments when 'the grass blade carries the universe upon its point' (only sometimes the universe is carried by the salmon in the pool, which the young boy has to catch with his bare hands), where 'the hailstone is the journeyman of God' (only more often it is the hazel-nut), but such moments are not in the last analysis isolated, for it is through them that the character – boy or man – perceives that 'there is a unity everywhere' and that 'everything fulfils a purpose that is not its own'. In Gunn's terminology they are 'moments of delight', and it is through such heightened moments that a character becomes aware of his true personality, which turns out to be not *merely* individual, but something independent of the accidents of education and culture, and even to a certain extent of time, though not, I think, of place. A person's true personality is archetypal, primitive – that of hunter or fisher, maker, searcher, or gazer on bright water; and if he is to retain his integrity it will remain the same for all his days, not changing or developing except in the most superficial of senses, but shining perpetually within him at the still point. Of course, there are other moments too – moments of anguish, moments of betrayal, that are equally significant; but it is moments of delight that seem most characteristic for Gunn, just as 'spots of time' were for Wordsworth.

In *The Silver Darlings* the childish moment that stands out above all others is not a moment of delight but of guilt, when little Finn acts out the Fall of Man, the end of innocence and the coming of evil. Like everything else in the book the incident has epical overtones. (Finn's name, of course, has epical significance – the name of the Celtic hero Finn MacCoull – and serves to link what at first sight appears a purely regional novel with a culture that goes back beyond that of any fully developed, post-Renaissance nation to the culture of the 'nationalities', as Stalin called them, and tribal groupings out of which modern nations were made). I am referring to Chapter V, 'Finn and the Butterfly', where the four-and-a-half-year-old boy's crossing the burn and his chase of the 'white fool' begin a delightful variation on the necessity of the chase for the epic hero. Finn's unmotivated killing of the butterfly is a moral archetype for the deliberate choice of evil, and it is given an extra twist by the parallel to another embryonic hero, the son of Coriolanus. In *Coriolanus* I.iii.60–5 Valeria, a visiting matron, tells Virgilia, Coriolanus' wife, how she saw her son run after a gilded butterfly:

and when he caught it, he let it go again; and after it again; and over and over he comes, and up again; catched it again; or whether his fall enraged him, or how 'twas, he did so set his teeth and tear it. O, I warrant, how he mammocked it!

Gunn's episode is not just a revelation of character, of *genetically* determined characteristics, as Shakespeare's is: it moves over into allegory and myth. When Finn rests after chasing the butterfly it is in the ruined church known as the 'House of Peace', where previously his mother Catrine and Roddie, the man she is later to marry, have had their first tentative communion; and when he rests there, he lies down on his right side, pulls his knees up into the foetal position, and 'hid his face with his arms and hands, whimpering as into his mother's bosom in the moment before sleep overtakes. The earth's bosom was warm with the sun and soon little Finn was sound asleep' (p. 95). Thus Catrine is identified with the Earth, just as in *A Scots Quair* Chris Guthrie is equated with the Land; Roddie in Gunn's book with the Sea; and the boy with epic heroism and hardship.

One of the most remarkable achievements of *The Silver Darlings* is the way in which its mythic structure does not obscure the developing personal relations between Kirsty (Finn's grandmother), Catrine, Roddie and Finn; between Finn and the girl in Lewis who had the same name as his mother; and between Finn and Una, the girl he is to marry. (The name Una is presumably Gaelic and Irish Oonagh; is 'one alone'; and may also carry associations from the romance-epic *The Faerie Queene*.) Even more remarkable is the way the mythic structure does not overwhelm the sense of *community*, of a rich and developing social entity which pervades the book, so different from the ingrown twistedness of Barbie in George Douglas Brown's *The House with the Green Shutters*. This is because Finn, in so far as he is representative, does not stand for 'the spirit of his race' in any mechanical, abstract way – nor does Catrine, nor does Roddie, but for the very best qualities of the community of Dunster itself – at work, at play, fighting the elements, worshipping God, and puzzling theology.

We notice this at an early stage, in chapters vii and viii, when the developing child is seen as in and of the community as well as in and of the family. Chapter VII begins with 'There were no fewer than five marriages that autumn'; with Roddie's toast to 'the silver darlings' (the herring) and his mocking statement 'I have married the sea' (p. 133): a positive assertion negated (but only tentatively) by his noncommittal meeting with Catrine later in the chapter and her slight nervousness. At that meeting, the dialogue is deliberately banal:

Catrine was waiting for them when they came out ['them' are Roddie, Don (one of Roddie's crew), and Finn. They have been drinking at a refreshment booth – the men whisky, Finn a ginger ale]. Her smile was a little awkward as she tried to dissemble her concern. 'I was frightened you had got lost,' she said, looking reproachfully at Finn.

'Why would he get lost?' asked Don. 'Surely the poor fellow can have a drink with the rest. Eh, Finn? Are you going home with your mother or are you sticking by Roddie and me?'

'Come, Finn,' said Catrine.

Finn hesitated. Roddie and Don laughed. 'That's the boy!' said Don. 'Away home, woman of the house, and leave the young man to enjoy himself. The fun hasn't started yet.'

'Come, Finn,' said Catrine firmly. She took his hand.

'Finn, Finn, my boy,' said Don, shaking his head,'that's what they do to you.'

'Have you sold?' asked Roddie [that is, has Catrine sold her produce].

'Yes, I'm glad to say,' replied Catrine. 'And at a good price.'

'Kirsty will be pleased!'

'Yes,' Catrine nodded.   (p. 143)

In spite of its extreme banality, Don's part of the dialogue hints with the greatest economy at the male and female roles in the community and how they are established. Immediately after the last piece of dialogue quoted, Catrine's monosyllabic 'Yes', there follows a description which presents her through the eyes of both men, but more particularly through Roddie's:

She was somehow a little constrained now and looked extremely attractive. Her eyes in the sun were not dark, they were nut-brown, a fathomless brown, shot through with light. Her mouth made any other woman's prim and pale. 'Thank you very much,' she said, flushing a trifle as she felt the men's eyes, 'and particularly for looking after Finn.'

'Really going?' asked Roddie.

'Yes, oh yes. I must.'   (p. 143)

We feel that although Roddie is responding in the same way as the other man to this female personality, so obviously *there*, there is an extra intensity to his reaction, and that it is *his* observation that 'her mouth made any other woman's prim and pale'; we feel that *his* perception of her has a richness denied to Dan, and to any others who may be standing around. And when, on the next page, Catrine and Finn have gone home, they have a dialogue about how nice Roddie is, how when Finn grows up he wants to be just like Roddie and be a skipper, and how Mama does not want him to go to sea because people who go to sea get drowned and the sea is an angry cruel place (p. 144). The personal and the archetypal are here blended with the greatest delicacy. The movement of the chapter has been from the community (five marriages) to Roddie's 'marriage to the Sea', to intimations of attraction between the Sea Hero Roddie and the Earth Woman Catrine, to the bitter tears she sheds at necessity and fate at the end of the Chapter (p. 145). It is not that the community is *background* for private feelings; it is rather a setting that is inseparably wedded to them – fate is at work in Caithness as it is in Hardy's Wessex. Another movement in the chapter has been from community to private feelings to these feelings as universal emotions within a predetermined condition of men; and it is, moreover, the movement of the book as a whole. There are only thirteen pages in the chapter, yet they manage very skilfully to convey the bustle and throng of the market, the excitement of haggling with dealers, all the fun of the fair. Connections are unobtrusively made with other things: the crowd is linked with the solitary landscape in which Finn has chosen an evil thing – he is just as afraid of the tumultuous dark forest of the crowd as he had been of the silent wood (p. 136). This moment of fear is overcome, through struggle; then there is a moment of awe when he sees the wonderful mound of trumpets, followed by a second moment of fear before the trumpet Roddie has bought him. But Roddie, his precursor as Hero, shows him how to blow, 'and the trumpet sounded loud and high, clearing a path for itself over the world' (p. 139). It is a moment of assertion – the assertion of the heroic personality against the background of the crowd, whose champion he will become. There are two other moments in the scene, each of delight; the first, when Finn wins a brooch, under Roddie's guidance, by putting a marble in the correct slot; the second, when Finn glories in Roddie getting his money back by hitting a knob with a hammer that causes an iron pointer to run up a mast and ring a bell at the top; the third, later, when Finn gives his brooch to his mother.

In *The Silver Darlings*, then, an all-pervading spirit of epic operates at many levels. It is there in the book as a whole at the level of history, in the struggle of the community to create the herring industry on the coasts of the Moray Firth – a community of crofters evicted from their inland glens and pastures. It is there in the individual episodes we have examined, and in almost every other chapter in the book. It is there in Catrine's journey into a strange country after her first husband, Tormad, is taken from her. It is there in her giving birth to Finn in the straw; it is there in Finn's barefoot tramp of thirty miles to fetch a doctor for Kirsty during the cholera epidemic. It is there in the first venture of the Dunster boat beyond the Moray Firth to Stornoway: Chapter XIV, 'Out to Sea', is a miniature Odyssey-episode encompassing Homeric parallels like the whirlpool of the Wells (p. 283) and Rob's old salt's tales; it is there in the chapter entitled 'Storm and Precipice' (Chapter XV), a little epic of the physical in which the antagonism between Roddie and Finn – between the son and the man who will later marry his mother – is played out against the rest of the crew; and the climax is Finn's ascent of a sheer precipice when they try to put in at a deserted island to get water for the thirst-tormented Callum. It is there (Chapter XVII) in the tremendous fight between Roddie and Big Angus, the Stornoway bully. It is there in Finn's extraordinary luck when he alone strikes a great shoal of herring at the end of the book: 'Now Finn felt like a great hunter, like the leader of hunting men. Assurance of his strength and power was in him like a song' (p. 57). But it is not *completely* there in the structure of the book as a whole, because its movement is from the heroic to the idyllic; it ends like comedy on the eve of marriage, in an almost pastoral atmosphere, on the knoll of the House of Peace where a ruined chapel stood; indeed, the House of Peace has a role rather like that of the Standing Stones in *Sunset Song*. And it ends on a beautiful note of irony. On the night before his wedding Finn has retreated there so that his comrades and crewman would not 'put him through certain heathenish practices', as Gunn puts it (p. 582). The great hunter has himself become the hunted. After visualising himself as an old man, the head of a tribe, he became aware of stealthy, climbing sounds. Finn's body drew taut, heaved up on to supporting palms. Whisperings, the movement of the top of a small birch-tree here and there whose trunk invisible hands gripped. The hunters in their primordial humour were closing in. Life had come for him.   (p. 584)

The life that comes for Finn is in part the happiness of Benedick the married man, the prelude to the founding of a clan; it is parallel to the ending of the greatest of all epic novels, *War and Peace*, when Pierre and Natasha, 'world-continuing' personalities like the peasants, settle down to their fecund marriage. At the end of each book we look beyond its action – in *War and Peace* to the Decembrist conspiracy of 1825 in which Pierre and Nicholas will probably take part, in *The Silver Darlings* to Finn's future as skipper, leader of men, and founder of a tribe. Whatever else it may be, *The Silver Darlings* is a glorious celebration of patriarchy.

LEWIS GRASSIC GIBBON, *A SCOTS QUAIR*

The whole *Scots Quair* trilogy is nothing if not tidily constructed. It is in three books corresponding to the youth, adulthood, and middle age of the heroine. Each has its characteristic husband (farmer, minister, poet-craftsman); each has its characteristic community – country estate with its farms and crofts, small town, commercial and industrial city. Each of these corresponds to three stages in the development not just of the north-east region nor of Scotland the nation, but of western Europe as a whole.

Each book has four sections. The four divisions of *Sunset Song* refer to the cycle of the farming year – ploughing, drilling, seed-time, harvest. Those of *Cloud Howe* indicate four increasingly sombre cloud formations – cirrus, cumulus, stratus, nimbus. And those of *Grey Granite* bear the names of minerals arranged in ascending order of hardness and purity – epidote, sphene, apatite, zircon.

The men in the heroine's life fit into these emblem groups. Chris's father, John Guthrie, and her first husband, Ewan Tavendale, are quintessential men of the land. In *Cloud Howe* the disillusion of her second husband, the Reverend Robert Colquhoun, follows the growing darkness of the clouds: and both his liberal Christianity and his social democracy have a cloudiness about them too. Her son, young Ewan, develops in *Grey Granite* all the stony hardness appropriate to the Communist Hero of the 1930s.

One major difference between the books is in the sphere of language. As far as possible Gunn uses an early twentieth-century colloquial Highland English to render the dialogue of his Gaelic speakers of 1825–40. But Gibbon in his prefatory note to *Sunset Song* brings the nature of his linguistic experiment squarely before the reader:

> If the great Dutch language disappeared from literary usage and a Dutchman wrote in German a story of the Lekside peasants, one may hazard he would ask and receive a certain latitude and forbearance in his usage of German. He might import into his pages some score or so untranslatable words and idioms – untranslatable except in their context and setting; he might mould in some fashion his German to the rhythms and cadence of the kindred speech that his peasants speak. Beyond that, in fairness to his hosts, he hardly could go – to seek effect by a spray of apostrophes would be both impertinence and mistranslation.
>
> The courtesy that the hypothetical Dutchman might receive from German a Scot may invoke from the great English tongue.

Gibbon is here claiming that the pages that follow are in a national language, not a regional dialect. The parallel to Scots is 'the great Dutch language'; though it may be dying, we are meant to think of it as equal to 'the great English tongue'. Gibbon creates a highly unusual medium in *Sunset Song*; instead of an absolute division between English for narrative and description and often fairly thick dialect for dialogue passages, so often the practice of Scott and Stevenson, lowland Scots is brought into every strand of the texture – narrative, description, and dialogue. A precedent is the rather thin Scots of the first-person narrative of Galt's *Annals of the Parish*.

With Gibbon, action and comment are not those of one person only but of several. In *Sunset Song* the main voices are those of the heroine, Chris Guthrie, and an anonymous folk narrator who often seems to embody the negative side of that rural community whose passing Gibbon is mourning – its narrow-mindedness, its meanness, its suspicion of those who are merely different and 'individual'.[6] In *Cloud Howe* Chris's voice and point of view are still dominant but, as W. K. Malcolm has pointed out, 'the rustic narrative voice, which in *Sunset Song* incorporated various – mainly unspecified – personae, now acquires a representative capacity which generalises the experience described'[7] – that is, there is *one* narrative voice, representative of a small-town petty bourgeoisie becoming united against the threat of the proletarian spinners. In *Grey Granite*, set in the industrial city of Duncairn, Chris's voice, though still heard, is not dominant, and – I quote W. K. Malcolm once again – 'the customary anonymity of the narrator who relates the experience of the typical "keelie" deliberately degenerates into a vague facelessness' (p. 154). Gibbon now has to deal with whole groups of people, such as factory workers on the job and a mass of marching demonstrators. Thus there are many voices in the proletarian sections, all of them, however, basically the same, as befits a class whose traditional virtue is solidarity during struggle. Again, the Scots words in the proletarian narrator's speech are interspersed with general political words like 'contingents' and 'marshalled', as in the description of the Communist march:

Jim Trease had planned the march for the Friday, Broo day, with all the unemployed of Paldy and contingents from Ecclesgriegs and Footforthie and a gang of chaps on the Kirrieben Broo. The main mob marshalled up in the Cowgate, the Communists crying for the folk to join up – *we'll march to the Council and demand admittance, and see the Provost about the P.A.C. ...* Right in front was Big Jim Trease, big and sappy in his shiny blue shirt, beside him the chap he'd been helping of late, Stephen Selden that had been an immigrant to Canada and come back from the starvation there to starve here. The two of them were in the lead of the march, wee Jake Forbes waddling behind, banging the drum, *boomroomroom*, he could play a one-man band on his own, a Red musician, and played at the dances with his meikle white face that had never a smile. And on and up you rumbled through Paldy, clatter of boots on the calsay stones, the sun was shining through drifts of rain, shining you saw it fall on the roofs in long, wavering lines and floodings of rain, queer you'd never seen it look bonny as that.   (*Grey Granite*, pp. 41–2)

That last sentence of urban description seems to lift the consciousness of the anonymous unemployed marcher to Chris's level – it's more like Chris's own voice than anything attained by the *narrators* of the two previous volumes. For that voice at its finest – Chris's – we have to go back to *Sunset Song* and listen to her as a young girl, as in the narrative of the Guthrie family's trek over the hills to their new croft in Kinraddie. The passage is an epic within an epic, a microcosm of the historical migrations of all Scotland's colonisers – and not only Scotland's. The emphasis is on the family unit, and Chris within it aware of her family as individuals. And the style of the first three sentences is hard and objective, epically outside Chris's consciousness.

> Wild weather it was that January and the night on the Slug road smoring with sleet when John Guthrie crossed his family and gear from Aberdeen into the Mearns. Twice the great carts set with their shelvins that rustled still stray binder-twine from September's harvest-home laired in drifts before the ascent of the Slug faced the reluctant horses. Darkness came down like a wet, wet blanket, weariness below it and the crying of the twins to vex John Guthrie.

Then we shift inside Chris's mind:

> Mother called him from her nook in the leading cart, there where she sat with now one twin at the breast and now another, and her skin bare and cold and white and a strand of her rust-gold hair draped down from the darkness about her face into the light of the swinging lantern: *We'd better loosen up at Portlethen and not try the Slug this night.*
> But father swore at that *Damn't to hell, do you think I'm made of silver to put up the night at Portlethen?* and mother sighed and held off the wee twin, Robert, and the milk dripped creamily from the soft, sweet lips of him: *No, we're not made of silver, but maybe we'll lair again and all die of the night.*

The pain and discomfort of their trek over the Slug Road is seen as Chris experienced it, with the emphasis on her freezing knees and aching breasts, until

> she fell to a drowse through the cold, and a strange dream came to her as they plodded up through the ancient hills.

For out of the night ahead of them came running a man, father didn't see him or heed to him, though old Bob in the dream that was Chris's snorted and shied. And as he came he wrung his hands, he was mad and singing, a foreign creature, black-bearded, half-naked he was; and he cried in the Greek *The ships of Pytheas! The ships of Pytheas!* and went by into the smore of the sleet-storm on the Grampian hills, Chris never saw him again, queer dreaming that was. For her eyes were wide open, she rubbed them with never a need of that, if she hadn't been dreaming she must have been daft. They'd cleared the Slug, below was Stonehaven and the Mearns, and far beyond that, miles through the Howe, the twinkling point of light that shone from the flagstaff of Kinraddie.   (*Sunset Song*, pp. 40–2)

The young girl's vision puts her own family in the same position as those Pictish inhabitants of the Mearns who saw the Greek explorers out at sea, and makes us see the Guthrie family expedition, spurred on by bitter economic necessity, in the context of the voyages of ancient adventurers. It also introduces the reverberations of prehistory and diffusionist anthropology which are part of the intellectual texture of the work. (The other main strand is a type of Marxian social analysis and prophecy.)[8]

The note about language which precedes *Sunset Song* makes implicit claims for the book as a national as well as regional novel. Young Chris's famous conflict of language, consciousness, and culture is put before us as a conflict of Scots versus English, not of 'Doric' versus English.[9] Of her father and mother she says:

you wanted the words they'd known and used, forgotten in the far-off youngness of their lives, Scots words to tell to your heart, how they wrung it and held it, the toil of their days and unendingly their fight. And the next minute that passed from you, you were English, back to the English words so sharp and clean and true – for a while, for a while, till they slid so smooth from your throat you knew they could never say anything that was worth the saying at all.   (Ibid., p. 37)

Gibbon means us to think of these words as national, not regional, it is clear. A statement by Robert, her second husband, has often been debated – 'Chris Caledonia, I've married a *nation*!' (*Cloud Howe*, p. 104) – especially when put beside Mowat's remark that when Chris looked at him 'he felt he was stared at by Scotland herself' (ibid., p. 79). Is Gibbon thinking allegorically, or is he not? If an observer says a person is 'Scotland herself', and if the remark applies to character, he can only mean that her personality reflects and embodies what the observer conceives to be the *national* character (see the Stalin definition, quoted above, to which 'national character ' is essential). And if she is 'the ultimate representative of her class', as W. K. Malcolm says she is (p. 171) it can only mean that in the novel the truest Scots – the only true Scots people – are the peasants, until such time as the peasantry are transcended and, as Marx and Engels put it, the proletariat 'constitutes itself the nation'.[10] I take it that the action of *Grey Granite* is an attempt to show us the proletariat constituting itself the nation, or rather a step along that road – a process which involves also what Lenin and others called 'proletarian internationalism'.

There is, then, allegory in *A Scots Quair*, but it is not naïve allegory: we should call it rather an 'allegorical dimension' coexisting with the dominant 'realistic' one. The book has to do with the years 1905–30, approximately, and not with the whole of Scottish history, as some have claimed; but the whole of Scottish history is there in the background, in the way both Kinraddie and Segget (the small town of *Cloud Howe*) are given histories that go back to the Middle Ages. The movement of the trilogy as a whole is not, as with *The Silver Darlings*, towards domesticity and the founding of a dynasty but *from* domesticity (Chris's three marriages) to an austere, intellectualised male asceticism that rejects marriage in favour of a hard renunciatory creed seen as historically necessary. Chris falls into the earth on Barmekin hill at the end: that earth with which, like Catrine, she is identified, for the very good reason that she represents a rural way of living and feeling that has no future. The nation is no longer embodied in the peasantry or the land, but in the industrial working class; and its interests pass beyond any former 'bourgeois nationalism' to a world federation of socialist republics. As Gibbon himself said in his essay on Glasgow, writing in the spirit of the founding fathers of Marxism and of Trotsky rather than of Stalin:

Glasgow's salvation, Scotland's salvation, the world's salvation lies in neither nationalism nor internationalism, those twin halves of an idiot whole. It lies in an ultimate cosmopolitanism, the Earth the City of God .... A time will come when the self-wrought, prideful differentiations of Scotsman, Englishman, Frenchman, Spaniard will seem as ludicrous as the infantile squabblings of the Heptarchians. A time will come when nationalism, with other cultural aberrations, will have passed from the human spirit, when Man, again free and unchained, has all the earth for his footstool.[11]

Diffusionism, class oppression, nationalism, Communism are not the whole story, however. There is another theme still, a more than Spenserian mutability which Chris often expresses – a conviction that the ding-dong through the ages of *male* creeds and ideologies is as nothing beside woman's fecundity and the pull of the land. Yet these values are themselves ultimately to be overturned and replaced by others – or so *Grey Granite* states, on one reading at least. 'Ill would change be at whiles, were it not for the change beyond the change.' Why is it that we can still respond to *Grey Granite* as a living experience when the Communist struggles depicted by Gibbon seem, for western societies at least, now relegated to what Marxists call 'the dustbin of history'? As W. K. Malcolm puts it: 'Where Ewan ends trying to conquer the future, Chris finally triumphs over all the forces of time' (p. 184). That 'trying' is crucial: in the text, we do not know the outcome for Ewan, but in Malcolm's view we know it positively for Chris, for on the Barmekin 'she ultimately recognises God in the constant working and reworking of her natural surroundings, identifying the power of Change which holds sway over life as the final truth' (p. 184). But that, it is important to realise, is the final truth for Chris – not for Ewan, and not, I would claim, for Gibbon.

CONCLUSION

The Silver Darlings and *A Scots Quair* are open-ended historical novels whose historicity consists in their union of paradigm and region, and whose universality is seen in their reaching out *through* the regional to dimensions other than the historic. *The Silver Darlings* unites the region with the universal without any obvious mediation of the nation. The people of Gunn's region are like those tribes or 'nationalities' that historically come together to form nations; they have a common language which is under threat, but which is not that of the majority of the Scottish nation. Finn's descendants, only two generations after the end of the novel, will no longer speak it, but Gunn does not seem to regard this as important. The people are distinct from the majority of the Scottish nation; their shared fate is different in many details from that of the lowlanders to the south. But that fate has a historical typicality similar to Kinraddie's in *Sunset Song*. In Gunn's case the typicality replaces the national factor and perhaps even transcends it; it is that fate, that typicality, which induced Marx to use the Highland Clearances as a prime example of 'primitive accumulation' in *Capital*.[12]

In spite of the obvious neatness of Gibbon's intended structures, his achievement is more uneven than Gunn's, and he has defects of taste and sensibility not found in Gunn; but in spite of these *A Scots Quair* is the greater achievement because of its greater depth of characterisation, particularly of Chris Guthrie who, though firmly rooted in her region, is given a *national* typicality not seen in Scottish fiction since Scott's Jeanie Deans.

NOTES

1. Quoted in Elie Kédourie, *Nationalism* (1960) pp. 80–1.
2. Ernest Renan, 'Quest-ce qu'une nation' (1882), in *Oeuvres Complètes* (1947) vol. I, p. 903.
3. H. M. Chadwick, *The Nationalities of Europe and the Growth of National Ideologies* (1945).
4. Lewis Grassic Gibbon, *A Scots Quair*, comprises *Sunset Song* (1932), *Cloud Howe* (1933) and *Grey Granite* (1934). All references are to the 1950 edition of the complete trilogy, in which each novel was paginated separately.
5. Neil Gunn, *The Silver Darlings*; all references are to the 1969 edition.
6. For the various narrative voices, see Graham Trengove, 'Who is you? Grammar and Grassic Gibbon', *Scottish Literary Journal*, vol. 2, no. 2 (1975) pp. 47–62.
7. William K. Malcolm, *A Blasphemer and Reformer* (1984) p. 148.
8. For diffusionism in *A Scots Quair*, see Douglas F. Young, *Beyond the Sunset* (1973); and for its Marxism, Malcolm, *A Blasphemer and Reformer*.
9. In Aberdeen and its hinterland the term 'Doric' is often used for the dialect of the north-east counties of Scotland.
10. Karl Marx and Friedrich Engels, *The Communist Manifesto*, in *Collected Works*, vol. VI (1976) p. 503.
11. Lewis Grassic Gibbon, *A Scots Hairst* (1967) pp. 92–3.
12. Karl Marx, *Capital* (Penguin ed.) vol. I, pp. 890–5.

9

Scoticisms and Cultural Conflict

DAVID HEWITT

The imaginative literature of Scotland in the eighteenth and early nineteenth centuries is of considerable significance for the literature of region and nation in that the compromise between English and Scots, of which the poetry of Burns and the novels of Walter Scott are the best examples, suggested to the writers of the nineteenth century ways of treating and presenting regional experience.

The Scottish literature in question is a product of the linguistic conflict between Scots and English in the second half of the eighteenth century – as the spelling of 'Scoticisms' in the title suggests. The topic is well known; indeed it has been so thoroughly explored that there is probably nothing new to discover. The aim here is not to challenge 'the facts', but rather the standard interpretation of them, which usually implies that the advent of English was 'a bad thing'. It is common to find the linguistic changes presented as the 'colonisation' or the 'takeover' of Scots by English, but the imperialistic and financial metaphors, with their variety of derogatory overtones, are restrictive, in that they direct attention only to the regrettable features of the changes – that Scots ceased to be an independent language, and that in the long term a rich vocabulary fell into desuetude as English terms displaced Scots. There were other consequences beneficial to literature: the conflict stimulated a reaction in favour of the use of Scots as a medium of poetic expression, and, in addition, Scots writers gained a second language. The enhanced linguistic resources available to Robert Burns and Walter Scott are the product of the linguistic conflict and are integral to their literary achievement.

In his essay, 'A History of Scots', which constitutes the Introduction to *The Concise Scots Dictionary*, A. J. Aitken writes:

The progressive anglicization of writings in manuscript (records, diaries, manuscript histories, and others) proceeded through the seventeenth century and into the eighteenth, until finally virtually every trace of Scottishness had disappeared from Scottish writing. In print, partly or largely as a result of commercial considerations by publishers and printers, the demise of literary Older Scots is far earlier and more sudden. After 1610, except for a few legal texts and one or two comic or satiric *tours-de-force*, all Scots writings in prose, whether printed in Scotland or, as often, in London, are in what can only be called English – with an occasional Scots locution only every dozen pages or so.[1]

Thus in the mid-eighteenth century, David Hume's well-known attempts to combat Scotticisms – he is said to have sent his *History of England* to an English friend to check for them, he published his own list of them, and he helped to edit them out of works by Robert Wallace and Thomas Reid – are not a new development but the culmination of an extended historical process.

Aitken also argues that by the late seventeenth century 'the formal or, in the language of the period, "polite" speech of the social élite of Scotland was ... expected to approximate to the southern English dialect'.[2] 'Polite' speech was certainly established as the ideal by this time, but few attained a southern English, upper-class pronunciation. No doubt some of the aristocracy and others accustomed to living or to transacting political business in London anglicised their speech, but the evidence suggests that until the mid-eighteenth century nearly everyone spoke Scots. Ernest Mossner quotes one of Hume's relatives to the effect that Hume

retained the accent, expression and vulgarity of his paternal stile on the Banks of the White Water & Tweed, in such a degree that you would have imagined he had never conversed with any person but the commonest farmer in the Merse.[3]

Even so, it is accepted that after 1745 the speech habits of the educated in Scotland changed rapidly; in 1764 James Boswell actually predicted the demise of Scots: 'The Scottish language is being lost every day, and in a short time will become quite unintelligible.'[4] Such a statement may be more emotional than analytic, but it does suggest that the changes were dramatic.

In the earlier part of the century the absorption of English lexis, and the modifications in pronunciation, were the natural consequence of greater traffic with England after the Union in 1707. William Robertson argues in his *History of Scotland* (1759) that before 1603 'the intercourse between the two nations was inconsiderable'[5] and he quotes in support two Elizabethan surveys of 'all the strangers within the cities of London and Westminster', showing a Scottish population of only 58 in 1567, and 88 in 1568. During the seventeenth century, contacts must have increased considerably as the politics of these islands became increasingly 'British'. They must have been very much greater after 1707; quite apart from social and business travel, 45 members of the House of Commons and 16 representative peers had to maintain establishments in London.

But the adoption of English forms was not just the passive consequence of a developing awareness of English; it was deliberately acquired. In 1761 *The Scots Magazine* published 'Regulations of the Select Society for Promoting the Reading and Speaking of the English Language in Scotland'. The opening paragraph explains:

> As the intercourse between this part of Great Britain and the capital daily increases, both on account of business and amusement, and must still go on increasing, gentlemen educated in Scotland have long been sensible of the disadvantages under which they labour, from their imperfect knowledge of the ENGLISH TONGUE, and the impropriety with which they speak it.[6]

The desire to participate in the administration of the country, or to shine in the field of letters, is very evident in the writings of the period. It seems to have been a prevalent view that the key to success lay in linguistic conformity, or in at least sufficient linguistic adjustment as to prevent any adverse response among those who 'counted'. But there was also an additional motive that is hinted at in the phrase 'sensible of the disadvantages', but is seldom fully articulated – the fear of ridicule. Ernest Mossner suggests that a linguistic disagreement led to Hume's being dismissed by Michael Miller from his counting house in Bristol in 1734, and that it was this that made Hume wish to expunge Scotticisms from his work: no Englishman would again have the opportunity to mock him.[7] Nearly 50 years later, John Sinclair, then an MP, published his *Observations on the Scottish Dialect*. Hidden in his text is a hint of the kind of personal experience that gave impetus to the learning of English:

> It is indeed astonishing how uncouth, and often unintelligible, Scotch words and phrases are to an inhabitant of London, and how much it exposes such as make use of them, to the derision of those with whom they happen to have any communication or intercourse.[8]

Ambition and fear of ridicule provided the thrust for the anglicisation of speech, and it is entirely natural and understandable that in the political circumstances of the enlarged kingdom people should have modified the way they spoke. But linguistic change became a cause. It was promoted by the lists of Scotticisms published by David Hume, James Beattie, Lord Hailes and John Sinclair, and after Thomas Sheridan lectured in Edinburgh on 'Elocution and the English Tongue' in 1761, the Select Society expressed the opinion that:

> Even persons well advanced in life may be taught, by skilful instructors, to avoid many gross improprieties, in quantity, accent, the manner of sounding the vowels, &c. which, at present, render the Scotch dialect so offensive.

The Society therefore decided:

> it would be of great advantage to this country, if a proper number of persons from England, duly qualified to instruct gentlemen in the knowledge of the English Tongue, the manner of pronouncing it with purity, and the art of public speaking, were settled in Edinburgh.[9]

Such statements are characteristic; the advocacy of English for what are often sensible, practical motives, is accompanied by a denigration of Scots as a corrupt form of the English language.

The 'cause' had significant support, to judge from the frequency with which articles and letters on the subject were published in *The Scots Magazine*, but its promotion seems also to have created a reaction. The practice of vernacular poetry, dormant since the heyday of Allan Ramsay in the 1720s and 1730s, was revived in the 1760s. Of course, the poetry itself constitutes a rejection of the arguments in favour of English, but within the poetry there are clear statements about Scots as the language of Scotland. The poets are inclined to echo enlightenment ideas about language, and employ them against the anglicisers. In writing his pastoral 'epic' *Helenore* (1768) Alexander Ross chooses not a great English poet, but Ramsay as a model. He is inspired by his muse Scota who gives the following advice:

> Speak may ain leed, tis gueed auld Scots I mean;
> Your Southern gnaps, I count not worth a preen.
> We've words a fouth, that we can ca' our ain,
> Tho' frae them now my childer sair refrain,
> An' are to my gueed auld proverb confeerin –
> Neither gueed fish nor flesh, nor yet sa't herrin.[10]

Scota advises Ross to *speak* her own 'leed'; 'leed' implies the spoken language, rather than the written, and so 'speak' is probably not just a way of putting it: Scota means that Ross should speak the language. And this is significant, for the experience of the overwhelming majority of people is that the spoken language is closer, more integral to them than the written. In the context of the Scottish Enlightenment debate on language it carries further significance, for the literati, in spite of their championing of English, found that they were employing a foreign tongue that restricted their self-expression.[11] Scota characterises her language as 'gueed auld Scots', a phrase that suggests both comfortable familiarity, and the dignity of age. She dismisses 'southern gnaps' (a derogatory description that implies a namby-pamby way of speaking) and asserts that Scots has a rich vocabulary and has no need to borrow foreign terminology. And finally she says that although her children now try to avoid using Scots, they have created something that is neither Scots nor English; in other words, they have contaminated the purity of an established language. Whereas the literati normally argue that Scots is a corrupted form of English, Ross suggests that the anglicisers have corrupted Scots.

Other writers, in their practice and in their deployment of ideas, also talk about Scots. Smollett's Lismahago voices a feeling of outraged national pride in *The Expedition of Humphry Clinker* (1771) when he comically inverts the arguments in favour of English; Jerry Melford tells his correspondent:

> He said, what we generally called the Scottish dialect was, in fact, true, genuine Old English, with a mixture of some French terms and idioms, adopted in a long intercourse betwixt the French and Scotch nations; that the modern English, from affectation and false refinement, had weakened, and even corrupted their language, by throwing out the guttural sounds, altering the pronunciation and the quantity, and disusing many words and terms of great significance.[12]

Smollett here mocks a nationalistic contribution to the language debate, but the reader inevitably wonders about the author's true position; perhaps he believes what Lismahago utters (not the specifics necessarily but the thrust of the argument), but is protecting *himself* from mockery by putting the views in the mouth of a comic character. Whatever Smollett's own feelings, there must already have been a recognised and established response to the anglicising movement that could be made fun of. It is possible too that Robert Fergusson was actuated by ideas of linguistic purity, for in spite of his command of English idiom, when he turned to Scots as the medium of his poetry, he used a language little 'contaminated' by English. In Burns's poetry there are many statements about language; in his second epistle to John Lapraik, 'To the Same', to choose but one example, he writes:

> Sae I've begun to scrawl, but whether
> In rhyme, or prose, or baith thegither,
> Or some hotch-potch that's rightly neither,
>   Let time mak proof;
> But I shall scribble down some blether
>   Just clean aff-loof.[13]

Burns's self-image reflects the new englitenment idea of the model poet, of a man inspired to pour forth spontaneously; it also criticises implicitly the literati's lack of spontaneity (by their own confession) in manipulating a learnt language.

Looking back from later in the century, John Ramsay of Ochtertyre, who records more about the speech of his contemporaries than any other commentator, comments on the whole anglicising cause:

> Servile imitation, unrestrained by judgment, is, however, such a confession of inferiority as one would hardly have expected from a proud manly people, long-famous for common-sense and veneration for the ancient classics.[14]

It is a most unsophisticated statement; but perhaps it utters bluntly the kind of irritation that the poets felt about the way in which the speaking of English was promoted, and explains their desire to assert their Scottishness by using Scots.

A second major consequence of the linguistic revolution was the enhancement of the linguistic resources available to Scottish writers. Those who acquired English did not lose their Scots; the two co-existed and became levels of discourse that could be varied appropriately, according to the situation. Ramsay of Ochtertyre says that after 1745 nobody doubted 'the possibility of a Scotsman writing pure, nay, even elegant, English, whilst he spoke his native dialect a little diversified'.[15] His description of Lord Kames explains the nature of the diversification; he writes that 'the language of this social hour was pure Scots, nowise like what he spoke on the bench, which approached to English'.[16] His censure of Lord Auchinleck (James Boswell's father) provides another indication of the expected speech habits of the educated in mid-century: 'he was one of the very few that never endeavoured to form an oratorical language half-way between familiar discourse and their style of writing'.[17] What was established as the norm among the educated and upper classes was the possession of both a full colloquial Scots and a more formal Scottish variety of English.

It could be argued that Scotsmen of the period exhibit the characteristic linguistic expertise of minority cultures – the ability to handle two languages efficiently. However, it is clear that the educated did not talk upper-class, southern English. Kames's legal language 'approached to English'; in another telling description, Ramsay again suggests that the English talked in Scotland only approximated to the southern variety in the period 1740–60:

> Besides the colloquial Scotch spoken in good company, there was likewise the oratorical, which was used by judges, lawyers and clergymen, in their several departments. In this, perhaps,

there was even greater variety than in the other; but it may be concluded, that such as wished to excel in their public appearances strove to bring their speeches or sermons some degrees nearer pure English than their ordinary talk.[18]

As English became acclimatised in Scotland (to become what we would now call Scottish English) many people became so adept at dialect switching that they fashioned a new kind of speech, and in so doing, greatly extended the rhetorical range of the language. Towards the end of the century, the situation had become naturalised, for Henry Cockburn's description of Scott's speech two generations on suggests habits similar to those of Lord Kames;

> No bad idea will be formed of Scott's conversation by supposing one of his Scotch novels to be cut into talk. It is not so much conversation as a joyous flow of anecdote, story, character, and scene, mostly humorous, always graphic, and never personal or ill natured.[19]

Out of the language conflict there developed a clear talking style, which was characterised by a highly rhetorical shifting of register. In the late eighteenth and in the early nineteenth centuries, this style went back into literature and became the matter of art – in poems like 'The Cotter's Saturday Night' and 'Tam o' Shanter', and in the novels of Scott and Galt. They too are characterised by a 'flexibility of speech and tones',[20] to use a phrase of Ramsay's.

The linguistic conflict in Scotland was thus productive; it stimulated a new literature, best illustrated by the Scots poetry of Alexander Ross and Robert Fergusson, and created a linguistic compromise that was exploited to great effect by Burns and Scott. It also left a legacy to the nineteenth century, for the compromise as exemplified by the novels of Scott offered a model to Emily and Charlotte Brontë, Charles Dickens, George Eliot, Thomas Hardy and even D. H. Lawrence in their representation of regional experience. The model was obviously efficient (common experience transmitted in English and particular regional experience in dialect); yet many of the peculiarities that were the result of historical evolution of the compromise were also transmitted to the nineteenth century and helped to create some of the ambiguities that are still inherent in the discussion of the literature of region and nation.

The nature of the compromise created a literary language whose social and political implications were significantly different from the impulse that had created it. In Burns, Scott, Hogg and Galt, standard written English is the medium of the narration and represents the speech of the educated, while the speech of more humble characters is frequently dialectal. This did not mirror actuality; the son of a small laird in seventeenth-century Scotland never talked English, as Henry Morton does in *Old Mortality*, or even anything that approached to English. And as we have seen, standard written English could not even be said to record the speech of educated Scots in the period of Burns and Scott. What in fact it does is reflect the latter's aspirations. In literature the use of the compromise offered a rhetorical way of representing a range of social perspectives – a greater range than had been achieved in English literature before this time, and it was this which appealed to the nineteenth-century novelists. But when seen from a different context, whether of time or place, it does look as though regional experience is peculiar to ordinary people, because in literature it is they who speak in dialect, while 'national' concerns are expressed in English. Furthermore, it emphasises the (linguistically unjustifiable) equation of the speech of the educated with standard written English; the educated appear to speak the lingua franca while the humble express themselves in some deviant form of the language. It would not be appropriate here to consider the political consequences of this linguistic configuration, but its symbolism has had an extraordinary hold on the national imagination.

Secondly, Scots poets had resisted the advent of English; they deliberately used Scots, because they considered it a national language, of equal status with English. When reviewing R. H. Cromek's *Reliques of Robert Burns* in *The Edinburgh Review* in 1809, Francis Jeffrey wrote:

This Scotch is not to be considered as a provincial dialect, the vehicle only of rustic vulgarity and rude local humour. It is the language of a whole country, – long an independent kingdom, and still separate in laws, character and manners. It is by no means peculiar to the vulgar; but is the common speech of the whole nation in early life, – and with many of its most exalted and accomplished individuals throughout their whole existence; and, if it be true that, in later times, it has been, in some measure, laid aside by the more ambitious and aspiring of the present generation, it is still recollected, even by them, as the familiar language of their childhood, and of those who were the earliest objects of their love and veneration.[21]

It was because at least some Scots thought of the language question as an international issue that the compromise was effected; but to the English, Scotland was merely a region of the British Isles. This perception no doubt made easy the application of the Scott pattern to the exploration of regional experience, but it also fuses the discussion of the regional and the national in a way that is still often felt to be unacceptable by Scots.

It is not possible in a brief essay to do much more than to raise issues, but I hope that what has been achieved is to show that at least some of the questions that arise in the contemporary discussion of the literature of region and nation have a strong historical dimension and are coeval with the literature itself.

NOTES

1. A. J. Aitken, 'The History of Scots', in *The Concise Scots Dictionary*, ed. Mairi Robinson (Aberdeen, 1985) pp. x–xi.
2. Ibid., p. xi.
3. Ernest Campbell Mossner, *The Life of David Hume*, 2nd edn (Oxford, 1970) p. 370.
4. James Boswell, *Boswell in Holland 1763–1764*, ed. Frederick A. Pottle (London, 1952) p. 161.
5. William Robertson, *The History of Scotland* (London, 1759) vol. II, p. 304.
6. *The Scots Magazine*, vol. XXIII (1761) p. 440.
7. Mossner, *The Life of David Hume*, p. 90.
8. John Sinclair, *Observations on the Scottish Dialect* (1782) p. 143.
9. *The Scots Magazine*, vol. XXIII (1761) p. 440.
10. *The Scottish works of Alexander Ross*, ed. Margaret Wattie, Scottish Text Society, 3rd series, vol. 9 (Edinburgh, 1938) *Helenore*, lines 56–61.
11. The best evidence of Scots finding the use of English difficult comes from James Beattie, but this is only one of many possible examples; he says that the greatest difficulty is 'to give a *vernacular* cast to the English we write. . . . We who live in Scotland are obliged to study English from books, like a dead language. Accordingly, when we write, we write it like a dead language, which we understand, but cannot speak.' (Quoted in William Forbes, *The Life and Writings of James Beattie* (Edinburgh, 1806) vol. II, pp. 16–17.)

12. Tobias Smollett, *The Expedition of Humphry Clinker*, ed. Lewis M. Knapp (Oxford, 1966) p. 199 (to Sir Watkin Phillips, July 13).
13. *The Poems and Songs of Robert Burns*, ed. James Kinsley (Oxford, 1968) vol. I, p. 91, no. 58, lines 37–42.
14. John Ramsay, *Scotland and Scotsmen of the Eighteenth Century*, ed. Alexander Allardyce (Edinburgh and London, 1888) vol. I, p. 5.
15. Ibid., vol. I, p. 310.
16. Ibid., vol. I, pp. 211–12.
17. Ibid., vol. I, p. 168.
18. Ibid., vol. II, p. 544.
19. Henry Cockburn, *Memorials of His Time*, new edn (Edinbugh, 1874) p. 393.
20. Ramsay, *Scotland and Scotsmen of the Eighteenth Century*, vol. II, p. 545.
21. Taken from *Robert Burns: The Critical Heritage*, ed. Donald Low (London, 1974) p. 186.

10

The Double Man

IAIN CRICHTON SMITH

First of all, as this paper will be devoted to an issue which concerns me closely; may I introduce myself? I come from the island of Lewis in the Outer Hebrides. Lewis, is, perhaps, with possible objections from some of the other islands, one of the strongest bastions of Gaelic at a time when the language is in decline.

Though I have written much in English, in both poetry and prose and to a limited extent in drama, my native language is Gaelic. I did not learn to speak English till the age of five, when I went to school, and when I had to learn all my other subjects in English. I cannot now remember the actual process but that I did learn to speak English is evidenced among other things by this paper. In school I spoke English, in the playground I spoke Gaelic. And of course, I spoke Gaelic at home. At the age of eleven I went to Secondary School in the Nicolson Institute in Stornoway and there I spoke English in the school, in the playground, and Gaelic at home.

It must, I think, be remembered that there was a social content here as well. To speak English to someone from the village which I grew up in was to make this person into a stranger, to make oneself in some significant way superior to him. The very fact that I had to learn English when I went to school was probably registered in some obscure corner of my psyche as an indication that English was superior to Gaelic. This is the point that the Gaelic poet Derick Thomson was making in his poem 'Coffins'.[1] Many years afterwards I tried to find an image for bilingualism, and I found it in the tunic of the medieval jester with its two colours, say, red and black. This is the origin of the idea of the double man and appears in the poem called 'The Fool' which I quote in translation:

> In the dress of the fool, the two colours that have tormented me,
> English and Gaelic, black and red, the court of injustice, the
> reason for my anger, and that fine rain from the mountains and

these grievous storms from my mind streaming the two colours together so that I will go with poor sight in the one colour that is so odd that the King himself will not understand my conversation.[2]

In Scottish literature there are many double men, including Dr Jekyll and Mr Hyde; these however are ethical double men. I am a linguistic double man.

Let me explore this linguistic dilemma a little further. When I read my Gaelic poetry I find that it is on the whole, though not exclusively, centred on the Highlands. Within that world it may refer to Gaelic songs, as for instance, and specifically, a Gaelic song called *An eala bhan* ('The White Swan'), a love song of the First World War. For a non-Gaelic speaker to understand my Gaelic poetry even in translation would be difficult. On the other hand this is how those in Scotland who speak only English understand Gaelic poetry – that is, in translation. Thus our most famous Gaelic poet of the present day, Sorley Maclean, has achieved much of his reputation by means of his translations, and essays are confidently written about him by those who don't know Gaelic.

We are here involved in the question of available audiences. For a Gaelic poet the audiences are as follows: first of all, those who read Gaelic in the Gaelic area; secondly, universities where there are Gaelic departments with scholars who can place such a poet in the Gaelic tradition; thirdly, intellectuals who speak English only and who achieve access through translations. For an *avant garde* poet such as Sorley Maclean, and one who was extending the limits of Gaelic poetry both thematically and formally, his audience is on the whole reduced to two types, the university one and the English-speaking one. Thus he is in a peculiar position – as I, too, am, as far as my Gaelic work is concerned – in that those who study him are the intellectuals outside the Gaelic area, some speaking Gaelic and some not. There is one other audience that I should perhaps have mentioned, and that is the city-based people who have, usually for economic reasons, exiled themselves from the Highlands. These are people who return from Glasgow or Edinburgh, for instance, once a year and who are on the whole conservative and wish things to remain as they are. They carry in their minds, as medieval people used to carry relics of saints, pictures of the islands of their youth which were ethically pure, eternally beautiful and wholly Edenesque. Such people will not welcome *avant garde* poetry. They are the natural inheritors of the kailyard.

When I am writing in English such considerations do not apply. My English, such as it is, is easily read and can be read by everyone in Scotland. Thus, for instance, I can refer to Wittgenstein and write a poem such as 'The Notebooks of Robinson Crusoe'. I can refer to great painters, musicians. I have referred to Freud in a Gaelic poem; but this was on the whole considered to be boastfulness.

There is also a further problem. There are many Gaelic speakers who do not read or write Gaelic. I do not know whether this is a common problem in other languages, but it certainly is as far as Gaelic is concerned.

Other difficulties exist. Thus, for instance, on the analogy that if certain English writers can write about countries outside England I could do the same with Gaelic, I wrote a Gaelic short story about an American President having to decide to release (or not) the nuclear deterrent. This was not considered a Gaelic theme. There is a conservative force which drives Gaelic writers towards writing on Gaelic subject matter, and this on the whole I have done in my poetry, though not in my prose. One wishes after all to be read by one's own people. Or again, if one is writing a play in Gaelic, how does one deal with the incomer who speaks English – the doctor, the lawyer? Should one, in fact, use Gaelic for such a person? Does this mean that parts of the play will be in Gaelic and parts in English? If one is a purist, one is naturally compelled to write plays which will involve only Gaelic speakers, and this in turn will limit the subject matter and tend to reinforce the larger mentality of the conservatives.

And this, of course, is one side of the coin. The other side is that linguistically Gaelic may not have the resources to deal exactly and naturally with certain subjects, for example, technological ones. It is the problem of a language which is weakening in face of an imperialist neighbour.

Thus when I am writing in Gaelic I am constrained in a way that I am not when I am writing in English. The constraints when I am writing in English are different. One of them is: can I attain my full potential when writing in English, even when all themes are open to me? MacDiarmid, of course, would say that one cannot. In addition, it is the case that the two major poets of this century in Scotland are MacDiarmid and Sorley Maclean. These poets wrote their best work in a language other than English. Whether, however, a major Scottish poet will ever again emerge whose language will not be some version of English is doubtful.

I think that, other things being equal, the poet who writes consistently in his native language is the one who is most likely to achieve greatness. In addition, it is possible that Gaelic poetry cannot be translated into English, and that the poet the Gaelic reader knows is not the same poet as the English reader knows. For myself, I have written in Gaelic, but at the same time I was drastically limiting my potential audience. Also I wanted to write novels and short stories, and these forms are relatively new in Gaelic and, as far as the novel is concerned, not strong. To all intents and purposes the Gaelic short story, though strong, is a twentieth-century phenomenon. Furthermore, I wished to develop thematically and not be constrained by the Highlands. On the other hand, even in my English work I am constantly turning back to Highland themes, such as the church, exile, and so on.

I do feel a nostalgia for my own country, for my own language. And it may well be that as a whole personality it may be impossible for me to operate either in English or Gaelic. If Gaelic had been a strong language able to include the whole spectrum of forms, and also linguistically, I would, I think, have been happy to write in Gaelic exclusively. But this is not the case. Therefore I do the next best thing, I write in an English which is probably, in some ways unknown to me, a Highland English. It is comprehensible, but is it allowing my whole personality to function as is absolutely necessary for the writing of poetry? Probably not.

The more I consider the whole question of language the more mysterious it appears. There are certain Gaelic songs which will reduce me to tears in a way that English songs will not do. I feel clumsinesses in my English which I am unable to eradicate. Carlyle apparently had a struggle with English and probably felt that the struggle was necessary. I, too, feel at times that the Gaelic world is not getting into my English, that some deep emotional power is missing. There is a way one can speak in Gaelic even now which is simple and piercing: and perhaps this is no longer possible in English; as there is a way of singing in Gaelic which satisfies a Gaelic audience though not perhaps a musical purist ignorant of the Gaelic tradition. I think that it is very hard to get into an alien language the direct emotions associated with one's deepest being. There is a simple piercing quality in Burns's Scots songs which is not present when he is writing in English. It may indeed be possible that the intellectual side of one's nature is emphasised in the speaking and writing of a foreign language, and that the emotional side loses its resonance.

For myself, the solution I have taken is to write in two languages but less and less in Gaelic, and this for a reason which may appear to you naïve. It is a fact that I am a full-time professional writer, and that there are too few openings in Gaelic for me to make a living from writing exclusively in that language. Economic factors govern cultural ones to an extent greater than we often dream of. And thus I am a double man riddled with guilt. A poem, 'The Second Island', by Derick Thomson recognises this doubleness, this time in what he sees.[3] It is this condition that I must live with as the double man. The complexities are enormous, mind-breaking. Only those who have lived through or are living through them can fully understand them. And it is not even a question of understanding, it is a question of feeling them on the pulse.

First, most of the poets who write significant work in Gaelic are not living in the Highlands. They have to earn their living elsewhere. They hardly speak any Gaelic in their daily lives. Secondly, a practical matter, if such a person marries and if he marries a non-Gaelic-speaking wife, what is to happen about the education of the children? Thirdly, why does such a poet write so that the ordinary people who speak Gaelic cannot understand him? And so on. These are problems which on the whole the writer not weighed down with bilingualism does not face.

Fourthly, if he were to return to the Highlands for patriotic reasons to live there, would he be diminishing himself as a person? Fifthly, should he be back in the Highlands saving the language at source instead of, for instance, being an academic in a city university? Sixthly, if he is not living in the Highlands can he have anything worthwhile to say about them? Does he lose his feel for what is happening there? There is no end to the questions. [At the conference Mr Crichton Smith then quoted another Gaelic poem by Derick Thomson entitled 'Water and Peats and Oats'.[4]] The mind free, the poet says, but the freedom bought at the expense of the feelings. Perhaps. Who knows? [Mr Crichton Smith then read sections (5), (6), (8), (13), (18) and (22) from his own poem 'Shall Gaelic Die?'[5]]

Now I turned to writing in English for two reasons. I was finding English easier for me to write in and also I wished to extend my range. Why did I progressively find that English was more and more easy for me to write in? There are various reasons for this. One of them is that when I was growing up, the books I read were in English. Thus I read *Kidnapped* and *Treasure Island* as other children did. There were then hardly any Gaelic books for children at all. Now there are, and indeed the members of a conference on the provision of Gaelic books were recently surprised at their range and quantity. I remember myself weeping over the death of an English boy in a public school while the sound of cricket bats hitting cricket balls was heard through his hospital window. I remember when I was in school in the Nicolson Institute in Stornoway visiting the Reading Room of the local library every dinner time and leafing over leather-covered copies of the *Tatler* and the *Illustrated London News* which showed photographs of the haggard aristocracy sharing a joke. What a joke indeed it was!

Now, too, I have left the island where Gaelic was my native language. I hardly ever speak it. First of all, I came to Aberdeen University, then I taught in Oban High School, and now I live in a small village called Taynuilt in Argyll. There are some Gaelic speakers there, but they tend to be among the very old who are systematically dying. Thus I hardly ever speak Gaelic.

It is possible, too, that the oral culture of Gaelic is dying. A poet like Sorley Maclean whom I have already mentioned was brought up in an environment which was exclusively Gaelic. His parents were inheritors of a treasury of songs and poems and stories. Now people of this kind no longer exist or only to a limited extent. English especially through television has dominated their world.

With regard to the second point, my own desire for expansion as a writer, it was almost necessary that I should develop my work through English. Most of the English writers that I admired wrote in English. I studied English in University. My mentors were people like Eliot and Auden and Lowell. English words now come more easily to me than Gaelic words do. I am able to enter a whole English world: the whole of English literature is available to me. I do not need to be limited by Gaelic constraints. I can write about anything I like, and I do. I can write about a night in the life of Kant (you might think that, too, is limited, but not the way I wrote it!). I can write about areas outside the Highlands and use the kind of dialect that they speak, which would be impossible for me in Gaelic. I can conduct arguments on Hamlet which would be difficult for me in Gaelic. It is true that some of my novels could have been written in Gaelic, but I would have been severely limiting my readership. However, not all my work could have been written in Gaelic for a lot of it depends on an English ambiance. I have already said that I have written a poem about Freud in Gaelic, but it somehow seems not Gaelic enough. I should like to read it to you in an English translation.

Great man from Vienna who opened the mind with a knife keen with sore efficient happy light, and who saw the seas sweating with the blue-green ghosts of plague and uncountable riches.

I follow the beasts with a joy that I cannot tell though I should be fishing from dungeon or from prison, as they move on that sea bottom in the freedom of truth with their great helmets. No one will bring them to shore.

Cancer took your jaw away but you were scanning with profundity the bottom of that sea where there are terrifying shadows. Father, mother and daughter fighting entwined together in a Greek play, in a strangling of forests.

The letter that I will not send, the letter that I will not keep, the poetry that my head cannot put together, the history that I would not want anyone to tell of my planets, the star is below in the seaweed of the skies.

Goodbye to the laughter of nature, and the seas, goodbye to the salt that will bring tears to thoughts, goodbye to death which opens valuable countries, our rings are early in the weddings of our gifts.

O miracle of the waves and I tirelessly scrutinising you like a gay porpoise in my country, it was you who gave us these new waves – your monument is at the bottom, and the seas are your pulpit.[6]

Certainly the imagery I have used belongs to the sea and to a certain extent to religion, but nevertheless I am not sure how far it is what I would call a Gaelic poem. It certainly does not fit easily with previous Gaelic poetry; it is not a subject that one would find there, it is not a subject that would be open to many traditional readers. Much more open to traditional readers would be the following, which I will read first in Gaelic and then in English. The title is 'Nighean Og', or 'Young Girl'. [Mr Crichton Smith read this poem.[7]]

It is possible that there is a Gaelic *blas*, or taste, in the second poem that the first one lacks. But to an English speaker there might not appear to be any difference. There is an inbuilt feeling for the limits and music of a language that only those who know that language can appreciate fully. It could be that it is the least Gaelic of Sorley Maclean's poems that an English reader will appreciate most. These, of course, are deep problems and mysteries of language.

Here is a little anecdote. When I was teaching in Oban High School my headmaster there for many years was a brother of Sorley Maclean. He was a very fine classical scholar with a First from Cambridge, and later studied in Vienna. He had to retire early because of bad health, and he was given a typewriter as one of his going-away presents. He began to tanslate the *Odyssey* into Gaelic and finished it very rapidly since he knew it practically by heart. He once told me that he thought the *Odyssey* would go more easily into Gaelic than into English because of the variety of sea terms in Gaelic, and also perhaps because of the tribal or clan background common to a certain extent to the Greek and Gaelic worlds. He may very well have been right for I have no Greek.

It is true, therefore, that I have written works which might have been written in Gaelic, but on the other hand there are things that I have written which depend on a literary provenance outside the Gaelic world. Some years ago I wrote a long poem called 'The Notebooks of Robinson Crusoe'. This section here could have been written in Gaelic.

> Island what shall I say of you, your peat bogs,
> your lochs, your moors and berries?
> The cry of your birds in the fading evening.
> Your flowers in summer glowing brightly where there
> are no thoroughfares.
> The perpetual sound of the sea.
> The spongy moss on which feet imprint themselves.
> The mountains which darken and brighten like ideas
> in the mind.

> The owl with its big glasses that perches on a late
> tree listening.
> The mussels clamped to the rocks, the fool's gold,
> the tidal pools filling and emptying.
> The coin that turns from pale green to yellow, my
> scarecrow rattling in the wind.
> The smoke that arises from my fire.[8]

That island could very well be Lewis. Its images are composed from my own island. The only line that would not be Gaelic in essence would be

> The mountains which darken and brighten like ideas
> in the mind.

All the other paraphernalia such as the mussels, the fool's gold, the owl, are indigenous. Even a line like

> The perpetual sound of the sea.

refers to a specific Gaelic poem.

However, the next section could not be considered Gaelic so easily. For my Robinson Crusoe is an intellectual.

> I have read them all, Sartre, Wittgenstein, Ryle. I have listened at midday to the actresses, pop stars, authors, on 'Desert Island Discs' speculating happily on islands among the traffic of London. (Am I allowed dettol and bandages? Voltaire?)
>
> And as I remember hell, the choice of staying by the communal inferno where we feed on each other or going alone into the middle of the dark wood leaving behind me forever the Pickwicks and the iced candles of Christmas, I hear now clearly in the hollow spaces of the valleys, in the roar of the waterfall, in the appearance of the birds of spring and their departure in the autumn the same phrase repeated over and over:
> Language is other people.[9]

Here, of course, there are references, not explicit, to Sartre and Dante and specific references to Dickens. We are very far from the Gaelic world here.

For I think every language has its own horizon, its ways of

speaking. And the problem of the bilingual is perhaps that leaving one language behind he cannot quite exactly get the ways of speaking of the new language. The writer himself cannot know this. The reader, however, can sense it.

There is a poem by Derick Thomson which is concerned with images drawn from a culture outside his own. It is called 'Changed Days'. [Mr Crichton Smith read this poem in translation.[10]] It is perhaps not odd that he should qualify the second symbol for he says, 'but for the fact that it looks false'. In other words it is not a traditional Gaelic image.

Here is another short poem by the same poet.

> The loom does not make the same music
> In Lewis and in Leeds.
> The Lewis looms have Gaelic.[11]

Again, there is a poem by the Reader in Celtic in this University of Aberdeen who is one of our major Gaelic poets. It is in translation and is called 'A Penny for the Guy, Mister ...'. [Mr Crichton Smith read this poem.[12]] You can therefore see that I am obsessed with language, and why. And you can see, I hope, the ravages that are made on the bilingual, his guilt and his sense of inadequacy.

I am, I suppose, indeed the double man, a kind of monster, an Incredible Hulk that slouches somewhere to be born. But where is that somewhere? I doubt very much that it is Bethlehem. It may be in a No Man's Land between the two languages. It may be where no one has been before. It may lie somewhere between Lewis and Wittgenstein.

[Mr Crichton Smith ended his paper by reading the whole of the poem 'Coffins' written by Derick Thomson.[13]]

NOTES

1. Derick Thomson, *Creachadh na Clarsaich* (Edinburgh: Macdonald Publications, 1982).
2. Iain Crichton Smith, *Selected Poems, 1955–80* (Edinburgh: Macdonald Publications, 1981).
3. Thomson, *Creachadh na Clarsaich*.
4. Ibid.

5.   Crichton Smith, *Selected Poems, 1955–80*.
6.   Ibid.
7.   Ibid.
8.   Ibid.
9.   Ibid.
10. Thomson, *Creachadh na Clarsaich*.
11. Ibid.
12. Donald Macaulay, *Seobhrach as a'Chlaich* (Glasgow: Gairm Publications, 1967).
13. Thomson, *Creachadh na Clarsaich*.

11

England: a Country of the Mind

G. J. B. WATSON

We all live in actual places, but we all equally inhabit, imaginatively, countries of the mind. I was born in a small town called Portadown, in County Armagh, and lived there until I was 21. I want to talk about the various ways in which I have been possessed by imaginative senses of England, a country which in some ways seemed more real to me than the Northern Ireland I grew up in. Inevitably, I will be talking about the effects of cultural imperialism on me, as an Irishman, but I hope to avoid the Hibernian tone so deftly characterised by Evelyn Waugh, when he spoke of the Irishman as 'carrying everywhere with him his ancient rancour and the melancholy of the bogs'. Perhaps, too, what I say may be of interest for the light it throws on the complexities of cultural arrangements and accommodations within the tiny archipelago which is called the British Isles.

Portadown is where the Orange Order was founded in the late eighteenth century, and has remained a bastion of Orange bigotry to this day. When Sir John Lavery wished to paint the strange tribal rite known as 'The Twelfth', when the Orangemen parade on 12 July with their drums, bands, sashes and banners through the streets in celebration of their domination over the sullen Papists, he chose – appositely – to site his picture on Portadown's main street. I could have been one of the small boys on Lavery's canvas, standing back on the edge of a Catholic street to watch the parade from a safely discreet distance. Catholic adults stayed indoors, but even Catholic boys found it hard to resist the appeal of the bands – accordion, flute and, best of all, the pipes in the 'kilty' bands. And watching those parades as a very small boy was where I first encountered a sense of England. The Orange phenomenon might have been a purely indigenous growth, but its iconography asserted the might of England. The Union Jack was everywhere;

the huge Lambeg drums which thundered ceaselessly the warning 'Catholics lie down' proclaimed 'God Save the King' on their gross swollen bellies; the banners portrayed the crown; on them King William of Orange urged his white charger across the Boyne to smash King James; on them, Queen Victoria, in full regalia on her throne, held out a Bible to a kneeling black African who kissed it, over the legend 'The Secret of England's Greatness' – a message easily translated and understood by Northern Ireland's negro population. The *Royal* Ulster Constabulary were out in force to prevent riot, revolvers in their shiny holsters and their oak-pale batons prominent, on their caps the insignia which emblematised our status – English crown above Irish harp. The Orangemen – indeed the whole state – was 'Loyalist'. Loyal to England. And the Orangemen hated us. So presumably England hated us too? I would never go to England: if it could be like this on its fringes, what must it be like at the centre?

In the home, however, things became more complex, and it was difficult to identify 'English Ulster' with 'England'. Every evening at nine, with the immutable regularity with which we said the family rosary, my father would switch on the wireless. And there would be a different England. The glorious solemnity of Big Ben filled our Irish kitchen: my very first sense of drama came from that moment of complete silence between the ending of the chimes and the first of the nine reverberating gongs. Then: 'This is the BBC Home Service, and this is Alvar Liddell with the nine o'clock news. Today, on Luneburg Heath, Field Marshal Montgomery accepted the surrender of all German forces. The war in Europe is over . . .'. The beautifully modulated voices, the rational moderation ('so far, these reports are unconfirmed' was a phrase which ran like a leitmotiv through the news bulletins of my boyhood), the largeness of the issues, all seemed totally unrelated to the tight bigotries of Northern Ireland's streets. For me, the BBC was quintessentially English – those accents! – and provided an enormous sense of security. I remember how particularly I loved the shipping forecasts, especially on stormy nights, when the wireless would bring into the warmth of the kitchen a comforting sense of other men's danger, but danger, the smooth voice always implied, under control: 'The meteorological station issued the following gale warning to shipping at 0600 hours Greenwich Mean Time: "Gales are imminent in sea areas Dogger, Rockall, Fisher, German Bight, Lundy, Fastnet, Faroes, Finisterre . . ."'. There was a kind of poetry in this; and also early on, I derived a strong sense of the poetry of English place names. I lived near places with beautiful names – Tanderagee, Banbridge, Slieve Donard in the Mourne mountains, Slieve Gullion, Slemish (where St Patrick fasted and prayed), Ballynahinch, Magherafelt, Magheramore – but, of course, I didn't see anything special about them. The place name is without honour in its own country. There is a wonderful moment in Brian Friel's fine play, *Translations*, which is about the imposition of English names on Irish places carried out by the Army Ordnance survey in the nineteenth century. One of the English officers falls in love with the music of Irish place names, and with an Irish girl. For her, however, his glamour is located at least in part, in *his* places:

> Winfarthing – Barton Bendish – Saxingham Nethergate – Little Walsingham – Norwich – Strange sounds, but nice; like Jimmy reciting Homer.

My responses to English names originated less romantically, but in its own way, just as strongly.

Once again, it was the BBC which at 5 pm every Saturday opened a casement on a magic land: 'Here are today's football results: Tottenham Hotspur 2, West Bromwich Albion 0; Wolverhampton Wanderers 1, Manchester United 1; Blackburn Rovers 1, Accrington Stanley 2; Brighton and Hove Albion 3, Nottingham Forest 2.' Wolves did wander, I knew, and Robin Hood lived in a forest near Nottingham, but who was Stanley? and could anything hit the ear, let alone the imagination, more finely than the tripping rhythms of 'Tottenham Hotspur'? (Our local football team was called, prosaically, Portadown.)

And England was the home of cricket. My mother was born in the province of Connacht, in Connemara, on Ireland's western coast, a beautiful but barren, boggy, rocky and mountainous region, its coastline deeply fretted by the huge Atlantic breakers which take their first bites at this last output of Europe on their voyage from North America. Like most people of that area at that time, she spoke the Irish language; and I know she never saw a cricket match – perhaps not even a cricket pitch – in all her life. The game's terminology – leg before wicket, silly mid on, long leg, the slips, the gully, the covers – remained obscure to her, as to me for many years. Yet I remember our mutual raptness as the wireless transmitted commentary on the Test Matches, especially those between England and Australia, from distant Lords, or the Oval. I suppose it was something to do with the very mysteriousness of the arcane terminology. 'And Bradman has swept Bedser down to fine leg for two runs.' Certainly it was to do with the round gravelly tones of John Arlott, whose deliberation was a byword and who seemed to *relish* all those moments – frequent in cricket – when nothing is happening. 'And Edrich just gives a little tug at his cap, while a small boy moves behind the sight screen. Probably on his way to buy a bottle of pop. It's certainly a hot enough day here at the Oval, with the famous gasometer shimmering faintly in the heat haze.' Most of all, the appeal of cricket on the BBC was precisely due to its suggestion of a world of harmless ritual, of endless sunny afternoons, of soporific torpidity – all of which contrasted so appealingly with the tension and latent violence of our lives in the North. England, as refracted through the BBC, with its dignified voices which highlighted the more our spiky hard-edged local accents, with its romantic names and its calm, was – most confusingly for me – the great good place.

We could also receive, of course, and did, the broadcasts of Radio Eireann, the radio service of the Irish Free State, lying a mere twenty miles south, where the famous border runs from Cross-maglen to Bessbrook and Forkhill. But Radio Eireann was a sponsored service, and even as a boy I thought that some of the dignity of its news bulletins seeped away when they were followed by advertisements for Donnelly's Pork Sausages (' is it true they're the talk of the nation?') or for Galtee and Mitchelstown Cheese ('keeps you slim, trim and brimful of energy'). Our relationship as a family with the Free State, which became officially the Republic in 1949, was in any case an uneasy one.

My father was born in Kilkenny in 1898, my mother in Connemara in 1900. Both Catholics. Both believed in Home Rule. Like many another southern Irishman, my father saw no incompatibility between believing in Home Rule for Ireland, and enlisting as an infantry private in the British Army during the First World War, where somehow he survived the carnage of Passchendaele. When he returned, lacking any real educational accomplishments, he joined the Royal Irish Constabulary. But the Ireland he returned to was a different place. In the aftermath of the Rising of 1916, Ireland had embraced the republican doctrines of Sinn Fein, and the IRA had begun a policy of harassment, intimidation – and indeed shooting – of members of the RIC, as these were seen as representative of the English Crown forces in the island. His family's house was burned down, and many of his comrades shot. Coincidentally, my mother's house was also burned down – her father was also a member of the RIC. And so, when the Treaty which partitioned Ireland was signed in 1921, they both came North to the new statelet, and my father made the worst mistake of his life – though what else could he do? – and joined the Royal Ulster Constabulary. His seven children were all born in the North. Externally, the conditions of our lives were not easy. It wasn't so much that we were poor, though we were (my father had a constable's wage); but we were Catholics in a Protestant state designed, as its first prime minister put it, for a Protestant people. (Indeed my parents gave themseles away every time they opened their mouths, because they retained their Southern accents.) Worse, our co-religionists regarded us with deep suspicion – the RUC was unquestionably a sectarian police force. My father wore his revolver and carried his baton as if the albatross was hung around his neck.

Internally, in terms of that imaginative sense of tradition and continuity which all of us need, I found it equally difficult. Even had I wanted to – for that matter, even had my father wanted me to – I could not identify with Northern Ireland as a state or polity. The Protestant boys whom we had to fight almost daily on our way back from primary school told us we were Fenian scum, and in a probably unconscious echo of Cromwell's words told us to get the hell back to Connacht. They were British, we were Irish.

Things improved slightly when I was sent to secondary school at St Patrick's College in Armagh, ten miles from Portadown (which did not, of course, have a Catholic secondary school). Armagh was a Catholic, nationalist town, and since the school served the arch-diocese of Armagh, I was surrounded by boys from South Derry, Tyrone, Fermanagh and even from across the border, from Dundalk and Dunleer and Ardee. For the first time in my life, I remember feeling that *we* outnumbered *them*, and that it was *our* Ireland.

But ... while I learned Irish, played Gaelic football and hurling, and found it easy enough to identify with nationalist Ireland, I could never go the whole hog. Partly it was to do with differing attitudes to the Second World War. Southern Ireland had remained neutral, and I knew Catholic boys from Belfast whose families deliberately left lights burning in skylights during the blackout in the hope that German bombers would spot them. As regards the war, I was firmly pro-British and even more so after seeing those first ghastly newsreels about the relief of the concentration camps. But mostly my internal complications about nationalism centred on feelings about my parents and their history. A youthful idealism and a love of eloquence in me responded powerfully to the canonical texts of the Republican tradition – to Robert Emmet's speech from the dock in 1803 ('When my country takes her place among the nations of the earth, then, and not till then, let my epitaph be written'); to the proclamation of the Republic in 1916 ('Irishmen and Irishwomen, in the name of God and of the dead generations, Ireland through us summons her children to her flag and strikes for her freedom'); and above all to the graveside oration delivered by Patrick Pearse in 1913 over the body of O'Donovan Rossa: 'They think they have foreseen everything. They think they have foretold everything. But the fools, the fools, the fools! They have left us our Fenian dead, and while Ireland holds these graves, Ireland unfree shall never be at peace!' But these texts, learned lovingly at school, could not be uttered in my home. They would have affronted my parents who had been driven into exile, in a very real sense, by the ideology which lay behind them. Indeed, my father never referred to Patrick Pearse without appending the bitter phrase 'that squinting idiot'. (Pearse had a cast in one eye.)

I think all boys hunger for heroic models. I could find nothing heroic in Ulster Protestantism, save perhaps in the memorials to those killed on the Somme and in Flanders, and I didn't see why these memorials insisted on giving the impression that only *they* had fought there. I found plenty that was heroic in the long nationalist tradition, but my access to that was hampered and thwarted by family *pietas*. Perhaps inevitably – however paradoxically – the simplest solution for me was to go for *English* heroic models, which were, emotionally speaking, uncomplicated. This applied particularly to one Sergeant Matt Braddock, VC, the eponymous hero of a serial story that appeared in the boy's comic, *The Rover*, every week. Strong of chin, blue of eye, Matt Braddock was co-pilot of a Lancaster bomber of the famous Tiger Squadron. Only a sergeant, note – part of the great appeal was Braddock's ordinary background. He wasn't just co-pilot – on its bombing missions into Nazi Germany, the plane was attacked usually by thousands of Messerschmitts (their pilots saying over the radio things like 'Jawohl, mein Führer, the English *Schweinhund* will be brought down before Bremen') and the flak was always most alarming. Matt therefore generally had to fly the plane single-handed – Squadron Leader Neville 'Tufty' Tufnell having taken some shrapnel over the Ruhr – and navigate it, *and* act as rear gunner, *and* drop the bombs (always spot-on, and always on a factory making tanks for the Waffen SS), *and* nurse the crippled Lancaster – G for George – back to Lincolnshire before the chip shop closed. I loved it – I had not heard of Dresden. It was all so black and white – Nazi Germany *was* evil, it had to be beaten – and such a relief from the complexities of the home terrain. I think it was the very simplicity of English heroicising that appealed. Even before I came to Matt Braddock, I had thrilled to the patriotic stanzas in the poems I found printed in Arthur Mee's *Children's Encyclopaedia* (a kind of handbook of empire), poems like Sir Henry Newbolt's:

> The sand of the desert is sodden red,
>   Red with the wreck of a square that broke; –
> The Gatling's jammed and the Colonel's dead,
>   And the regiment blind with dust and smoke.
> The river of death has brimmed its banks,
>   And England's far, and Honour a name,
> But the voice of a schoolboy rallies the ranks:
>   'Play up! play up! and play the game!'

I took that imperial England for a heroic dream. I could see no connection between it and the circumstances of my boyhood life. We were not, as it seemed, threatened by British soldiers or gunboats. The threat lay in the flintfaced Calvinism of Stormont, in the Orange bigot ranting his hatred, in the B-Special waving down your bicycle at night with his squat Sten-gun.

In his famous essay, 'Boy's Weeklies', George Orwell remarks that 'the worst books are often the most important because they are usually the ones that are read earliest in life'. Later in life, when I read English literature at Belfast University, I was to encounter the genuine cultural wealth of one of the world's greatest literatures. 'The gaunt thorns all bent one way as if craving alms of the sun' in *Wuthering Heights*, the district where the young Wordsworth was 'fostered alike by beauty and by fear', the heroic pathos of Milton's Satan – 'If thou be'est he, but O! how fallen, how chang'd ...', the creamy sensuousness of Hardy's Tess, the laconic effrontery of Jonson's knaves and Shakespeare's Edmund, and so much more, became part of my mental furniture forever. However, I think Orwell has a point. I was an avid reader of public school stories, my favourite being a book called *Teddy Lester and His Chums*. It was prototypical of thousands of pages I read of a similar kind. Teddy Lester himself was superb at all games, and preternaturally fair in competition, but with a disarming weakness at French irregular verbs. Conversely, Ivor ('Bat') Robinson was the school genius, absorbing vast amounts of knowledge through thick spectacles, completely unco-ordinated at Rugby football, but with one special talent, for bowling devilish googlies. Lord Edward Ponsonby was a real sport, and constantly treated the chums at the tuck shock with fivers sent him by his 'pater'. Need I go on?

Orwell suggests that the great attraction of the public school lies in its snob-appeal, the overall class glamour of the thing. This was not what appealed to me, and I doubt if any Irish boy would have felt that particular attraction – the niceties of the English social register were well beyond us. Mainly, I think, the appeal lay in the notion of codes and rules, especially as those applied to enmity. You might have to fight, that is, but if you did, it would be with boxing gloves in a ring, with a proper referee, and afterwards hands would be shaken. Even the cads and bounders subscribed to the notion of 'fair play'. In that world, you would not see, with that sickening lurch of the heart, three shadowy figures detach themselves from a wall and saunter towards you, while you realised that your mental navigation – Matt Braddock, where were you? – had let you down, and you had blundered into an Orange street. In *Teddy Lester* you would not get a half-brick on the head because you were a 'Papish'.

Orwell describes sardonically the mental world of the public school story.

You are sitting down to tea in your study on the Remove passage after an exciting game of football won by an odd goal in the last half-minute. There is a cosy fire in the study and outside the wind is whistling. The ivy clusters thickly round the old grey stones. The King is on his throne and the pound is worth a pound. Over in Europe the comic foreigners are jabbering and gesticulating, but the grim grey battleships of the British fleet are steaming up the Channel and at the outposts of Empire the monocled Englishmen are holding the niggers at bay. Lord Mauleverer has just had another fiver and we are all settling down to a tremendous tea of sausages, sardines, crumpets, potted meat, jam and doughnuts.... Everything is safe, solid and unquestionable. Everything will be the same forever and ever.

Exactly. As a boy, I would not have had worries about the comic foreigners of Europe or the black or yellow peril. But what this England of the mind offered, in its atrocious way, was an image of security so powerful that the rubs of sad experience and the much greater literature I read subsequently could never quite expunge it. Perhaps it was because the Orangeman with the half-brick was such an immediate danger; but there was also in that cosy study and that English public school world of *Teddy Lester and His Chums* a more metaphorical kind of security – a security of cultural identity. A complacency, even. Perhaps an arrogance: the English were so obviously the master race that they didn't have to argue about it: they had the effortless superiority of the Balliol man. How I envied that confidence! At a simpler level, the physical comforts were not to be sneezed at: one of the reasons why I enjoyed middle-class English children's fiction, from Enid Blyton's Famous Five series through Richmal Crompton's William stories, to the works of Arthur Ransome where the girls were called amazing names like Titty – one of the reasons, apart from the fact that William and Co. had to *invent* their enemies, why I enjoyed them so much was that nearly everyone had a bedroom to himself or herself. And tents. And boats. And the church clock stood at 10 to 3 and there was honey still for tea. No world is as timeless as the world of our first reading, especially if that work is itself *deliberately* nostalgic, as I began to see that it was when I graduated to P. G. Wodehouse, in whose work the Drones Club, Blandings Castle and Mr Mulliner's bar are simply immortal, places out of time.

I had, then, lived quite intensely in various Englands of the mind before I arrived, aged 21, in Oxford, as a graduate student. Perhaps that almost farcically beautiful city is not the best place to begin an encounter with the real England; but so, for me, it was. The first shock to my system was to discover how completely secular a country England was, compared to my own. I remember my first Sunday walking to mass and wondering where everyone was, until I began to notice various manifestations of the most sacred English religion of today: the Worship of the Car. Everywhere machines were being washed, polished, buffed, hoovered, dusted, adored. Religion in England had dwindled, I saw after a while, to what I might call secular rituals – the weekly car-wash, show-Saturdays, race-meetings, seaside outings, weddings at Whitsun: the secular rituals celebrated so beautifully, yet with such characteristic English agnosticism, in the poetry of Philip Larkin. I perceived this secularism with a kind of contempt; I was sufficiently Irish to consider the worship of material things vulgar. Further, I could see that England had not really excised intolerance: there was no religious intolerance, true, but that was only because religion was a dead duck in England; what there was was plenty of racial intolerance.

The second major shock was to encounter, even in the sacred colleges of Oxford University – or perhaps – I should say *especially* in the colleges of Oxford? – condescension and ignorance. The condescension was well meant in the sense that it was friendly, but all the more alarming for being so: one was made to feel like a monkey in the zoo. I would not have minded so much being a monkey in the zoo if I could have felt that the spectators were rather more informed about the monkeys. Precisely because I had lived imaginatively in England I expected (unreasonably?) that the English might have devoted a little thought, a little imagination, to their oldest colony. They hadn't – as was made quite clear in the desperate flailing scramble of the editorial writers to clarify 50 years of total neglect, when the Northern Irish time-bomb finally exploded in 1968–9.

The wheel had come full circle. The trials and tribulations of life in Ireland, plus the proximity and sheer bulk of English culture had helped to turn me into a kind of exile in my own country, who responded to versions of Englishness. Living in England, explaining myself, and watching my little province tear itself apart, I found I was driven back on my Irishness. Further, I have asked myself: What does it all mean?

There is a famous paradigmatic moment in Joyce's *Portrait of the Artist* where Stephen Dedalus experiences the shadow of imperialism falling across his conversation with an English priest:

He felt with a smart of dejection that the man to whom he was speaking was a countryman of Ben Jonson. He thought:

The language in which we are speaking is his before it is mine. How different are the words *home, Christ, ale, master,* on his lips and on mine! I cannot speak or write these words without unrest of spirit. His language, so familiar and so foreign, will always be for me an acquired speech. I have not made or accepted its words. My voice holds them at bay. My soul frets in the shadow of his language.

Speaking the English language, listening to the BBC, reading English school stories, considering soccer and cricket superior to Gaelic football and hurling, more interested in the Battle of Britain than in the Battle of Clontarf, wanting to go to Oxford rather than to University College, Dublin – I might be a perfect specimen of the colonised, if the index of that condition is the degree to which the coloniser's value system is internalised. But how intensely do I feel 'the smart of dejection'? Or, in general terms, how evil *are* the effects of cultural imperialism? To answer that question would require the best efforts of political theorists, sociologists and anthropologists. Indeed, it may not be possible to give a comprehensive answer. That would be part of my point. For it is certainly easy to dramatise, even sentimentalise, and over-generalise about, the condition of the colonised.

Thus, I can easily sympathise with, even identify with, those Irish writers who seek to restore in their art the consciousness of 'the dispossessed', the consciousness of the Gaelic civilisation of Ireland which began to die in the eighteenth century, and which received its mortal wound in the calamity of the Great Famine. My sense of deprivation is there, and it is real, as I recall some of my mother's Irish phrases and turns of speech. But there is also the question of realism. I would agree with the Irish poet Thomas Kinsella's remarks on the vanished Gaelic world: 'The inheritance is mine, but only at two enormous removes – across a century's silence, and through an exchange of worlds.' The broken tradition, the fragmented culture is a reality, and it is only honest (if painful) to accept that this is so. To pretend otherwise, to imagine that the clock can be turned back, is a mistake; and the sterilities (and the dangers) of a strident assertion of the purity of the national identity – 'little Irelandism' – are sufficiently obvious in the island today.

I see now all the faults in my youthful embrace of the simplified stereotypes and clichés of Englishness, which the English manufacture with such facility and export with such success, what might be called 'Masterpiece Theatre England' (*Brideshead* and all that) in all its ineffable silliness. But I must ask myself: was I wrong to feel that to respond to England's involvement in the Second World War with the traditional phrase 'England's difficulty is Ireland's opportunity' was to respond narrowly and myopically? Would I have received a university education if I had not had the benefits of the British university grants system? Was it a bad thing to be opened to English culture, and through it, to the culture of the Anglophone world, whether American or Australian or West Indian? Was it not useful, certainly instructive, to grow up even in Northern Ireland, where I learned early the oppression, discrimination and bigotry which is the fate (at more frightening levels) of so many people of the world? Cannot an admiration for Irish cultural traditions coexist with an admission of the relevance of the modern world? I learned many useful things from my encounter with 'Englishness'; and on balance, I would say the benefits outweighed the very real drawbacks: ethnic political resentment is a fact, but so is a sense of cultural enlargement.

I understand the feelings and motivation of those who would insist on the purity, or the purification, of their own cultural traditions. The homogenisation of the world – MacDonalds in Munich, Coca-Cola in Khartoum, 'Dallas' in Dublin – is not a pretty sight or a pretty prospect. But I have more faith in the unquenchable, individualising diversity of cultures, despite the levelling forces at work in our modern world, than those who, even for laudable ends, would erect *cordons sanitaires* around their own ethnicities. And clearly, as the history of the twentieth century shows with depressing clarity, cultural nationalism can be a very dangerous force indeed.

A final point. One of the dangers of cultural nationalism is its insistence on the absolute uniqueness of the cultural experience, whether German, Japanese, Iranian or Irish. But we who are modern live increasingly in a discontinuous, polyglot world, and what is now clear to me is that the experience described in this essay, of confused loyalties and uncertain identity, is not, as I once thought, aberrant. In a world often politically and culturally disrupted it is an experience which becomes increasingly typical. I end with part of a letter to Herbert Read, written by that great defender of tradition, stability and continuity, T. S. Eliot:

I want to write an essay about the point of view of an American who wasn't an American, because he was born in the South and went to school in New England as a small boy with a nigger drawl, but who wasn't a southerner in the South because his people were northerners in a border state and looked down on all southerners and Virginians, and who so was never anything anywhere and who therefore felt himself to be more a Frenchman than an American and more an Englishman than a Frenchman and yet felt that the U.S.A. up to a hundred years ago was a family extension. It is almost too difficult even for [H]enry J[ames] who for that matter wasn't an American at all, in that sense.

12

'The Most Wonderful Foreign Land I Have Ever Been In': Kipling's England

NORMAN PAGE

Conrad, Joyce, Eliot, Nabokov, Beckett, Kipling. As the advertisements say, what do these men have in common? Or, to pose the question perhaps less teasingly, in the manner of an old-fashioned IQ test, which of the names on this list is the odd one out? Faced with the latter question, most people, I imagine, would promptly nominate Kipling as the cheeky interloper, the incongruous intruder in this small gathering of academically venerated modernist and post-modernist writers. I would like to suggest, however, that he has more in common with them than is sometimes supposed. Unavoidable or voluntary exile, the loss or renunciation of homeland and sometimes also of mother tongue, is a recurring feature of twentieth-century literature, though case-histories can display a variety of patterns. Joyce quits his country by an act of will but continues to write about it; Nabokov is forced to flee from his. Conrad, having jumped out of Poland, adopts first one country and then another, and at last chooses an alien language as his literary medium; Nabokov writes first in his native language and then, after a second flight in middle life, in an adopted one; Beckett, somewhat similarly, writes first in English, then in French, completing the circle by becoming a self-translator. These representative figures of the twentieth century, the age of emigration and exile, exemplify the fate of millions in their loss or surrender of country, family, culture and even language.

What can Kipling possibly have in common with the likes of these? The popular image of him is scarcely that of the exile, isolated and ill at ease, but of one aggressively, even oppressively self-confident, a pillar of the establishment, a friend of royalty, unofficial Poet Laureate and spokesman for the Empire, strident and hectoring, a sort of up-market Alf Garnett in manner as well as moustache – and, in most present-day academic circles, irredeemably unfashionable. Like other popular images, however, this one ignores the complexities of a writer whose nature was full of contradictions, tensions and enigmas, and whose work sometimes reflects these qualities. It also relies too exclusively on the public man of the later years – a common failing on the part of popular images, as the examples of Tennyson and Hardy among many others confirm. A glance at some of the circumstances of Kipling's early life suggests that the experience of exile and rootlessness was something he knew intimately enough to turn to creative account.

Born in Bombay, he spent most of his first five years there, and his earliest remembered impressions were of tropical sunlight and colour and an Eden-like cornucopia in the fruit market to which his ayah took him. She was a Goanese Roman Catholic who sometimes stopped with her small charge to pray 'at a wayside Cross';[1] the other family servant with whom he spent much of his time was the bearer Meeta, who took him to the Hindu temples; so that alien forms of worship were implanted in his young mind as early as the Christianity of his parents. With Meeta the child spoke Hindi, and (as he recalled near the end of his life) when he appeared before his parents had to be reminded to 'speak English now to Papa and Mama'. 'So', Kipling adds in his autobiography, 'one spoke "English", haltingly translated out of the vernacular idiom that one thought and dreamed in.'[2] When at the age of sixteen, after eleven years in England, he returned to India, the long-unused vernacular came flooding back; and an Indian scholar has said that Kipling in his writings uses Indian words with greater 'ease and understanding' than any other Anglo-Indian writer.[3]

In the hot afternoons of his early childhood they all slept; then, as the light faded, they walked 'by the sea in the shadow of palm-groves', and Kipling always remembered 'the menacing darkness of tropical eventides, ... the voices of night-winds through palm or banana leaves, and the song of the tree-frogs'.[4] I take these phrases, again, from *Something of Myself*, Kipling's last major prose work, the opening pages of which bring his life full circle. It sounds like, and surely was, a setting of Conradian romance and exoticism for what Dickens in *Great Expectations* refers to as a child's 'first most vivid and broad impression of the identity of things'. But when Kipling recalled and recreated it in his seventieth year, he had not seen India for well over forty years and wrote as an exile from a world that, like Nabokov, he preserved in scrupulous and detailed memory but never chose to revisit – one could go further and say chose not to revisit – in the flesh.

For Kipling's parents, as for all Anglo-Indians, it was England that was 'home'; and the usage, somewhat paradoxical to a child born and reared in the tropics, must have been part of Kipling's early experience. It did not, however, prevent the cold and sunless northern land from coming as a severe shock to him when he saw it, 'a dark land'; and the syntax of the passage in the autobiography that recalls the journey to England and arrival there evokes the world of the child in a way that recalls the opening page of Joyce's *Portrait of the Artist as a Young Man*:

> There was a train across a desert (the Suez Canal was not yet opened) and a halt in it, and a small girl wrapped in a shawl on the seat opposite me, whose face stands out still. There was next a dark land, and a darker room full of cold, in one wall of which a white woman made naked fire, and I cried aloud with dread, for I had never before seen a grate.[5]

A year or two before Kipling wrote these words, Jean Rhys rendered a very similar experience in her novel *Voyage in the Dark* (1934), whose heroine comes to England from the West Indies:

> It was as if a curtain had fallen, hiding everything I had ever known. It was almost like being born again. The colours were different, the smells different, the feeling things gave you right down inside yourself was different.

And she registers 'the difference between heat, cold; light, darkness; purple, grey' just as the young Kipling must more intuitively have done.

There followed for him the seven years hard in 'The House of Desolation' in Southsea with the Holloways of Lorne Lodge (could invention possibly improve on the symbolic rightness of those actual names?) – an experience that was, as Edmund Wilson suggested long ago, Kipling's more prolonged equivalent of Dickens's blacking-factory, and one that left no room for doubt about his expulsion from India-Eden, since at a blow he was deprived of land, climate, home, parents, friends, the reassuring deference of servants, and the language in which he had 'thought and dreamed'.

Then came four and a half years at the United Services College in North Devon, where he was not unhappy but, as the only boy in the school wearing spectacles and as the son of an artist in a school dominated by army families, he was inevitably something of an alien.

I have perhaps gone far enough in recalling these aspects of Kipling's early years to suggest that leaving behind the land of his birth and its culture and language was a part of his most deeply rooted experience. But he had turned thirty before he made England his permanent adopted home, and even then only with important qualifications; and we need to glance at the extensive wanderings of the fourteen years between his leaving school and his eventual resettlement in England in 1896. His return to India at the age of sixteen initiated his period of apprenticeship as a writer, spent working for newspapers in Lahore and Allahabad. During this time, and while he was still only twenty, *Departmental Ditties* appeared, followed less than two years later by *Plain Tales from the Hills*. In these twin débuts, in verse and prose, it is of course India, Indians and Anglo-Indians that furnish his material; and perhaps the most impressive quality of these youthful writings is the expertness of Kipling's knowledge of his material. (It was Joyce who said, after reading the *Plain Tales*, 'If I knew Ireland as well as R. K. seems to know India, I fancy I would write something good.')[6]

Not surprisingly, success engendered the desire to test his talents in a wider sphere; and this prodigy who already looked middle-aged but was in fact only 23 travelled the long way home (though he can hardly have thought of it as such), to England via the Pacific and the United States. What he was returning to, in personal terms, was the scene of an unhappy childhood and a rather isolated boarding-school life; in professional terms he was moving from the fringes of the civilised world (as many of his contemporaries would have seen it) to its very heart. He made some efforts to adopt protective coloration – by joining the Savile Club, for instance – but remained a discontented outsider in the London of the day. As Kingsley Amis has written, 'With all his knowledge of the outside world, he was a colonial in the London of the English Decadence, on the eve of the Nineties and *The Picture of Dorian Gray*.'[7] The first of Max Beerbohm's series of hostile caricatures, which place the emphasis on Kipling's provincialism and populism, follows only a few years later (1896), while Kipling gives as good as he takes in combative verses such as 'The Rhyme of the Three Captains', in which this upstart outsider quarrels publicly with the middle-aged Hardy and other established figures in the literary world.

All this suggests an only partially successful attempt to settle happily in London: it is surely significant that during this period Kipling's closest friend and collaborator was an American, and that he soon married that friend's sister, for his inclinations were still cosmopolitan and his impulses towards globe-trotting, the life of the roving journalist rather than that of the man of letters. Just before his marriage he set off to go round the world (and in the course of that voyage saw India for the last time); immediately after it the couple set off on another global trip. As it happened, both circumnavigations, for different reasons, proved abortive; but the idea of settling down was evidently still far from Kipling's thoughts. The loss of his savings took him back to Vermont, where his wife's parents had an estate; and thus began a four-year period of residence in the United States that, but for family unpleasantness, might have been lifelong. Kipling stayed there long enough at any rate to consider taking out citizenship and to acquire the beginnings of an American accent; but for the quarrel with his brother-in-law, he might have belonged to American literature; and he left the country with the hope of returning some day and with a strong sense of loss and deprivation. He is reported to have said on the day before his departure that there were 'only two places in the world where I want to live – Bombay and Brattleboro [Vermont]. And I can't live at either.' Exiled from India in childhood, he now, as the father of young children, suffered exile a second time.

It was in these inauspicious circumstances that Kipling once again came to England in 1896, and he might have been dismayed as well as surprised if he had been told on arrival that he was to remain there for the next forty years. Not that his globe-trotting quickly ceased: on the contrary, the Kipling family remained great travellers, revisiting the United States (disastrously) and spending many winters in South Africa. But he never returned to India, and came to write about it less and less.

The creative vacuum was filled by a preoccupation, limited at first but growing steadily, with recording and celebrating his discovery of England – an England, it is as well to say at once, partly observed, partly recreated from the historical past, but also to an important extent idealised or invented. Speaking of his second career, as a novelist in the English language, Nabokov wrote in his essay 'On a Book Entitled *Lolita*': 'It had taken me some forty years to invent Russia and Western Europe, and now I was faced by the task of inventing America.' Kipling's self-imposed task was to invent England, and he did it most notably in a series of stories of which I want to discuss the best and most characteristic examples in some detail.

But first let us consider for a moment the process by which Kipling, now thirty years old and returning yet again to England – a country that both was and was not 'home' – eased himself into English life. During the mid 1890s, in the course of what may be called his American period, he had visited England twice to see his parents, who had by that time left India to spend their retirement in a Wiltshire village; and a little later I shall draw attention to a story that reflects those visits. But the return from America in August 1896 was not a holiday but, as it turned out, a permanent and final change of his country of residence; and it saw the beginning of his association with a series of houses in southern England that were to play a part in his work. A rented house near Torquay was the Kipling family's first English home and appeared long afterwards in the story 'The House Surgeon'. Within less than a year, though, they had moved to Sussex; and this was the county that Kipling adopted – though perhaps appropriated or annexed would be a better word, since there was something fiercely proprietorial in his attitude towards it, the jealous possessiveness of the outsider who needs to assert his status as insider (for emotional rather than social or economic reasons, it should be added). This conspired with Kipling's lifelong addiction to in-groups of all kinds: schools and clubs, the army and the freemasons, every kind of craft or calling from the ship's engineer to the writer that has its own techniques and jargon and professional mysteries. He was capable of turning any human group – those who had lost a child, or those suffering from cancer or shell-shock – into a kind of secret society; and his newly acquired status as a resident of Sussex quickly became a badge and a boast. The audacity of that favourite anthology piece, his poem 'Sussex', is almost breath-taking:

> God gave all men all earth to love,
>   But, since our hearts are small,
> Ordained for each one spot should prove
>   Belovèd over all;
> That, as He watched Creation's birth,
>   So we, in godlike mood,
> May of our love create our earth
>   And see that it is good.

In other words, each man – at least, if he happens to belong to the club formed by those who feel a deep affection for England – does God's work over again for his private purpose.

Actually, the boasting had begun even earlier. In, for instance, the story 'A Matter of Fact', written during his American residence, he had indulged in that favourite pastime of the British of putting those from younger countries in their place by drawing attention to the superior antiquity of the English scene. A nice example of this gambit, in an elegant and subtle form, turns up in Rupert Brooke's *Letters from America* (1916):

> I travelled from Edmonton to Calgary in the company of a citizen of Edmonton and a citizen of Calgary. Hour after hour they disputed. Land in Calgary had risen from five dollars to three hundred; but in Edmonton from three to five hundred. Edmonton had grown from thirty persons to forty thousand in twenty years; but Calgary from twenty to thirty thousand in twelve.... 'Where' – as a respite – 'did I come from?' I had to tell them, not without shame, that my own town of Grantchester, having numbered three hundred at the time of Julius Cæsar's landing, had risen rapidly to nearly four by Doomsday Book, but was now declined to three-fifty. They seemed perplexed and angry.   (pp. 128–9)

In Kipling's story, when an American journalist in England asks 'How old is that farmhouse?' he is told, 'New. It can't be more than two hundred years at the most'; and this is echoed in the autobiography, in a passage in which Kipling relates his first sight of the Jacobean house that was to become his final home and comments, 'the "new" end of her was three hundred years old'.[8] And yet what Kipling had behind him, of course, was not Brooke's Rugby and Cambridge but the United Services College, a brand-

new public school, and the *Civil and Military Gazette* of Lahore; and
for all his assertions of profound Englishness he remained, for
better or worse – or more precisely for better *and* worse – an
outsider.

Soon after he settled in England he wrote from the genteel town
of Torquay:

> I have been studying my fellow-countrymen from the out-
> side.... We are a rummy breed – and O Lord the ponderous
> wealthy society. Torquay is such a place as I do desire acutely to
> upset by dancing through it with nothing on but my spectacles.[9]

That declaration involves a curious balancing-act: he is studying
the English 'from the outside', as he is well qualified to do, but it is
'we', not 'they', who are 'a rummy breed': he evidently has a sense
of being simultaneously inside and outside the English scene. And
a recurring figure in his English stories is the foreign visitor,
usually an American, who is variously baffled or seduced, made
ridiculous or enchanted, by England and the English: a figure who
is at times at least semi-autobiographical (as the Kipling family was
semi-American), but is at other times seen with callous objectivity.

From the beginning of the 1890s, Kipling uses English themes
and settings in his stories, and over the ensuing years he uses
them with increasing frequency. An early instance, 'My Sunday at
Home', takes place on 'an English May-day', and the narrator-
observer is a returned exile who loves his country 'with the
devotion that three thousand miles of intervening sea brings to
fullest flavour'. His response to the landscape of the south of
England is the idealised one of the summer visitor and the English
Tourist Board:

> And what a garden of Eden it was, this fatted, clipped, and
> washen land! A man could camp in any open field with more
> sense of home and security than the stateliest buildings of
> foreign cities could afford. And the joy was that it was all mine
> inalienably – groomed hedgerow, spotless road, decent greysto-
> ne cottage, serried spinney, tasselled copse, apple-bellied
> hawthorn, and well-grown tree.

Again, the stance is that out of outsider-insider: the 'intervening
sea' surely alludes to Kipling's own American residence, and the

'stateliest buildings' that offer no 'sense of home and security' seem to be those of New York. And again the note of possession, and possessiveness, is unmistakable: 'all mine inalienably'. What is interesting is that the story was written *before* Kipling's return to England: its composition belongs to one of those holiday visits to his parents in Wiltshire; and this is perhaps hinted at in another passage in which the narrator comments,

> There was a beautiful smell in the air – the smell of white dust, bruised nettles, and smoke, that brings tears to the throat of a man who sees his country but seldom – a smell like the echoes of the lost talk of lovers; the infinitely suggestive odour of an immemorial civilisation.

This seems to anticipate (for the date is 1894) the Georgian poets, but the exile's sadness is Kipling's own.

The other characters in this story are a guileless American visitor and a Chaucerian and Falstaffian English navvy; the narrator's role is that of mediator and his position clearly falls between these two national identities. A final point of interest is that the story includes a reference to *Tess of the d'Urbervilles* (a novel that opens on a day in May), was originally published while the serialisation of *Jude the Obscure* was in progress, and is partly set in Wiltshire, which is, of course, included in Hardy's Wessex. It is difficult not to read the closing words of the story – 'And the seven forty-five carried me on, a step nearer to Eternity, by the road that is worn and seamed and channelled with the passions, and weaknesses, and warring interests of man who is immortal and master of his fate' – as a calculated retort to Hardy's tragic vision in language that comes close to parodying Hardy's own language and imagery; and it is striking (though also characteristic) that Kipling, as a visitor to England, is prepared to take on the great novelist of the English landscape and to offer a rival view of man's nature and destiny.

Of the series of stories with English settings that belongs to Kipling's Sussex years, I want to draw attention to just a handful. So far my discusion has been mainly of the Victorian Kipling (his life, neatly and aptly, is almost exactly equally divided between the nineteenth and the twentieth centuries); the stories I now turn to are by the Edwardian and the Georgian Kipling, and cover the two decades from 1904 to 1924. Kipling settled in Sussex in 1897 and moved to Bateman's, where he spent the rest of his life, in 1902. His father had come from Yorkshire; his mother's family were Scots; he had been to school in Devon, and as a young man had lived in London; but, as his autobiography relates (or claims), he gravitated 'almost by instinct' to Sussex, where he had spent boyhood holidays with his aunt and uncle and had passed his 'very last days before sailing for India' fourteen years earlier.[10] In Bateman's, a Jacobean house, Kipling consciously inhabited history. His description of the house as being reached 'down an enlarged rabbit-hole of a lane' has an *Alice in Wonderland* flavour of magic; and he struck up acquaintance with Sussex characters who seem to have been survivors from a vanishing age of folklore and superstition, including a woman who 'would range through a past that accepted magic, witchcraft and love-philtres', and who 'described [a] midnight ritual at the local "wise woman's" cottage, when a black cock was killed with curious rites and words'.[11] In his autobiography Kipling renders her dialect speech as he does for some of his fictional characters. Another acquaintance was a poacher who was 'more "one with Nature" than whole parlours full of poets'.[12] Kipling had begun his career as a journalist of genius, recording the exotic and alien scene in the country of his birth; now he had come 'home', in Anglo-Indian terms, to a country he did not know well and that had for him its own exotic strangeness. Hence his remark to Charles Eliot Norton: 'England is a wonderful land. It is the most marvellous of all foreign countries that I have ever been in' – echoed in another letter to Rider Haggard: 'I am slowly discovering England, which is the most wonderful foreign land I have ever been in.' These statements have the form of a Wildean epigram but for Kipling embodied a profound truth.

It is tempting to read his story 'An Habitation Enforced' as an allegory of Kipling's own settlement or resettlement in England. The theme of sickness and healing that is later to become so prominent in his work makes an early appearance in this story of 1905. A youngish American tycoon – and Kipling himself was, after all, a very successful man in his own line of business, who had nearly become an American – has suffered a complete breakdown and resorts to travel in quest of spiritual health. He and his wife find themselves by chance in an English village, they fall in love with a derelict eighteenth-century house, become absorbed in the task of restoring it to its former splendour, and discover that they are also becoming absorbed into the social fabric of rural England. Ultimately they learn that they have unwittingly come home, since it emerges that the wife's ancestors had originally emigrated to the New World from this very spot. (It may be relevant to recall at this point that some of Kipling's maternal ancestors had fled across the Atlantic after Culloden.) The couple are at first bewildered by the English attachment to place – as the millionaire says, 'People don't seem to matter in this country compared to the places they live in' – but they are educated into a realisation of the duty they owe to the land and a reverence for tradition and history: as he later tells his wife, 'It's *not* our land. We've only paid for it. We belong to it, and it belongs to the people – our people they call 'em.' The story ends with the birth of a son and heir and the assurance of continuity; America and the pursuit of wealth seem to have been entirely forgotten.

The rural social order depicted is archaic, hierarchical, almost feudal, and yet adaptable enough to absorb an American couple into the gentry once they have demonstrated their commitment to house, estate and community (the favourite Kipling motif of the qualifying test). What makes them different from certain *nouveau riche* neighbours is that they are moved entirely by love and not by social aspirations; perhaps only those from outside English society itself, as the Americans are and as the Kiplings must have seen themselves as largely being, could have bypassed all considerations of social rising. It seems possible that Kipling's wish to be accepted as a member of English upper-class society, and for his American wife to accept England as her home, is behind this story. Certainly the poem 'The Recall', which stands as a pendant to it, has an autobiographical application:

> I am the land of their fathers,
>   In me the virtue stays;
> I will bring back my children
>   After certain days.
>
> Under their feet in the grasses
>   My clinging magic runs.
> They shall return as strangers,
>   They shall remain as sons.

Arnold Bennett complained that 'An Habitation Enforced' relies on 'a terrific coincidence', but if he had read it more carefully he would have found that Kipling confronts and responds to this objection. When the couple attend the village church and are shown into the pew that belongs to their house, the wife, kneeling in prayer, finds her mother's family name carved on the floor. 'Coincidence?' asks her husband; to which she replies, 'perhaps . . .'. But for Kipling it is clearly the result of a kind of 'leading' (a word his heroine has used earlier in the story): a guiding of human actions by some means inexplicable in rational or Arnold Bennett terms. It is not for Bennett's reason that I am myself uneasy about this powerful story. The American woman's discovery that she has unwittingly (though perhaps with an unconscious sense of direction) returned to her roots is disturbing not because it relies on coincidence, which is unimportant, but because it is superfluous and needlessly confuses the issue. Kipling's central theme surely runs something like this: whom does England – rural England – belong to? (That rural England is for him the 'real' England is a consideration, some will think a disabling one, to which we must return.) His answer is that it belongs to an aristocracy: not (to paraphrase a famous passage by E. M. Forster) an aristocracy of birth but one of love, duty and responsibility. The American couple pass this test; so (to show that the hereditary aristocracy are not necessarily disqualified at the outset) does Lady Conant, a Lady Bountiful who is bossy and eccentric but whose heart is in the right place; so do not the social climbers. But Kipling goes beyond this to show that the American woman is the real thing, with upper-class Sussex blood in her veins, in any case and after all; and this belt-and-braces argument seems to weaken the force of the story. Conceivably Kipling is uncomfortably close in this story to his own anxieties and longings: as the owner of freehold in Sussex, he wanted to be accepted as an English gentleman even though he had been to the wrong school, was too short-sighted to shoot, and was that dubious thing, a professional writer; but he also felt that he was entitled to it anyway. The clear fictional pattern has perhaps been distorted by autiobiographical pressures; and once again the uneasy role of the insider-outsider is in evidence.

At the end of this story, the couple are 'down at the brook . . . to consider the rebuilding of a footbridge carried away by spring floods'; and I want next to consider two stories that take up this motif of the flooded brook and use it for their own purposes. Both are included in the volume *A Diversity of Creatures*, and both are accompanied by poems that present the central ideas of the stories without their rich fictional circumstantiality.

'Friendly Brook' returns to the theme 'Whom does the land belong to?' in somewhat purer form than we have seen it in 'An Habitation Enforced'. A Sussex farmer is blackmailed by a ruffian from the city; but the forces of nature are kindly disposed towards countryfolk, and the invader is drowned by the flooding of a brook. Thereafter the farmer tries to repay his debt of gratitude to the brook by allowing it in floodtime to carry away the occasional haystack. The story is set in a frame of work on the land: as they labour at hedging, one countryman tells the anecdote to another, and this point of view has the effect of heightening the contrast between town and country. London is a place where people maintain an existence without engaging in 'real' work: when his listener asks 'Hadn't that man no trade or business, then?' the storyteller replies, 'He told me he was a printer. I reckon, though, he lived on the rates like the rest of 'em up there in Lunnon.' One feels that even if he had genuinely been a printer, the dissemination of words could hardly be regarded in this context as productive toil. The joke is, of course, that in another sense the context is the printed page and that the ultimate storyteller is Kipling himself, who has assigned to a printer the task of giving permanent and public form to his gibe against printers. As often – and increasingly – in these stories, the country world is enclosed and unchanging, but we are made aware of the other England of change and hurry just beyond its boundaries. At one point in the narrative, the speaker points 'up-hill, where unseen automobiles and road-engines droned past continually', and he comments: 'A tarred road, she shoots every drop o' water into a valley same's a slat roof. 'Tisn't as 'twas in the old days, when the waters soaked in and soaked out in the way o' nature.' Kipling's evocation of 'the way o' nature' is blended with a poignant awareness that tarred roads and traffic have come to stay, and with them a way of life that will inevitably destroy what has survived from the past.

The poem 'The Land' that accompanies 'Friendly Brook' conducts a brisk survey of English history from the Roman occupation to the reign of George V in order to make the point that, no matter who owns title-deeds and pays taxes, the real owner of the land is the English yeoman. The theme of both poem and story recalls that of Forster's *Howards End*, published a few years earlier; but although there is a touch of Kiplingesque mysticism in Mrs Wilcox's recognition of Margaret as a kind of spiritual heiress, Forster is more heavily committed to the nineteenth-century tradition of realism and in the end it is, as in *Mansfield Park*, through marriage and the laws of property and inheritance that the question of spiritual inheritance is settled. Kipling's background – and perhaps also his temperament and the nature of his genius – makes him less committed to what Q. D. Leavis called 'the Englishness of the English novel', and he is bolder in his depicting of instinctive loyalties and inexplicable acts of justice: the wilful child who used to 'walk down the village street muttering "Ruddy is coming, Ruddy is coming" '[13] turned into a writer equally ready to strike out on his own.

Like many of his later stories, 'Friendly Brook' is about the restoration of health after disorder: the flood is only apparently destructive, and is more truly healing and creative, or, like Shelley's west wind, both a destroyer and a preserver. Kipling, incidentally, did not have to go far from home for his symbol: the Kiplings' governess, Dorothy Ponton, later recalled that the stream flowing through her employers' Sussex property, 'hardly more than a trickle of water' in fine weather, was quickly transformed into 'a rushing torrent' by a storm and on occasion even flooded house and grounds.[14] Yet it was the same stream that helped to supply electric power to the house, which also depended on a well for its water supply. Like the river in Eliot's *Four Quartets*, the stream was for Kipling a 'reminder / Of what men choose to forget. Unhonoured, unpropitiated / By worshippers of the machine, but waiting, watching and waiting', and the parallel is not a desultory one, for Eliot's debt to Kipling in his poetry is pervasive, as Robert Crawford showed recently in an impressive essay published in *Essays in Criticism*.[15]

Another story written at about the same time, 'My Son's Wife', uses a flood for a similar purpose; and indeed the two stories have other elements in common. Town and country are again set in contrast: this time the feudal society of Sussex, the customs, conventions and codes of which are observed and recorded by Kipling with the fascinated and informed curiosity of an anthropologist, is contrasted with the metropolitan intelligentsia; and the timeless world of tradition is set against the brief and silly London fashions. When the central character returns to town after a period in the country, we are told that 'His three months' absence ... had put him hopelessly behind the London field. The movements, the allusions, the slang of the game had changed.' Kipling's examples are not idly chosen: there is dialect in Sussex, but not slang; immorality, but not casual, experimental promiscuity; and his phrase 'the London field' is surely ironic.

Like 'An Habitation Enforced', 'My Son's Wife' is a story of conversion, another favourite Kipling theme. Inheriting a house in the country, a member of the left-wing smart set samples life in Sussex and in spite of initial resistance is seduced by it and ends by marrying a hearty girl with a passion for hunting. It seems to me a less satisfactory story than the last two I have referred to, partly because its unexamined assumptions are not only unacceptable but cannot have been seriously held by Kipling himself. That it is better to kill a pheasant than to attend a literary tea-party, better to go cubbing than to go to the theatre, hardly command universal assent; and there would surely be no place for a writer like Kipling himself in this loud-voiced, red-faced and heavily perspiring society in which Surtees is a cult author. The interesting question is why someone as intelligent as Kipling should for a moment have been tempted to offer for admiration this picture of what Forster in one of his short stories calls 'the brainless life'; and the parallel is a close one, for Forster in his 'Ansell' and elsewhere (most notoriously in the conclusion of *Maurice*) offers a version of pastoral that he himself seems able to accept only by an effort of will.

What are we to make of what seems to be a gesture of disloyalty to the craft Kipling pursued with such devotion and for so long? Is he perhaps registering a protest, however short-lived, at the isolation of a life spent in a world of words? This would be consistent with his passionate interest in the life of action, in all kinds of work and in knowing *how* all kinds of things work. (One of the most charming and revealing anecdotes of Kipling is of his causing offence to his hostess during a country-house weekend by being discovered in the servants' quarters, interrogating the staff on their duties and functions.) But we need to note precisely what it is that he is rejecting: a complacent and self-regarding metropolitan literary-cum-political coterie – in a word, perhaps, Bloomsbury. In his early years in London he expressed his impatience with the artistic fashions of the 1890s, and in his later years he cultivated the friendship of public men such as Stanley Baldwin and Cecil Rhodes rather than literary men. It is surely revealing that, while writers were thick on the ground in his corner of south-east England, with Conrad, Ford, James, Wells and others within easy reach, Kipling was not at all prominent in the close network of relationships that developed between them.

It might be supposed that the negative message of 'My Son's Wife' is that expressed by the anti-hero of one of Philip Larkin's poems: 'Books are a load of crap'; though it is not in fact literature as such but intellectual modishness that is rejected. In any case, though, the positive message is more important, and this is a celebration of country life: not a life of studious retirement but one of vigorous physical activity. This, after all, is a story of conversion, and allowances ought to be made for the convert's inevitable disparaging of what he has abandoned as well as his immoderate enthusiasm for the new life into which he has been born.

I have not so far mentioned the most famous of all Kipling's stories with a Sussex setting, the tender autobiographical ghost story 'They', written in 1904 to commemorate the death of his daughter five years earlier. The lost child died in New York, but it was Sussex that she haunted; and for Kipling her memory was powerfully associated with a sense of place. He told his mother that 'he saw [Josephine] every time a door was opened, every time a place was empty at table, saw her in every green corner of the garden, radiant and heart-breaking'.[16] In the story, the first-person narrator recounts a journey from 'the other side of the county' and the discovery of a hidden country house set in a lush Sussex countryside full of history: a Roman road, Norman churches, a medieval smithy, a Tudor house. The intersection of place and history that Kipling evokes makes it almost inevitable that this story should have been in Eliot's mind when he wrote 'Burnt Norton', with its 'rose-garden' (there was a rose-garden at Bateman's) and its 'shrubbery' and 'leaves ... full of children'. As in some of the other Sussex stories, the Sussex of 'They' is both the place of the date of composition and publication, traversed by the narrator in his new-fangled motor-car, and a place of history and tradition where the past is vividly present and faith, folk-beliefs and superstition and the supernatural are a living reality.

This is no less true of the last of the stories I want to discuss: the last in date of composition, and perhaps the finest of all the group associated with Sussex. 'Rud at his new story,' wrote Kipling's wife in her diary in 1924; 'Rud quite hopeless with depression.

Nerves and Nerves.... Rud wretched.'[17] Out of this black misery came a story of remarkably controlled sadness, 'The Wish House', and in it Kipling heightens the contrast between new and old, present and past, more than in any of the earlier stories in this group. It is Saturday afternoon in a Sussex village situated on the main road to the coast. Outside the door of a cottage a stream flows past – not a 'friendly brook' of unpolluted water but a stream of motor vehicles, stinking and roaring, private cars and motor coaches, an invasion from the city for whom the village is not a living community but just another sight glimpsed, or ignored, on the way to the coastal resorts. Inside the cottage, a few feet from the traffic, two elderly women, childhood friends who have met only infrequently in the intervening years, sit and recall the past. One of them, a former cook, has a sore on her shin that refuses to heal, and that turns out to be cancerous; the unostentatious allusion is to the cook in Chaucer's General Prologue and its point seems to be to emphasise the traditional, almost medieval England into which the old women were born and whose near-vanishing they have lived to witness. (The theme of cancer occurs in other stories of the 1920s; Kipling had been ill and had undergone surgery in 1922, and his subsequent depression seems to have originated at least partly in a fear of that disease.)

The old women's memories, shared through the dialect speech that constantly reminds of us of their Sussex origins, return to the world before the twentieth century and the advent of the internal combustion engine: one of them recalls a summer in Victorian London, when it was 'hot an' windy for weeks, an' the streets stinkin' o' dried 'orse-dung blowin' from side to side an' lyin' level with the kerb' – the kind of graphic detail that can convey more than a chapter of social history and that is in its sensuous exactness a kind of Kipling trade-mark. As the speaker adds, 'We don't get that nowadays.' Elsewhere a man is recalled who began his career as a carter and later took to driving a lorry: a microcosm, in a single representative life, of an England transformed and of, in Peter Laslett's eloquent phrase, a 'world we have lost'. The old women have survived to see an England in which the grandson of one of them, a wireless enthusiast, asks her for money 'for them aireated wash-poles folk puts up in their gardens to draw the music from Lunnon, like'.

Still, their age and their proud independence enable them to stand aside from the sweeping changes of the new age: the transformed England just outside the cottage door, an England of technology and fast travel and instant communication, hardly touches their inner lives, and the patchwork quilt that one of them is making is a symbol for the patchwork of memories contrived by their conversation. They have lived narrower lives than the trippers for whom the village is no more than a milestone on the road to a crowded coast (in his autobiography Kipling was to write of the 'horror' of the developed Sussex coast); but they have lived with passionate intensity; and the central idea of the story, the way in which one of them has through magic and faith taken upon herself the physical sufferings of the man she has loved, insists upon the reality of the pre-scientific world that is dying with these two friends who are, it becomes plain by the end of the story, now meeting for the last time.

Between them, the stories I have referred to delineate the Sussex that Kipling part discovered and part created: a region of intoxicating natural beauty that is, until the later stories, still largely unspoilt, and a pre-industrial society in which traditional crafts are practised and transmitted, most people contentedly accept their places in a still stable and largely unchallenged rural hierarchy, peasant loyalty is as strong as *noblesse oblige*, and a sense of the past – not so much of 'history' as conventionally understood as of a land continuously inhabited – broods over the present. London is still at a distance, an alien place from which people come or to which they return if they do not know better. Especially in 'The Wish House' this Sussex world is under threat from social and technological change; but the old way of life is preserved by the older generation (to which Kipling himself, of course, by the mid-1920s belonged), and Sussex can still represent a haven or retreat, a place to which exiles and wanderers can come home (as in 'An Habitation Enforced'), neuroses can be cured, conversions can take place, order can be restored, and faith in magic and miracles is justified. If some of the elements in this account sound like a sentimental refashioning of the myth of the golden age, there is not much doubt that Kipling is also a historian of 'change in the village' (to borrow the title of a book by his contemporary, George Sturt) during a period that has the Great War as its centre and turning-point.

This group of stories occupies an important place in Kipling's vast output, includes some of the best of his short fiction, and suggests that Kingsley Amis's glib epigram that 'Kipling develo-

ped early and he went off early'[18] tells less than the whole truth.
Hilton Brown declared forty years ago that with 'They' and 'An
Habitation Enforced' Kipling 'struck a vein of incalculable richness
which he must subsequently work', and that with them 'the latest
– and in many ways the finest – Kipling had been born'; and for
Angus Wilson more recently 'Friendly Brook' and 'The Wish
House' are 'arguably the best individual stories of [Kipling's] later
years'.[19] More might have been said in this essay about Kipling's
masterly evocation of the physical world of Sussex: landscape and
weather, buildings and people, including his painstaking and
wholly convincing use of dialect. And more might have been said
about the way in which these stories register a changing England:
Kipling started out as a Victorian, and some of the stories I have
discussed are Edwardian, but 'The Wish House' recognisably
belongs to the period of *The Waste Land*. Kipling is a contemporary
of the Georgian poets, but he has a much more poignant sense
than most of them that in the upheavals of early twentieth-century
England something precious is being lost for ever. Perhaps
enough has been said, however, to suggest that these stories, like
many others in his output of two hundred or more, richly repay
reading and rereading; and that, in assessing Kipling's place as
one of the greater writers of regional fiction, it is worth considering whether Sussex, where he ended, is not nearly as important as
India, where he started.

NOTES

1.   Rudyard Kipling, *Something of Myself* (London: Macmillan, 1937) p.
     2.
2.   Ibid., p. 3.
3.   K. Bhaskara Rao, *Rudyard Kipling's India* (Norman, Okla.: Universi-
     ty of Oklahoma Press, 1967) p. 21.
4.   Kipling, *Something of Myself*, p. 2.
5.   Ibid., p. 4.
6.   *Letters of James Joyce*, ed. Richard Ellmann (London: Faber, 1966) vol.
     II, p. 205.
7.   Kingsley Amis, *Rudyard Kipling and his World* (London: Thames &
     Hudson, 1975) p. 58.
8.   Kipling, *Something of Myself*, p. 178.
9.   Quoted in Lord Birkenhead, *Rudyard Kipling* (London: W. H. Allen,
     1980 [Star Book reprint]) p. 172. The passage continues in terms that

are echoed in some of the later stories: 'Villas, clipped hedges, and shaved lawns; fat old ladies with obese landaus – the Almighty is a discursive and frivolous trifler compared with some of 'em. But the land is indescribably lovely and I am making friends with the farmers.'

10.   Kipling, *Something of Myself*, p. 136.
11.   Ibid., p. 183.
12.   Ibid., p. 182.
13.   Birkenhead, *Rudyard Kipling*, p. 12.
14.   Harold Orel, *Kipling: Interviews and Recollections* (London: Macmillan, 1983) vol. II, p. 333.
15.   Robert Crawford, 'Rudyard Kipling in *The Waste Land*', *Essays in Criticism*, vol. XXXVI, no. i (January 1986) pp. 32–46. Crawford's observation that 'If old men should be explorers, Kipling too became the explorer of Sussex' (p. 33) is relevant to the present essay.
16.   Birkenhead, *Rudyard Kipling*, p. 199.
17.   Ibid., p. 298.
18.   Amis, *Rudyard Kipling and His World*, p. 91.
19.   Hilton Brown, *Rudyard Kipling* (London: Hamish Hamilton, 1945) p. 168; Angus Wilson, *The Strange Ride of Rudyard Kipling* (London: Secker & Warburg, 1977) p. 281.

13

Williams and Stevens: the Quest for a Native American Modernism

A. WALTON LITZ

William Carlos Williams was born in Rutherford, New Jersey, in 1883, and died there in 1963. In 1883 Rutherford was a small village across the Hudson River from New York; today it is a suburban extension of New York, and from some vantage-points you can see the skyscrapers of Manhattan. But Rutherford still retains the atmosphere of a pre-Second World War small town, and to visit Williams's home at 9 Ridge Road, where he lived from 1913 until his death, is to enter a fold in time. The late Victorian three-storey house, which contains the office where Williams saw his patients, looks much the same as it did in 1916, when Williams, Marcel Duchamp, Man Ray, Alfred Kreymborg and other members of the New York avant-garde had their photograph taken on the lawn. Williams's first son, now over seventy, still practices medicine in his father's office. The whole scene, countrified and comforting, could have inspired a cover for the *Saturday Evening Post* in the 1930s. To a non-American, and to many Americans, it is a scene that calls for the label 'local colour', provincial and picturesque.

This sense of provinciality is part of the received portrait of Williams, and it is reinforced by the deliberately unsophisticated, know-nothing voice that one often hears in Williams's prose and poetry: the voice that in his 'Portrait of a Lady' says 'Agh! what / sort of man was Fragonard? / – as if that answered / anything'. Unfortunately, many of Williams's critics have chosen this voice in their attempts to cast Williams's thoughts – real and supposed – in a kind of free indirect discourse. The result could only confirm the worst fears of a British reader, such as *The Times Literary Supplement* reviewer of 1959 who spoke of an 'aggressive nativeness in American poetry, the sort of thing illustrated so determinedly (and for British readers so bewilderingly) in the poetry of William Carlos Williams'.[1]

I shall try to modify this portrait somewhat by talking about what the notion of the 'local' actually meant to Williams and to his sometimes near-collaborator Wallace Stevens. In 1955 a young critic wrote to Williams asking for his opinion of the Southern Agrarian writers, the Fugitives, logically assuming that Williams had been following their work with close attention. But in his reply, which has never been published, Williams said that he had never kept up with the Fugitives or Southern writing in general. He then went on:

> My eyes have been so unfailingly directed toward Europe, toward what has come out of Paris especially, that I had little interest in anything else. You may be surprised to hear a man who has so identified himself with American beginnings say this but it is so. The very shock of America to my nerves has made me the more European in my instinctive reactions.[2]

A few years ago I would have read this letter with great scepticism, but now I take it as a simple statement of fact. Having been brought up on Eliot and the metaphysical tradition, for many years I thought of Williams as R. P. Blackmur did in his magisterial essay 'Lord Tennyson's Scissors': a poet who remained fettered by the assumptions of the Imagist manifesto long after Eliot and Pound had left them behind, a poet who sacrificed 'tact' in his desperate search for contact with the local environment. Here is the heart of Blackmur's criticism:

> the counterpart heresy [to that of *a priori* correct form] is William Carlos Williams' notion, which rises from his intense conviction that the only value of sound or sense is in direct perception, that forms are themselves incorrect when they are not unique. To him beauty is absolute and falls like the rain, like the dream of rain in a dry year. He is, if you like, the imagism of 1912 self-transcended. He is contact without tact; he is objectivism without objective; *l'anima semplicetta* run wild, with all the gain in the zest of immediate wonder, with all the loss that strikes when memory and expectation, the double burden of the true music, are both gone.[3]

But over the last few years, in reading Williams and, more recently, in editing his poetry, I have come to see him as a man of relatively deep culture and learning. His command of Spanish and French was more precise than Pound's, his knowledge of modern art in some ways more comprehensive than Stevens's. In annotating his poems I had to go far beyond matters of local topography and history (although there's plenty of that) to, for example, the poetry of Metastasio and the more arcane details of the history of the Lutheran church. As cultural possibilities and historical events fade from memory, the poet who mocked the notes to *The Waste Land* may someday need a greater freight of annotation.

The key to Williams's poetic psychology is that he always felt 'belated'. He was still trapped in the style of academic romanticism when Pound was making his breakthrough of 1912–14. 'I am late at my singing', the refrain of the first poem in *Sour Grapes* (1921), is the refrain of Williams's entire career. The history of modernist American poetry is the history of attempts at a 'poem of some length', and here too Williams was belated: coming after *The Waste Land* and *Four Quartets* and most of the *Cantos* and most of Stevens's long poems, *Paterson* must constantly resort to imitation and parody in order to assert its special identity. Sometimes the 'belatedness' takes pathetic forms, as when in his *Collected Earlier Poems* Williams places his 'Portrait of a Lady' (written in 1920) in his 1913 volume *The Tempers*, hoping to claim priority over Eliot's poem that was first published in 1915 (of course, we now know that Eliot's 'Portrait of a Lady' was written much earlier). Sometimes the belatedness takes on tragic overtones, as in Book V of *Paterson* where Williams, meditating on the Brueghel nativity scene, identifies himself with Joseph, who played no part in creating the Word. But whatever form it takes, it is the key to the aggressive tone that so troubled the TLS reviewer. And since Williams, not Eliot or Pound, was the major influence on the American poets of the generation after Berryman and Lowell, we need to understand him for reasons that go beyond his own poetry.

Wallace Stevens and William Carlos Williams came to maturity at a time when American art, and especially American fiction, was most concerned with celebrating the regional. The new areas of regional experience explored by post-Civil War writers were numerous; America seemed a growing confederation of distinct regions, each with its local voice. The problem Stevens and

Williams faced was how to preserve this interest in the local without becoming a 'local colour' writer, with all the limitations that implies. The assumption they both worked from, at the time when they were virtually collaborators (that is, during and just after the First World War), was summed up by Williams in 1921: 'If Americans are to be blessed with important work it will be through intelligent, informed contact with the locality which alone can infuse it with reality'.[4] This is really the ground-base of American aesthetics at the end of the First World War: everywhere you look, in literary or art criticism, you can find its equivalent.

For a time, Stevens and Williams felt they had found a common solution to the problem of how to be 'local' without being provincial: it lay in the methods of modernist art and the new poetry. The 1913 Armory Show had introduced post-Impressionist painting to New York, while the early issues of the *Egoist* and *Poetry* magazine had liberated both Stevens and Williams from stale poetic forms. While Pound in London felt that the Great War had cut short a poetic renaissance, Stevens and Williams believed that the centre of power had shifted to New York. 'In New York in the spring of 1915, one was feeling a strange quickening of artistic life', wrote Williams in a letter to the *Egoist*, a letter which concluded: 'America has triumphed!'[5] This was the moment when Stevens and Williams were following the same programme and exchanging poems, the moment that produced the more direct landscape poems of *Harmonium* and the poems of Williams's *Al Que Quiere!*, which invite the reader

> to come with me
> poking into negro houses
> with their gloom and smell!
> in among children
> leaping around a dead dog!
> Mimicking
> onto the lawns of the rich!
> You!
> to go with me a-tip-toe,
> head down under heaven,
> nostrils lipping the wind
> ('Sub Terra')

But this sense of discovery, and of a shared enterprise for the two poets, was short lived. In the 1918 prologue to his improvisations,

Kora in Hell, Williams is once again unsure and defensive, feeling that Eliot's *Prufrock and Other Observations* has tipped the balance toward Europe, that American poetry will go the way of 'La Figlia Che Piange' rather than the way of his own poetry. The title *Kora in Hell* sums up Williams's feeling: the brief springtime of native American poetry has given way to darkness.

The prologue to *Kora in Hell* elicited three letters from Pound in which he shrewdly (and I think rightly) turns the tables and places Williams in the role of the foreigner, the first-generation American of exotic origins who is desperately looking for 'roots'.

> you can idealize the place (easier now that Europe is so damd shaky) all you like, but you haven't a drop of the cursed blood in you, and you don't need to fight the disease day and night; you never have had to. Eliot has it perhaps worse than I have – poor devil.
>
> You have the advantage of arriving in the milieu with a fresh flood of Europe in your veins, Spanish, French, English, Danish. You had not the thin milk of New York and New England from the pap; and you can therefore keep the environment outside you, and decently objective.[6]

From the 1918 Prologue to *Kora in Hell* to the end of his life, Williams was to cast Eliot as the enemy in his personal demonology, and *The Waste Land* would be his symbol of poetry that goes against the American grain (for this reason *Paterson* contains more dogs than any other poem I know, most of them rebukes to the poet who said 'Oh keep the Dog far hence, that's friend to men'). But it is the divergence between Williams and Stevens, not the one-sided quarrel with Eliot, that tells us more about Williams's (and Stevens's) ultimate uses of the local. By 1919 Stevens was resisting Williams's notion that poetry should fix on the object alone: we see this in his 'Nuances of a Theme by Williams', where he insists on 'interpreting' Williams's stark imagist poem 'El Hombre'. More subtly, we also find Stevens's critique of Williams in the famous anthology piece 'Anecdote of the Jar', which – like Frost's 'The Road Not Taken' – is seldom recognised as parody.

> I placed a jar in Tennessee,
> And round it was, upon a hill.
> It made the slovenly wilderness
> Surround that hill.

The wilderness rose up to it,
And sprawled around, no longer wild.
The jar was round upon the ground
And tall and of a port in air.

It took dominion everywhere.
The jar was gray and bare.
It did not give of bird or bush,
Like nothing else in Tennessee.

Here the ordinary American mason jar that has replaced the Grecian urn may represent the 'value of order' (that is the usual interpretation), but as Martha Strom has pointed out it is also an ironic comment on the tyranny of things in Williams's poetry:

> It cuts off the hill from the surrounding wilderness and is itself alien and sterile.... As Stevens wrote to Harriet Monroe in 1921, 'Whatever Dr Williams may say about being ... adrift, finding a place in abstraction sensually realized through CON-TACT – there can be a little too much of it.'[7]

Stevens carries his critique of Williams farther in 'The Comedian as the Letter C', where the ephoebe Crispin goes through a 'Williams phase' of revelling in the literalness of the local. This is most apparent in some passages that were excised from the original 'Journal of Crispin', the first draft that was not published until 1980.[8] In 'The Comedian as the Letter C', which rehearses the ten-year making of *Harmonium* (1913–23), Stevens says farewell to Williams's 'rude aesthetic', which for a brief time was his own. When he returned to the writing of poetry nearly ten years later his treatment of the native landscape was very different from Williams's, which may account in part for their growing estrangement. In fact, Stevens's thinking seems to have paralleled in a curious way that of Eliot in the period 1928–34 which led him to a new appreciation of Yeats as a 'regionalist' who transcends the local; to the comments on regionalism in *After Strange Gods*; to the little landscape poems, such as 'Virginia' and 'Cape Ann'; and finally to that most 'American' of his poems, *Little Gidding*.

Wallace Stevens's poems can be roughly divided into two kinds, those of 'making' and those of 'finding'. ('Tea at the Palaz of Hoon' and 'The Snow Man', which were first published facing each other, are good early examples.) In his later career the poems of place and region tend to be poems of 'finding', in which the attentive mind abstracts the idea of a place and then expresses it. To give you a sense of what I mean by a poem of 'finding', here is one of Stevens's most moving late poems, 'The Course of a Particular'. Its title, flat and pseudo-scientific, prepares us for a poem of discrete physical sensations. The word 'course' means both the progress of the particular sound as it is refined by the mind and a 'curriculum', a lesson to be learned.

> Today the leaves cry, hanging on branches swept by wind,
> Yet the nothingness of winter becomes a little less.
> It is still full of icy shades and shapen snow.
>
> The leaves cry ... One holds off and merely hears the cry.
> It is a busy cry, concerning someone else.
> And though one says that one is part of everything,
>
> There is a conflict, there is a resistance involved;
> And being part is an exertion that declines:
> One feels the life of that which gives life as it is.
>
> The leaves cry. It is not a cry of divine attention,
> Nor the smoke-drift of puffed-out heroes, nor human cry.
> It is the cry of leaves that do not transcend themselves,
>
> In the absence of fantasia, without meaning more
> Than they are in the final finding of the ear, in the thing
> Itself, until, at last, the cry concerns no one at all.

The word *cry*, repeated magically nine times through these intolerably long, three-line stanzas, would seem on first hearing to contradict the poem's overt meaning, its rejection of the pathetic fallacy in favour of 'the final *finding* of the ear'. But *cry* is one of Stevens's special words: the primitive utterance of a discrete moment in reality (in another late work Stevens says that the poem is 'the cry of its occasion').

We find the same incantatory use of the word *cry* in a 1948 prose tribute to 'John Crowe Ransom, Tennessean':

One turns with something like ferocity toward a land that one loves, to which one is really and essentially native, to demand that it surrender, reveal, that in itself which one loves. This is a vital affair, not an affair of the heart (as it may be in one's first poems), but an affair of the whole being (as in one's last poems), a fundamental affair of life, or, rather, an affair of fundamental life; so that one's cry of O Jerusalem becomes little by little a cry to something a little nearer and nearer until at last one cries out to a living name, a living place, a living thing, and in crying out confesses openly all the bitter secretions of experience. This is why trivial things often touch us intensely. It is why the sight of an old berry patch, a new growth in the woods in the spring, the particular things on display at a farmers' market, as, for example, the trays of poor apples, the few boxes of black-eyed peas, the bags of dried corn, have an emotional power over us that for a moment is more than we can control.[9]

These comments on Ransom are really comments on Stevens's own late career, where he sought to locate his persistent sense of fact in the remembered landscapes of his native land, Pennsylvania, and the present landscapes of his adopted home, Connecticut. Beginning in 1942 with 'Dutch Graves in Bucks County' Stevens re-entered the Pennsylvania of his youth, and in poems such as 'Credences of Summer' (1946) he recalled the landscape of Eastern Pennsylvania in words which try to reach beyond the secondary (that is, Romantic and pathetic) senses of the eye and ear.

> One of the limits of reality
> Presents itself in Oley when the hay,
> Baked through long days, is piled in mows. It is
> A land too ripe for enigmas, too serene.
> There the distant fails the clairvoyant eye
>
> And the secondary senses of the ear
> Swarm, not with secondary sounds, but choirs,
> Not evocations but last choirs, last sounds
> With nothing else compounded, carried full,
> Pure rhetoric of a language without words.

No American poet has written more or finer poetry after the age
of sixty-five than Wallace Stevens, and much of this poetry of old
age is a supreme poetry of 'making' which fleshes out the shape of
a final aesthetic. But some of the very best late poems are counter-
poems of 'finding', in which the particulars of his adopted land,
Connecticut, are given such loving attention that they become part
of what Stevens called his 'mythology'. In a brief essay on
Connecticut, written for the Voice of America in the year of his
death but never delivered, Stevens declared that 'we live in the
tradition which is the true mythology of the region and we breathe
in with every breath the joy of having ourselves been created by
what has been endured and mastered in the past.... It is a
question of coming home to the American self in the sort of place in
which it was formed'.[10] In one of his very last poems, 'The River of
Rivers in Connecticut', the old poet draws back from his clear
vision of Stygian night ahead and contemplates another river, the
mythic river of human intelligence which – like all Stevens's
abstractions – can only be imagined through the particulars of one
time and one place.

> There is a great river this side of Stygia,
> Before one comes to the first black cataracts
> And trees that lack the intelligence of trees.
>
> In that river, far this side of Stygia,
> Thee mere flowing of the water is a gayety,
> Flashing and flashing in the sun. On its banks,
>
> No shadow walks. The river is fateful,
> Like the last one. But there is no ferryman.
> He could not bend against its propelling force.
>
> It is not to be seen beneath the appearances
> That tell of it. The steeple at Farmington
> Stands glistening and Haddam shines and sways.
>
> It is the third commonness with light and air,
> A curriculum, a vigor, a local abstraction ...
> Call it, once more, a river, an unnamed flowing,

Space-filled, reflecting the seasons, the folk-lore
Of each of the senses; call it, again and again,
The river that flows nowhere, like a sea.

In contrast to Stevens, whose poetry of place is a special
modification of the familiar Romantic landscape poem, Williams
never abandoned his belief in the power of unmediated local
details. As Bram Dijkstra has said, one of Williams's dominant
characteristics was his 'curiously literal mind, which made him
capable of seeing poetry almost entirely in terms of painting'.[11]
Another characteristic was his belief that the American language is
fundamentally different from English. Working together, or
perhaps against each other, these two beliefs determined the shape
of his poetic life. I think Williams was partially mistaken on both
counts, although the growing inability of American readers to
'hear' contemporary British verse, and of British readers to 'hear'
contemporary American verse, is evidence on his side. *Four
Quartets* may be the last great poem that can be heard equally well
by American and British readers; and of course, Williams would
have taken that as a sign of failure.

In Book Five of *Paterson* Williams inserts part of an interview
with a journalist. He has just been shown one of e. e. cummings's
typographical experiments, and has rejected it as poetry. The
interviewer responds by reading one of Williams's own poems: '2
partridges / 2 mallard ducks / a Dungeness crab / 24 hours out / of
the Pacific / and 2 live-frozen / trout / from Denmark'. Now, says
the interviewer, 'that sounds just like a fashionable grocery list!'
Williams: 'It is a fashionable grocery list.'
Interviewer: 'Well – is it poetry?'
Williams: 'We poets have to talk in a language which is not
English. It is the American idiom. Rhythmically it's organized as a
sample of the American idiom. It has as much originality as jazz ...
it forms a jagged pattern. It is, to my mind, poetry.'

Here, in the simplest and therefore best form, is the poetic that
governed Williams's career. He made many more elaborate
attempts to explain it, as in his murky theory of the 'variable foot',
but these rationales strike me as too defensive. In practice his
poetic enabled Williams to write his greatest short poems, in which
the typography – the picture on the page – tells us how to perform
the poem. In the 1920s, in the experimental collage poems of *Spring*

and All and the later associative, surrealist poems, Williams is trying to reproduce in words the effects of modernist painting; later he tended to organise his poems in more regular stanza forms, finally settling into the three-step line we find in parts of *Paterson* and in the best short poems of the 1950s. In all these forms of the short poem we find the same qualities: 'the photographer's close-up attention to the thing at a precise moment of illumination [combined] with the modern painter's dismemberment of his means, or syntax'.[12] But this poetic proved counterproductive when it came to the construction of a long poem – hence the protracted deferral of *Paterson*.

The approach to *Paterson* begins in 1914 with 'The Wanderer', Williams's first attempt to include the ordinary and often sordid details of contemporary life in a poem of some length, to be – in his words – a mirror to modernity. Here the form and language are those of a conventional Romantic quest poem, and are constantly at odds with the subject (this at a time when Eliot had learned from Baudelaire and Laforgue one way to map the urban landscape). The next step is *Spring and All* (1923), the most neglected of the major works of early literary modernism, where some of Williams's most successful painterly poems are embedded in a context of Dadaist prose that meditates discontinuously, but I think very effectively, on the difference between prose and poetry. Although the thrust of *Spring and All* is to disclaim all connections with the past – it is on one level an anti-*Waste Land* poem – Williams is indirectly, and very consciously, rehearsing Coleridgean notions about the imagination and the distinctions between prose and poetry.

In fact, from *Spring and All* onward Williams was seeking for a large, architectural form that could accommodate both prose and poetry. Between 1923 and 1944 he made several attempts at a long construction of prose and poetry. *The Descent of Winter* (1928), which was mined out of a much larger journal of poems and prose entries, carries on the form of *Spring and All* but with the difference that Williams has recently visited Paris and is even more deeply indebted to Gertrude Stein and the surrealists. The marvellous poetic sequence of 1930, 'Della Primavera Trasportata al Morale' (which I would translate as 'a moral interpretation of springtime'), was originally a prose/poetry construction, but the prose never reached print. The same thing is true of *The Wedge* (1944), where the prose was cut at the last moment on the advice of Zukofsky.

Meanwhile Williams had been writing a great deal of very distinguished fiction (he is just now being recognised as one of the major short story writers of his time).

The problem was how to combine the two complementary modes, and that problem is acutely evident in a curious production of the late 1930s, largely unpublished, called 'Detail & Parody for the poem *Paterson*', a collection of a number of short poems based on 'found objects'. One of the most fascinating of these is Mrs Williams's reply to her husband's poem 'This Is Just to Say', the poem about stealing the plums from the icebox that was recently featured on the London Underground. What Williams has done is to take her note, found crumpled on her desk, and set it up as a 'poem'.

> Dear Bill: I've made a
> couple of sandwiches for you.
> In the ice-box you'll find
> blue-berries – a cup of grapefruit
> a glass of cold coffee.
>
> On the stove is the tea-pot
> with enough tea-leaves
> for you to make tea if you
> prefer – Just light the gas –
> boil the water and put it in the tea
>
> Plenty of bread in the bread-box
> and butter and eggs –
> I didn't know just what to
> make for you. Several people
> called up about office hours –
>
> See you later. Love. Floss.
>
> Please switch off the telephone.[13]

The entries in 'Detail & Parody for the poem *Paterson*' remind one of Joyce's epiphanies, but they lack the crisp dramatic structure and the high lyricism that mark Joyce's two kinds of epiphanies. How to make a long poem out of material such as this? How, to paraphrase Randall Jarrell on *Paterson* Book One, was

Williams to fashion a long poem which is neither – in a conventional sense – logical, dramatic or narrative? In making the original *Paterson* (the first four books) I think Williams relied on three models, none of which quite worked. One was the collage structure derived from his favourite painters, where the printed page itself, not the metrical line, becomes the poetic unit.[14] This proved inadequate for so large a design. A second model was Joyce's mythopoetic structures in *Finnegans Wake*: the use of archetypal figures that blend into the landscape, the circular four-part structure, the multiplication of variants on a few basic types – these are all right out of Joyce. But Williams simply did not have the architechtonic imagination that animates most of *Finnegans Wake*.

The third method was the musical orchestration of themes and motifs, learned I believe from *Four Quartets*. But Williams in the first four books of *Paterson* lacks Eliot's strong control of voice, and the method is also problematic because it is inextricably involved with parody. It is very difficult in *Paterson* to hear whether Williams is parodying Eliot or imitating him; I'm not sure Williams knew, or whether the distinction between parody and imitation makes any sense in a 'postmodern' work like *Paterson*.

Nor am I sure whether closure is possible in an open work like *Paterson*, and therefore we have *Paterson* Book Five, which I take to be almost wholly successful. It is infused with the strong lyric voice that we hear in the best poems of *Pictures from Brueghel* and *The Desert Music*, and its success is directly related to its major theme, failure: the failure of the poet to produce a finished masterpiece that can compete with the greatest works of the past. Like *The Pisan Cantos*, Book Five of *Paterson* possesses an eloquence and a curious nobility that validate the entire poem.

NOTES

1. Quoted in Charles Tomlinson, *Some Americans* (Berkeley, Calif. and London, 1981) p. 21.
2. William Carlos Williams to Henry W. Wells, 22 November 1955, General Manuscript Collection, Rare Book and Manuscript Library, Columbia University.
3. R. P. Blackmur, *Language as Gesture* (New York, 1952) p. 435.
4. William Carlos Williams, 'Sample Critical Statement', *Contact*, no. 4 (Summer 1921) p. 18.

5. *The Selected Letters of William Carlos Williams*, ed. John C. Thirlwall (New York, 1957) pp. 30–3.

6. *The Letters of Ezra Pound, 1907–1941*, ed. D. D. Paige (London, 1951) p. 223; letter of 11 September 1920.

7. Martha Strom, 'Wallace Stevens's Earthy Anecdotes', *New England Quarterly*, vol. 58 (Sept. 1985) pp. 427–8.

8. See Martha Strom, 'Wallace Stevens' Revisions of Crispin's Journal: a Reaction Against the "Local"', *American Literature*, vol. 54 (May 1982) pp. 258–76.

9. Wallace Stevens, *Opus Posthumous*, ed. Samuel French Morse (New York, 1957) p. 260.

10. Ibid., pp. 295–6.

11. Bram Dijkstra, *The Hieroglyphics of a New Speech* (Princeton, N.J., 1969) p. 194.

12. Jay Bochner, 'New York Secession', in *Modernism: Challenges and Perspectives*, ed. Monique Chefdor, Ricardo Quinones and Albert Wachtel (Urbana, 1986) p. 206.

13. *The Collected Poems of William Carlos Williams*, vol. 1, ed. A. Walton Litz and Christopher MacGowan (New York, 1986) p. 536.

14. See Marjorie Perloff, ' "To give a design": Williams and the Visualization of Poetry', in her collection *The Dance of the Intellect* (Cambridge, Mass., 1985) pp. 88–118.

14

The Local is the Universal: William Carlos Williams and Neil Gunn

ROBERT LAWSON-PEEBLES

Elsewhere in this volume Walton Litz and Thomas Crawford have discussed the separate contributions of Williams and Gunn to the richness of regional writing. In the next few pages I will try to demonstrate an ideological connection between the two writers, and sketch the expression of the ideology in the motifs to be found in one of Gunn's novels and much of Williams's work.

At first sight it might seem capricious to attempt to link the two men. Gunn's contacts with America were limited to a few meetings, in Scotland, with American publishers; and a few essays, on Scotland, aimed at tourism and published in American magazines. If Williams ever read any of the essays, he resisted their blandishments. He never visited Scotland. He came to Europe on four occasions, but set foot in the British Isles once only, in 1909, when he spent an uncomfortable week in London with his unpredictable, domineering friend, Ezra Pound. By the 1920s it had become a point of honour for Williams *not* to visit England, and throughout the rest of his life he expressed an intense dislike of his father's homeland. 'I don't want to go to England,' he spluttered in 1932, 'I don't care to hear their language spoken.' He remained as firmly rooted in New Jersey as did Gunn in Northern Scotland.[1]

However, a letter in the Special Collections of Aberdeen University Library shows that Williams travelled imaginatively if not physically to Scotland. The letter had been filed by Gunn in a signed first edition of Williams's *Collected Earlier Poems*. It was included late in 1971 in an exhibition devoted to Gunn at the National Library of Scotland, but has not been previously published, or otherwise noticed. It is typed, and its many errors confirm Williams's frailty. In the interests of clarity I have omitted the errors:

9 Ridge Road, Rutherford N.J.
Sept. 11, 1959

Dear Neil Gunn,

I'm very happy to be writing to you – out of an illness for which I had to be sent to the hospital from which I am now recovering. But I had to communicate with you to tell you how much Mrs. Williams and I enjoyed the reading of your novel 'The Drinking Well' – which Raymond Silvers had sent to us from Inverness. That was a beauty! If I had my full strength back I could go on for several pages in praise of the novel, its technical as well as its general aspects. Well done, I'm proud to make your acquaintance and to call you a friend. The final pages, how you made the final phase turn out, without redundancy, to a heart-satisfying conclusion filled me with satisfaction.

Within the next couple of weeks you'll be getting the 2 most plainly written books of my verse, the most satisfactory to give you an introduction to what I am attempting. Modern poetry makes as many enemies as friends, especially as I am an American completely given to the local idiom, you being a Scotchman will understand that in contradistinction to being stamped with the authority of the 'establishment.'

I'm getting tired and when I get tired I make errors in my typing [at this point, comically, Williams makes a typing error] – I write only with my left hand. Look for the 2 volumes of my verse in which I ardently hope you'll be able to find enough to enjoy to make the reading worth while.

Cordially yours,
William Carlos Williams

The identity of Raymond Silvers remains an enigma. He appears in none of the standard reference books, and the biographies of Williams and Gunn do not mention him. But clearly his gift of *The Drinking Well* impressed Williams so much that he not only wrote to Gunn at a difficult time but also sent him the major part of his published work, the *Collected Earlier* and (presumably) *Collected Later Poems*. Such 'ardour' indicates more than mere liking for the novel.[2]

The reason is not hard to find. It appears in the second paragraph of Williams's letter, where he rails against those who are 'stamped with the authority of the "establishment"'. We have here, I believe, the key terms for understanding the relationship between the two writers; for understanding, indeed, the essential unity of much of Scottish and much of American writing. Williams's words repeat the complaint of his predecessor, Edgar Allan Poe. In an 1836 essay Poe compared literature with law and imperialism. In each case, he said, 'an established name is an estate in tenure, or a throne in possession'. In other words, writers with an established name served to dispossess those who had none. Authors without tenure were stripped of their authority.

The tenured authors can be quickly identified. They are those who are wedded to a metropolis; those who, like Matthew Arnold, equate the terms 'provincial' and 'second-rate'. To get some idea of the seductive appeal of a metropolis and the authority associated with it we need only recall Johnson's assertion that 'when a man is tired of London, he is tired of life', or Henry James's remarks when visiting Johnson's home town:

> Lichfield in general appeared to me indeed to have little to say about her great son beyond the fact that the smallness and the sameness and the dullness ... may help to explain the Doctor's subsequent almost ferocious fondness for London.[3]

There are several strategies available to those who are dispossessed by their provincialism and who cannot or will not decamp like Johnson and James. One is to withdraw into a conservatism at odds with the environment. Another is to seal up the doors surrounding the self and populate the prison with an imaginary alternative audience. This was the method adopted by Emily Dickinson. A third strategy is outgoing. It involves constructing an alternative tradition comprising those authors who have complained of a similar fate. Such a strategy is the reverse of Harold Bloom's 'anxiety of influence' because it creates imaginative space, not by misreading predecessors but by relying on them.

This was the strategy adopted by Williams. In his 1925 collection of essays, *In the American Grain*, he constructed a Pantheon that eschewed the imperial influence of England. An important member of the Pantheon was Poe. When, in the late 1930s, Williams began sustained work on *Paterson*, the long poem which would occupy him for the remainder of his life, he drew on another long poem about New Jersey which he had discovered through Poe's criticism, Thomas Ward's *Passaic* (1842). Now, in 1959, *The Drinking Well* provided a further increment to the alternative literary tradition.[4]

The Drinking Well is not generally regarded as the best of Gunn's fiction. Nevertheless, it was important to Williams in part because it showed that Gunn adopted precisely the same strategy in response to the establishment. The novel contains two overt references to texts which help to validate the case that it makes. One is well known. It is Goldsmith's *The Deserted Village* (1770):

> *Ill fares the land, to hastening ills a prey,*
> *Where wealth accumulates, and men decay;*

The other is quite obscure. It is *The Grampians Desolate*, published in 1804 by Alexander Campbell. Campbell had been the singing teacher of Sir Walter Scott, but Scott was not an apt pupil and Campbell gave up his thankless task to devote himself to writing. His books reveal a concern for maintaining a viable Scottish culture in the face of English domination. He published histories and anthologies of Scottish poetry and song, and sketches of Scottish rural life. *The Grampians Desolate* is Campbell's best work. It presents his own poetry, supplemented by extensive notes on the depopulation of the Highlands following the introduction of sheep-farming. In doing so it too draws on *The Deserted Village*.[5]

Gunn had read *The Grampians Desolate* in preparation for his 1934 novel, *Butcher's Broom*, one of several to deal with the Clearances. *The Drinking Well* brings the story almost up to date. First published in 1947, it is set shortly after the First World War, which it calls 'the Great War'. The label is historically accurate. It is also ironic, because it becomes apparent that 1918 has not brought an end to strife. There are a number of suggestions that the troubles which scar the Highlands present a microcosm of a larger discord. The troubles are seen in close focus, through the life of Iain Cattanach, the youngest son of a crofting family. The structure of the novel is one often used by Gunn. Like *The Silver Darlings* (1941), for instance, *The Drinking Well* is a *bildungsroman* set at the conjunction of history and myth and in the context of a broken family. Iain's father is a silent man, shattered after a snowstorm destroyed his flock of sheep. His mother is terminally ill. She has already exported her two elder sons to North America and her daughter to London. Now she completes her task by arranging work for Iain in an Edinburgh law office. Her death symbolises the death of the community. It seems that the only option for the young is escape. Escape, however, is illusory. This is made clear in the sequence of settings, which place Iain firstly in the Highlands, then remove him to Edinburgh only to return him to his natural environment.

Three motifs are developed within this structure. The first is self-conscious and concerns the relation of writing and society presented in two competing models. One expresses Edinburgh and, in Gunn's view, the tempting but false values of any metropolis. It is to be found in the documents written in any law office, documents which record the ownership of property and which authenticate the exercise of power. This is the kind of writing rejected by Williams and Poe, and Iain expresses their point of view when he asserts that 'raising sheep and crops was at least as important as being office boys and copying letters and writing out deeds *about* sheep and crops'. At its worst, this form of writing is susceptible to perversion. Iain discovers that a senior clerk in the office is suppressing information which would maintain a crofter's claim against his landlord. It leads to a fight with the clerk, after which Iain forsakes the law and returns to his father's croft. But, even when legal documents reveal the truth (which is, of course, their aim) they uphold an oppressive, hegemonic system which ruins the crofters and forces young men like Iain off the land and into its service.[6]

It is here that Gunn's political vision emerges in its full force and sophistication. The legal system upholds and abets the landlords who, with one exception, are more interested in shooting game than in supporting the crofters. In the process the landlords destroy the delicate financial and ecological balance on which crofting depends. Because the crofters do not have adequate finance, they are forced into a one-animal economy which both destroys the land and renders them subject to the middlemen who manipulate the market prices. Because the landlords are interested in rough shooting, they encourage the bracken which acts as a refuge for the parasites which attack the crofters' sheep. It is little wonder that Iain calls the landlords and their kind the maggot-men (pp. 412, 454).

The exception to the parasitic type of landlord is David

Henderson, who emerges as a surrogate father for Iain. Significantly, he made his money in the colonies, far away from the corrupt metropolis. He is one of those benign capitalists who sometimes appear in Gunn's fiction. (In *The Silver Darlings* the publican, called 'Special' after his whisky, is another.) They leave Gunn open to the charge of political naïveté, but in *The Drinking Well* he responds that cynicism is the refuge of those who have given up the fight (p. 462). Henderson's influence is widespread. It was his lawyers who employed Iain in Edinburgh. When Iain returns he plans to use him as a leading figure in his schemes to regenerate the land. And it is to Henderson that Iain recommends *The Grampians Desolate* (p. 438).

The Grampians Desolate is an example of the other relationship between writing and society. Such writing tends towards literature rather than the law. It is both diagnostic and expressive: diagnostic because it reveals the ills which afflict the local community, and expressive because it reveals the folk culture which is an integral part of the community. Of course, *The Drinking Well* is within this category. Its diagnostic elements bring *The Grampians Desolate* up to date by drawing on the theories of Major C. H. Douglas, which were very popular in the 1920s and 1930s. Major Douglas's economic panacea, known as Social Credit, left the capitalist system intact, and through the device of subsidies insulated production from the market system. In Britain, Social Credit was opposed by the Labour Party, but it was adopted for a while in Alberta and had a number of American supporters, amongst them William Carlos Williams.[7]

However much the social and economic diagnoses of *The Drinking Well* may have appealed to Williams, there is no doubt from his letter that its expressive elements appealed to him more. These are contained within the other two motifs of the novel, nature and music. Both are to be found in Williams's work, too. Williams insisted again and again on the primacy of the earth. He asserted in *In the American Grain*, for instance, that 'unless everything that is, proclaim a ground on which it stand, it has no worth'. He treated nature in a post-Romantic manner, not as a screen on which to project emotions but rather as an entity with its own qualities. This led to some striking reformulations of the natural process. An example is to be found in the title poem of his 1923 collection, *Spring and All*, where the first growth of plants is seen from a plant's-eye-view:

> the profound change
> has come upon them: rooted, they
> grip down and begin to awaken.

Likewise, music is a central element of Williams's work. He was interested in folk music, particularly in the re-emergence of New Orleans Jazz in the 1940s – hence his poem devoted to the group led by the veteran trumpeter Bunk Johnson, 'Ol' Bunk's Band'. In a broader sense, Williams was interested in the folk music of American speech, and spent his entire career developing a poetic form which would capture it. As he said in a letter to Richard Eberhart, 'By its *music* shall the best of modern verse be known and the *resources* of the music.'[8]

The motifs of nature and music are united at the opening of Part 1 of *The Drinking Well*, in the image of birdsong. In a fine evocation of dawn in the Highlands, 'invisible oyster catchers' shoot 'arrows of dark sound', and the fluting of a curlew marks the arrival of daylight. The growing light is treated theatrically as a protagonist that firstly picks out the horizon, then the terrain (a river valley), and then the animals that will become actors in this drama: sheep, cattle and horses. Finally and appropriately the light picks out the homesteads; appropriately, because human beings are latecomers to this scene and their relation to it is problematic. The treatment of nature thus resembles that of Williams, and it allows Gunn to portray mankind in a critical 'light'. Hence the first reference to human inactivity:

> But man himself, the queer fellow, had blinded windows. He kept his face shut until the mood moved him. He went about, creating or killing on his own, and what he would be up to next was a thing the light never knew.   (p. 9)

The method of presentation suggests an organic natural unity from which man is alienated. This is confirmed at the beginning of Part 4 of the novel. We now know that man has been 'up to' no good, and the motifs of nature and music therefore appear in significant variations:

> The notes were not the notes of any bird that sang. In savage and disconnected scenery they fell like drops of water, round and pellucid, and turned into pure sound as they struck and

vanished. Note after note, in curves of sound that rose and fell like the onflowing branches of a creeper, of a flowerless honeysuckle, so pure in line that the line itself was the flower. He waited for it to stop. But it didn't stop. It could not. Just when it was going to stop, it began to rise again, to rise higher, to reach up for some final unimaginable hold on the branch of pure space, and, in the very instant of attainment, there it was, curving over and down again, but onward, festooning in aerial lightness the dark, fathomless chasm.   (p. 419)

These are the half-conscious fantasies of Iain as he lies in bed, badly concussed after a road accident. The denotative elements of the passage are carefully structured, the irregular, unsteady reachings of Iain's consciousness conveyed through an antinomy of continuity and closure, and an oscillating rhythm of short and long sentences. The connotative elements are, if anything, even more carefully conveyed. The relationship with the opening of Part 1 is signalled by the first sentence and the essential difference by the second. Instead of an organic unity suggested by direct appeals to sense-experience, the chimeras of disorder are described through the disjunctions of synaesthesia. The result is a landscape of perversity and terror.

As befits a novel with four sections, and in accord with its motifs, *The Drinking Well* is symphonic in form. A résumé of the contrasting themes of the first three sections is given by the opening figures of the fourth before a final development and summation is made. The first and third sections are set in the Highlands. The second section provides a counterpoint and is set in Edinburgh. It opens as Iain walks along Princes Street, ironically called 'the first street in Europe'. This may be the centre of civilisation, but Iain is far from happy in it. This is conveyed in two ways. The first resonates from the opening of Part 1 and draws on the motif of nature. It is sunrise again, but this time the growing light is described not as a natural process, but rather as a battle. Although the novel is set after the First World War, the imagery reveals that it was written after the Second:

The sun was carrying on an aerial battle with the vapours produced by its own heat. Silent explosions, molten red at the core, sent wreaths curling upward in fantastic gyres.

Riding this primeval warfare, its dark battlements showing

immovable amid the wreaths, was the Castle, high on its invisible rock ... contending with the sun and its fiery elements, dominant, and, even as he watched, taking the sun's first shafts and splintering them on turret and keep.   (p. 107)

Iain's unease, secondly, looks directly forward to the disease of Part 4 in the depiction of extravagant 'aerial' shapes. This is confirmed in the next paragraph, which anticipates Iain's accident in images of musical discord. These, clearly, are not the notes of any bird that sang:

Jostled, he moved on, and heard, for bugles, the clanging of tramcars, the grinding of their wheels as they took the curve, the hooting of dark, squat, swiftly-moving motor-cars, and glimpsed pale faces over shoulders before they hurried from one safe spot to the next, as a man leaps from one boulder to another in a dangerous current.   (p. 107)

The images of discord fall into place with the images of warfare to present Edinburgh, with its imperial Castle at its heart, as a paradigm of a 'savage and disconnected scenery'. Princes Street resembles Eliot's London Bridge. The people are 'intent and hurrying', and they act like amoebae, momentarily and nervously coagulating at kerbsides, then disintegrating to cluster briefly elsewhere. There is none of the calmness, none of the coherence and continuity of the countryside.

The images of discord are particularly appropriate because Iain perceives Edinburgh through the eyes and ears of a musician. He is an accomplished fiddler, the acknowledged lord of the dance at home. In Edinburgh, however, music is at the periphery of his life. The civic music of the city, a brass band which plays in Princes Street Gardens, is of a piece with the city and has no meaning for him. 'Each "classical excerpt" was a solemn irregular wall of sound, matching in sombreness the dark wall of the rock' (p. 130). Such discords are contrasted with the moments in Iain's room when he recreates his 'lost kingdom of life' by playing his fiddle (p. 133).

They also contrast with the most memorable moment in the novel. Iain is in an Edinburgh pub with a fast set who have been discussing the relation of nationalism, cultural heritage and art. Their talk is interrupted by the sounds of 'a street musician scraping Scots melodies from a violin'. Iain is sent out with a shilling to send the man packing, but when he hears the old man's 'country voice' he takes pity on him, tunes his fiddle and starts playing himself. The effect is electrifying. The dead music comes to life and a crowd gathers. An Irishman appears, demands a jig, and begins to dance:

> Iain, who knew only the graceful body-swinging and upward-curved arm of the Highland dance, knew also and in a moment that here was the classic way of the Irish dance. Within a couple of bars of the music, he had the dancer's own time, and, unison being complete, he could emphasise with an extra sweep of the bow those notes or beats which only the blood knows, and the Irishman, responding, was lifted off his feet to a clearer grace, a finer accuracy, and toes tapped and kicked the air, side-stepped and came together again, with the lightness of a youth in his twenties. Only once did he permit himself a gesture and that was when he caught his cap, which was slipping from his head, and with a sweeping forcefulness in perfect time to a descending rhythm of the jig, threw it flat on the street. And the crowd, caught by a nameless grace and strength in this act, by its wild, solemn humour, laughed and cheered. Whereupon the Irishman was driven to excel himself, and finally brought his dance to an end with a foot that hit the street with the sharpness of a gun-crack. Iain had seen the end coming and finished on the explosive crack.   (pp. 185–9)

Here, in the centre of the Scottish metropolis, the members of two despised provincial societies demonstrate the importance of a cultural heritage that the people in the pub have been merely prating about. The old musician (who is presented as another surrogate father for Iain) goes home with his cap full of coins, a direct legatee of the demonstration.

In 1932 William Carlos Williams had recognised that American and Irish literature should both assert their independence of English literature. The street-scene in *The Drinking Well* now showed him that Irishman and Highlander could unite to prove the superiority of the provincial life. The novel itself added further authority to the tradition of 'the local idiom', as Williams called it in his letter to Gunn. Several thousand miles away and in a quite different landscape and context from New Jersey, *The Drinking Well* proved to Williams the truth of his remark, in a 1939 essay, that 'the local is the universal'.[9]

NOTES

1. William Carlos Williams, 'Reply to Gorham Munson', *New English Weekly*, vol. I, no. 14 (21 July 1932) p. 331. The standard biographies of Williams and Gunn are: Paul Mariani, *William Carlos Williams: A New World Naked* (New York: McGraw-Hill, 1981), and Francis Russell Hart and J. B. Pick, *Neil M. Gunn: A Highland Life* (London: John Murray, 1981).

2. William Carlos Williams, *Collected Earlier Poems* (Norfolk, Conn.: New Directions, 1951); typescript letter 11 September 1959 to Gunn; both in Aberdeen University Special Collections, shelf reference CH Will c. *Collected Later Poems* has not been located, and must have been sold elsewhere when Gunn's library was dispersed. Background information from S. M. Simpson, National Library of Scotland, telephone conversation with Lawson-Peebles, 12 September 1986; and J. B. Pick, letter to Lawson-Peebles, 10 September 1986.

3. Edgar Allan Poe, 'Letter to B—', in *Essays and Reviews*, ed. G. R. Thompson (New York: Library of America, 1984) p. 6. Matthew Arnold, 'The Literary Influence of Academies', in *Complete Prose Works*, ed. R. H. Super (Ann Abor, Mich.: University of Michigan Press, 1962) vol. III, p. 240; James Boswell, *The Life of Johnson* (Harmondsworth, Middx.: Penguin, 1979) p. 233; Henry James, *English Hours* (1905; rpt. London: Heinemann, 1960) p. 47.

4. Harold Bloom, *The Anxiety of Influence: A Theory of Poetry* (New York: Oxford University Press, 1973) p. 5. Edgar Allan Poe, 'Our Amateur Poets – Flaccus', in *Essays and Reviews*, ed. Thompson, pp. 992–1003. Flaccus [Thomas Ward], *Passaic, a Group of Poems Touching That River* (New York: Wiley & Putnam, 1842). On the influence of Ward on Williams and for selections from *Passaic*, see Mike Weaver, *William Carlos Williams: The American Background* (Cambridge: Cambridge University Press, 1971) pp. 13–15, 165–200. On conservative responses to a provincial environment, see Albert J. Von Frank, *The Sacred Game: Provincialism and Frontier Consciousness in American Literature, 1630–1860* (Cambridge: Cambridge University Press, 1985). On Emily Dickinson see Michael Allen, *Emily Dickinson as an American Provincial Poet* (Brighton: British Association for American Studies, 1985).

5. Oliver Goldsmith, 'The Deserted Village', in *Works*, ed. Arthur Friedman (Oxford: Clarendon Press, 1966) vol. IV, p. 289; John Lockhart, *Memoirs of the Life of Sir Walter Scott* (Edinburgh: Robert Cadell, 1837) vol. I, pp. 52–3; Alexander Campbell, *The Grampians Desolate: A Poem* (Edinburgh: Manners & Miller, 1804), *An Introduction to the History of Poetry in Scotland* ... (Edinburgh: Andrew Foulis, 1798), *A Journey from Edinburgh through Parts of North Britain* ... (London: T. N. Longman & O. Rees, 1802). For assessments of *The Drinking Well*, see Douglas Gifford, *Neil M. Gunn and Lewis Grassic Gibbon* (Edinburgh: Oliver & Boyd, 1983) p. 38; *Essays on Neil M. Gunn*, ed. David Morrison (Caithness: John Humphries, 1971) pp. 30, 60; and George Bruce, 'Handling the Unbearable: *The Serpent* and

The Drinking Well', in *Neil M. Gunn*, ed. Alexander Scott and Douglas Gifford (Edinburgh: William Blackwood, 1973) pp. 220, 235, 238.

6. Neil M. Gunn, *The Drinking Well* (1974; rpt. London: Souvenir Press, 1978) p. 165; Gunn's emphasis. Further references to this text will be given parenthetically.

7. See, for instance, C. H. Douglas, *Credit-Power and Democracy* (London: Cecil Palmer, 1920). For a contemporary socialist critique of Douglas, see W. R. Hiskett, *Social Credits or Socialism* (London: Victor Gollancz, 1935). For the influence of Social Credit on Williams, see Weaver, *William Carlos Williams*, pp. 103–7.

8. William Carlos Williams, *In the American Grain* (1925; rpt. Harmondsworth, Middx.: Penguin, 1971) p. 122; 'Spring and All', in *Collected Earlier Poems*, p. 242; 'Ol' Bunk's Band', in *Collected Later Poems* (revised edn, New York: New Directions, 1963) p. 236; letter 23 May 1954 to Richard Eberhart, in *Modern Poets on Modern Poetry*, ed. James Scully (London: Fontana, 1966) p. 71; Williams's emphases.

9. William Carlos Williams, 'Letter to the Editor', *New English Weekly*, vol. II, no. 4 (10 November 1932) pp. 90–1, 'Introduction to Charles Sheeler', in *Selected Essays* (1954; rpt. New York: New Directions, 1969) p. 233.

15

Les Murray and the Poetry of Australia

BRUCE CLUNIES ROSS

> Exile's a rampart, sometimes, to the past,
> a distiller of spirit from bruised grains;
> this is a meaning of the New World.

These lines are from Les Murray's 'Elegy for Angus Macdonald of Cnoclinn', one of a set called *Five Gaelic Poems* in which he reverts to the Scottish theme that runs intermittently throughout his work. According to Murray's note on the poem, Angus Macdonald, born in North Uist in 1900, died in Sydney, Australia, 1975, 'was almost certainly the last fully-trained *seanachaidh* (English: *shenachie*, remembrancer) in Gaelic Scotland'. In the 'Elegy' his fate is associated with that of Murray's ancestors to reveal a new insight into what a slightly older Australian poet, Judith Wright, called 'the reality of exile', in her view one of the two determinants of the creative imagination in Australia.[1]

The Australian sense of exile no doubt has its origins in the remoteness of the continent from European civilisation and its use as a place of transportation for British criminals. Yet even when the convict system ended after about fifty years of settlement, many native-born Australians who had neither the opportunity nor intention of visiting Britain continued to call it 'home'. The exile's perspective became part of their outlook, and was sustained by the idea that culture came from somewhere a long way away. It was, of course, 'high' culture (as it is sometimes called) from which they felt removed, and distance encouraged the conflation of its disparate elements into a single entity called 'European culture'; something to be admired, but unlikely to be created, in Australia. This was the attitude which the phantom Australian poet Ern Malley called 'Culture as Exhibit'.[2]

The complaint of exile is heard in A. D. Hope's famous poem 'Australia' (1939):

> A Nation of trees, drab green and desolate grey
>
> . . .
>
> She is the last of lands, the emptiest,
>
> . . .
>
> Without songs, architecture, history:
> The emotions and superstitions of younger lands,
> Her rivers of water drown among inland sands,
> The river of her immense stupidity
>
> Floods her monotonous tribes from Cairns to Perth.
>
> . . .
>
> And her five cities, like five teeming sores,
> Each drains her: a vast parasite robber-state
> Where second-hand Europeans pullulate
> Timidly on edge of alien shores.[3]

The last lines quoted possibly suggest the qualification that Australia is not actually devoid of culture, but inherits it at second-hand. This hand-me-down conception of Australian culture is pervasive; it is implicit (to take a random example) in Robert Hughes's youthful *The Art of Australia* which rests on the assumption that Australian painting is a 'pendant' to European painting. Australians who share this idea keep one eye on Europe, or more recently, the United States, to judge how their culture reflects, with a happily decreasing time-lag, developments overseas.[4]

A. D. Hope's poem actually concludes with a preference for Australia, with all its drawbacks, over 'the chatter of cultured apes / Which is called civilization over there' and expresses a hope that 'still from the deserts the prophets come'. Yet this does not mitigate what he clearly regarded, when he wrote the poem, as the essential cultural barrenness of Australia. It has not always been seen in this way, however, and Les Murray's 'Elegy' offers a different, and in some respects contrary, idea.

The poem implicitly denies the assumption that Australia is distantly removed from some conglomerate called European (or British) culture, and suggests by example that it is a different mixture of regional cultures, often transplanted to specific parts of the New World. The Scots, who settled all over Australia, might be cited as a typical example, and Murray specifies his own ancestors, who took up land around Bunyah, on the north coast of New South Wales:

> but my fathers were Highlanders long ago
> then Borderers, before this landfall
> –'savages' once, now we are 'settlers'
> in the mouth of the deathless enemy –
> but I am seized of this future now.
> I am not European. Nor is my English.

Angus Macdonald, with his inheritance of Gaelic culture, was probably unique for his time in Australia, but like him, Murray's ancestors, and settlers from other regions, brought to Australia cultural traditions which were relegated or largely ignored by those who thought in comprehensive terms of a predominantly European culture. This, indeed, was often a reason for emigrating, for the new country offered scope for cultures which were being pushed to the margin in Europe. The settlement of Australia was not always by emigration from the centre to the periphery, but from one margin to another further out. These regional cultures survived, with modifications, sometimes for generations, until they submerged 'like a tendon a man has no knowledge of in his body / but which puzzles with his bending', as Murray put in in 'Lachlan Macquarie's First Language', or became, according to the 'Elegy':

> ancestral, a code of history,
> a style of fingering, an echo of vowels,
> honey that comes to us from the lost world.

These lines allude particularly to poetry, an art in which, Murray once suggested provocatively, the Scots played a disproportionate role in Australia in relation to their percentage of the population. According to this view, Australian poetry would be distinguished from other poetry in English by the prominence of certain features – 'a style of fingering, an echo of vowels' – which derive, without the author being any more aware of them than of a twinge, from Scots, and perhaps Gaelic, or the attempt to write 'Gaelic in English words'. Murray's own verse, which combines colloquial ease with the unforced but often elaborate chiming of sounds within the line and across longer passages, certainly exemplifies this.[5]

More generally, however, the lines refer to the way that cultures which were marginal or moribund in Europe became central in the substratum of Australian culture, and by a process which Murray aptly describes with the metaphor of distillation, produced not a remote off-shoot of Europe, but a culture which – to sustain the metaphor of distillation – is *essentially* different, even while it preserves deceptive resemblances to the Old World. This conception is directly opposed to the idea that Australian culture reflects that of Europe, for the latter would relegate once more elements which on Murray's view are central, though by now barely noticeable.

If ancestry explains what might be called, according to Murray's understanding of it, the essential but implicit distinction of Australian culture, environment accounts for many of the problems which influenced its development. The Australian sense of exile preserved and possibly heightened an awareness of the disjunction between the culture inherited from Europe and the Australian environment, which at its most extreme could amount to an alienation from the landscape. According to Judith Wright: 'our landscape threatened our identity . . .; it offered nothing to get a grip on with the instruments provided by English language and literature.[6]

This was an obstacle in the way of an authentic Australian poetry which some found almost insuperable. Barron Field, who claimed the honour of being the first Australian poet, recorded in his *Geographical Memoirs of New South Wales* (1825)

All the dearest allegories of human life are bound up in the infant and slender green of spring, the dark redundance of summer, and the sere and yellow leaf of autumn. These are as essential to the poet as emblems, as they are to the painter as picturesque objects; and the common consent and immemorial custom of poetry have made the change of seasons, and its effect upon vegetation, a part, as it were, of our very nature. I can therefore hold no fellowship with Australian foliage, but will cleave to the British oak through all the barrenness of winter.[7]

It is unlikely that there was anywhere in the region of New South Wales known to this author where winter is barren, but his observations about the way in which assumptions about culture and nature were embedded in the language and conventions of English poetry were perceptive, and foreshadowed the arguments of Judith Wright and others who found that the artistic conventions they inherited not only failed to engage with the Australian environment, but sometimes seemed to work against it. A simple example is the hostile rather than benign, effect of the sun in Australia, which the early settlers noticed, of course, but which artists only began to capture after a century or more; another, as we shall see in a moment, is the awe inspired by the boundless silence of the Australian wilderness, which early writers tried to describe, but which is artistically embodied in Les Murray's 'Noonday Axeman'.

The problem which Barron Field realised made a poetry founded in Australian nature impossible for him (as his verses on the kangaroo sufficiently demonstrate) became compelling for subsequent generations, for in order to continue living in Australia its white inhabitants had to take possession of the country in their imaginations, otherwise, as Judith Wright pointed out, their sense of identity is threatened, and, she went on in the same lecture, 'It is identity ... that we want our poets to affirm'. Coming to terms with the environment, and specifically with the landscape, thus became the driving force of Australian art, not just poetry, but notably painting, which is predominantly a landscape tradition, and even music. In an early notebook, the composer Percy Grainger set out his plans for an 'Australian Bush Style', inspired, amongst other things, by the dramatic effect of the Adelaide Hills after the 'broad uneventfulness of the scrubbed desert', and much of his life was devoted to trying to create a completely new set of musical principles and conventions to express the style he imagined. More recently, Peter Sculthorpe, who is convinced, apparently, that Australia is essentially a visual country, managed, in his sequence of pieces called *Sun Music*, to create equivalents in sound for the harsh, shimmering effects of Australian sunlight.[8]

When these artists succeeded, it was because they were able to renovate basic aspects of their craft so that it meshed with the antipodean environment. For poets this involved recasting the language and conventions of English verse without cutting it off from the literature from which it was ultimately derived. An interesting attempt to do this was made by a group of mainly South Australian poets in the 1930s and 1940s, who adapted an

Aboriginal word meaning 'to join' and called themselves *Jindywor-obaks*. Their preoccupation with Aboriginal matters, inspired by their belief that the Aboriginal people lived in harmony with nature in Australia, has resulted in a popular misconception that they wanted to amalgamate the Aboriginal and European literary traditions, though what they aimed to join was the rift between culture and environment in white Australia. They argued that poetry should embody 'environmental values'; specifically, that its diction and images should reflect the environment of the poet, rather than import inappropriate European associations. Unfortunately, their practice did not always advertise their theory successfully, and they were sometimes seduced into an excessive use of Aboriginal words which their critics lost no opportunity of mocking. Their work is largely forgotten, but their analysis of Australian culture remains valid. It has been reaffirmed by Les Murray, who once slightly facetiously called himself 'the last of the Jindyworobaks', and in a recent interview restated the idea quite seriously. Some of Murray's poems exemplify Jindyworobak principles beautifully. In the opening lines of the recent 'Flowering Eucalypt in Autumn', the tree is imagined as a 'slim creek out of the sky', an image which kindles a cluster of appropriate associations, not only through the use of the word 'creek' in its Australian sense, but also through the perception, which we owe to the Aborigines, that in a parched landscape water may be present vertically in the trees. The closing metaphor of the same poem illustrates Murray's development of the Jindyworobak idea by linking the flowering of the tree to the annual round of up-country agricultural shows.[9]

Murray's prose book *The Australian Year* (1985) is, amongst other things, a re-examination of the problem which impelled the Jindyworobaks, and he begins by pointing out that 'the four traditional seasons of the northern world are themselves perhaps the greatest and most significant cultural import the continent has seen'. However, the seasonal cycle which Europeans have imposed upon the Australian environment hardly fits it. Besides the absence of seasonal indications like budding growth and falling leaves, there are major natural events, such as fire and drought, which are recurrent but not seasonal. Murray goes on to argue – in a passage which echoes the observations of Barron Field – that transposing the seasonal cycle, with its rich cultural accretions, to the antipodes undermine[s] the ancient sense of consonance, ... the sense of intricate linkage between nature and the supernatural, the life of the seen and unseen realms. These links all have to be recast in the southern world of European settlement, and the great transitions given emblematic reality. This essentially poetic job has been under way for a long time already, both formally and informally.[10]

This recognition that the Australian poet has a well-defined and necessary occupation is important. The task is to assimilate the environment imaginatively and create a regional, and by extension, national (though not nationalistic) literature through which Australians can establish an harmonious sense of place and resolve their sense of exile. As he acknowledges, Murray is far from being the first to do this, but he has succeeded better than his predecessors in discovering the poetry in a continent Europeans long found alien.

One source of this sense of alienation was, as I have mentioned, the silence of the wilderness, particularly at certain times of the day. The first important colonial poet, Charles Harpur, noticed it in his 'Mid-Summer Noon in the Australian Forest':

> Not a bird disturbs the air,
> There is quiet everywhere;
> Over plains and over woods
> What a mighty stillness broods.

The poem illustrates Harpur's unsuccessful struggle to find a mode apposite to his subject. Even these opening lines contain the word 'woods', which along with 'rill' which occurs later would be a sure sign to the Jindyworobaks of a failure to observe 'environmental values'. There are no rills in the mainly arid Australian continent, and the open canopy of the park-like Australian forests gives them a pervasive lightness just the opposite of the shade connoted by the word 'wood'. Yet despite the failure of this poem, it conveys that fact that Harpur was impressed by the 'mighty stillness' – the limitless silence – which continues to inspire his successors. Les Murray evoked it in his early poem, 'Noonday Axeman':

Axe-fall, echo and silence. Noonday silence.
Two miles from here, it is the twentieth century:
cars on the bitumen, powerlines vaulting the farms.
Here, with my axe, I am chopping into the stillness.[11]

The poem is impelled by the ringing sound of the axe, and the way this heightens the silence, which is musically composed through tactful repetitions of the opening phrase, and by the crashing tree at the centre of the poem, which leaves the stillness 'there as ever'. Instead of simply asserting the silence, like Harpur, Murray incorporates in the language and rhythms of the poem a succession of sounds, climaxing in the stanza describing the collapse of the tree, all of which fail to disturb the effect produced by the subdued pulse of the words 'silence' and 'stillness' through the poem.

The opening lines (which I have just quoted) exactly define contemporary Australia in relation to the boundless 'inhuman silence'. The axeman is a typical pioneering figure, familiar from colonial literature and impressionist paintings around the turn of the century, but here he is at the edge of modern civilisation, at a point where history verges on space. His efforts, and those of his predecessors

have made this silence human and familiar
no farther than where farms rise into foothills.

Whereas the colonial poets and painters celebrated the attempts of the pioneers to subdue the land, Murray's poem, a meditation on silence, civilisation and nature, engages with the problem of human subjugation to nature, and celebrates (if that is the right word) the difficult virtue of living in the presence of overwhelming silence.

Though I go to the cities ...
... for the sake of belonging
for months and years at a time to the twentieth century
... I will be always
coming back here on the up-train, peering, leaning
out of the window to see, on far-off ridges
the sky between the trees, and over the racket
of the rails to hear the echo and the silence.

The cities – and civilisation – are envisaged as a retreat from the pervasive silence and the overpowering presence of the land which has to be faced by Australians, and the position of the axeman reveals the way white settlement remains a margin on the edge of interior space. Civilised Australia reflects the charts of the early navigators; the discontinuous outlines have just moved inland by no more, perhaps, than a hundred miles.

'Noonday Axeman' is centred on a place which is evoked through many precise details in the poem. Though it is not named, it is recognisably in the Bunyah region, familiar from much of Murray's other work. The poem is not, however, simply a piece of regional writing, created for the sake of local colour. As is usually the case in Murray's poetry, Bunyah is the vantage-point for a review of human history and geography, and the point is not random; the axeman is placed exactly where the history of Western civilisation runs out. This view from the edge casts new perspectives on human culture which Murray's poetry is in the process of elaborating.

It is developed, for example, in 'The Fire Autumn' which is concerned with a recurrent natural event in Australia which transcends the seasonal cycle. In the opening lines of the poem, fire is seen as producing an intermittent autumn, otherwise a barely noticed seasonal transition in much of Australia, except where there are stands of imported trees. From a distance, the effect of fire is like 'Autumn in the Jura', and this comparison becomes the springboard for the speculation that European civilisation has entered a 'great autumn'; a fall evident from its production of junk. Australians find the outer ripples of this washing up on their shoreline, but it is the place where civilisation runs out. Beyond the shoreline is 'the limitless country', 'too near for speech'.[12]

The final paragraph of the poem returns to the actual fire, and the rebirth it presages, for there are seeds in Australia, notably of some varieties of acacia, which only germinate after fire, and the eucalyptus trees have epicormic buds which send out new shoots

> claret, cerise, liquid green,
> faint blues fat with powder, new leaves clustered thick
> down the length
> of charcoal stiff bark.

'Noonday Axeman' and 'The Fire Autumn' both illustrate Murray's development of a flexible Australian poetic language, not restricted, as it is in much recent Australian literature, to a kind of stage Australian for broad characterisation and comic purposes. Murray has stripped the idiom of these associations to create a distinct language very much his own, and unmistakably Australian, yet continuous with the rest of English.

The 'Buladelah-Taree Holiday Song Cycle', along with the 'novel sequence' *The Boys Who Stole the Funeral* (1980), illustrate this better, perhaps, than any of his poems. The long lines of the Song Cycle use a cadential verse which Murray based upon Professor R. M. Berndt's translation of the Aboriginal Wonguri-Mandjiikai Song Cycle of the Moon Bone, and they capture the tone and rhythms of idiomatic Australian speech while retaining underlying hints of the original source, through such things as development by repetition (a typical characteristic of oral poetry) and catalogues of place names. Their rhythmic contours are reinforced by assonance and alliteration which enhance, rather than detract from, their idiomatic tone:

> The people are eating dinner in that country north of
>   Legge's Lake;
> behind flywire and venetians, in the dimmed cool,
>   town people eat Lunch.
> Plying knives and forks with a peek-in sound, with a
>   tuck-in sound
> they are thinking about relatives and inventory, they are
>   talking about customers and visitors.
> In the country of memorial iron, on the creek facing
>   hills there,
> they are thinking about bean plants, and rings of tank
>   water, of growing a pumpkin by Christmas;
> rolling a cigarette, they say thoughtfully Yes, and their
>   companion nods, considering.

As these opening lines suggest, the Song Cycle is, amongst other things, a poem of place, and it is rich in passages in which the region implied in many of Murray's poems, from 'Noonday Axeman' onwards, is charted and named according to its attributes, in the Aboriginal manner:

for this is the season when the children return with
    their children
to the place of Bingham's Ghost, of the Old Timber Wharf,
    of the Big Flood That Time,

the country of the rationalized farms, of the day-and-night
    farms and of the Pitt Street farms,
of the Shire Engineer and many other rumours,
    of the tractor crankcase furred with chaff,
the places of sitting down near ferns, the snake-fear
    places, the cattle-crossing-long-ago places.[13]

It could be argued that Aboriginal song is the authentic literature
of region in Australia, for like Aboriginal painting and the oral
narratives recently recorded, it reveals an intimate spiritual
connection between man and his environment, quite the reverse of
the disjunction between the two which results from the sense of
exile embedded in white Australian culture. As they come to terms
with the land, white Australians will, in Murray's view, borrow
something of the Aboriginal attitude; it is inevitable in a country
which white settlers have been unable to make conform to their
cultural inheritance. 'The Buladelah-Taree Holiday Song Cycle'
illustrates this 'convergence' (as Murray calls it) both in its form
and subject. The return to the country touched on in the closing
lines of 'Noonday Axeman', and a pervasive topic in Murray's
poetry, is expanded in the Song Cycle into a parallel with the
Aboriginal custom of revisiting spirit places in the land. In an essay
called 'Some Religious Stuff I Know about Australia' Murray
suggests that 'we have come to the sense, which the Aborigines
had before us, that after all human frenzies and efforts there
remains the great land. . . . We know in our bones that the land is
mightier than we are'.
    The three or four poems considered here are from what can now
be regarded as the first part of Murray's career. They are, like most
of his poems, centred in a region and concerned with what Murray
regards as the essential 'poetic job' of encompassing Australia
imaginatively through resolving some of the problems which beset
its inhabitants when they envisage their country as a nation. Yet he
is not simply a poet of region and nation. From Bunyah he deepens
our understanding through a vision which reaches back to the
primeval past:

> Far back as I can glimpse with descendant sight
> Beyond roads or the stave-plough, there is a boy on
>   cold upland,
> Gentle tapper of veins, a blood-porridge eater,
> His ringlets new-dressed with dung, a spear in his fist,
>
> It is thousands of moons to the cattle-raid of Cooley
>
> But we could still find common knowledge, verb-roots
> And noun-bark enough for an evening fire of sharing
> Cattle-wisdom.[14]

Like another regionalist, William Faulkner, though his art and vision are completely different, he realigns our perspectives on the whole of human culture precisely because he sees it from the edge. He has been able to take advantage of the fact that Australia remains a frontier of Western civilisation at a time when that whole phenomenon is being revalued.

From 'Noonday Axeman' onwards, and increasingly in his splendid recent poems like 'Equanimity', he has been a meditative, and ultimately religious, poet. Even one of his most characteristically Australian books, the 'novel sequence' *The Boys Who Stole the Funeral* – a story about an old digger's wish to be buried in his spirit country – is essentially concerned with the waverings of the human spirit in a world where it is denied apposite rituals for expression.

At the centre of his work, however, there is a vision, like that revealed to Kevin Forbutt in *The Boys Who Stole the Funeral*, of the 'great land'; his poetry continues to transform its strangeness and enhance our understanding of what he called in a recent poem, 'Louvres':

> the three quarters of our continent
> set aside for mystic poetry.[15]

NOTES

1. The *Five Gaelic Poems* were published under that title in Les A. Murray, *Ethnic Radio* (Sydney, 1977). The note is on p. 62 of that book. The quotation from Judith Wright comes from her *Preoccupations in Australian Poetry* (Melbourne, 1965) p. xi.

2. *Ern Malley's Poems*, with an introduction by Max Harris (Adelaide, n.d.) p. 36.

3. A. D. Hope, *Collected Poems* (Sydney, 1972) p. 13.

4. Robert Hughes, *The Art of Australia* (Harmondsworth, Middx., rev. edn, 1970) p. 19.

5. The attempt to write 'Gaelic in English words' is mentioned in the seventh stanza of the 'Elegy'. On the Scottish influence in Australian poetry, see Les A. Murray, 'The Bonnie Disproportion', in *Persistence in Folly* (Sydney, 1984) pp. 61–85.

6. Judith Wright, 'Some Problems of Being an Australian Poet', in *Because I Was Invited* (Melbourne, 1975) p. 50.

7. Quoted in Brian Elliott, *The Landscape of Australian Poetry* (Melbourne, 1967) p. 19.

8. Percy Grainger, 'Book of Intentions' (MS., c.1903–4, Grainger Museum, Melbourne); Michael Hannan, *Peter Sculthorpe: His Music and Ideas* (St Lucia, 1982) pp. 9–10, 12, 15, 78–94.

9. Brian Elliott, *The Jindyworobaks* (St Lucia, 1979) pp. 283, 300–8; Carole Oles, 'Les Murray: an Interview', *American Poetry Review*, March/April 1986, p. 28; Les A. Murray 'Flowering Eucalypt in Autumn', in *The People's Otherworld* (Sydney, 1983) p. 51.

10. Les A. Murray, *The Australian Year* (North Ryde, 1985) p. 5.

11. 'Noonday Axeman' appeared in Murray's first book, with Geoffrey Lehmann, *The Ilex tree* (Canberra, 1965). It is reprinted with a cut, in *The Vernacular Republic: Poems 1961–81* (Edinburgh, 1982) pp. 3–5.

12. 'The Fire Autumn' appeared in Murray's second book, *The Weatherboard Cathedral* (Sydney, 1969). It is reprinted in revised form in *The Vernacular Republic: Poems 1961–81*, pp. 36–9.

13. 'The Buladelah-Taree Holiday Song Cycle' appeared in Les A. Murray, *Ethnic Radio*, pp. 28–38. It is reprinted in Murray, *The Vernacular Republic: Poems 1961–81*, pp. 159–70, and *Selected Poems* (Manchester, 1986) pp. 52–63.

14. 'The Names of the Humble', one of the poems in the cycle *Walking to the Cattle Place*, originally published in Murray's third book, *Poems Against Economics* (Sydney, 1972). Reprinted with cuts in *The Vernacular Republic: Poems 1961–81*; printed as a single poem in *Selected Poems*.

15. 'Equanimity' was the titular poem in a rare pamphlet *Equanimities* (Copenhagen, n.d. [1982]); reprinted in Murray, *Selected Poems*, pp. 84–6, where 'Louvres' also appears, pp. 133–4.

16

The British Columbian History of Place

MARK S. MADOFF

John McLoughlin, chief factor of Fort Vancouver and superintendent in the Columbia district, set the tone by the 1830s for relations between the north-west coast of America and the nations which have claimed it. Though Canadian-born and Scottish-educated and agent of a company licenced by the British Crown, he strove to encourage more intensive Yankee settlement of Oregon. The Hudson's Bay Company viewed his behaviour with alarm, but in modern Oregon McLoughlin is revered; a West Coaster might see that he was behaving like a West Coaster;[1] that is, he was more concerned about pursuing a vision of the local territory than about the aims of distant corporations or nation states. Such obliviousness of the imperatives of nationality has endured as a feature of the West Coast man's imagination. About 150 years after McLoughlin's 'treachery', Ernest Callenbach imagined his ecological utopia, *Ecotopia*, stretching up the north-west coast against the grain of boundaries, along the grain of climate, conservational economics, devolutionary politics and appropriate culture.[2] Robert Sund, a poet, proposes to rename the coast the Ish Nation, after a common geographical suffix of the native Salish language.[3] Many have taken to calling it a 'bioregion', a 'geographical terrain and the terrain of consciousness ... a place and the ideas that have developed about how to live in that place'.[4] A bioregion is a denial of nationhood. There is an east-west line between Canada and the United States, but many have experienced and imagined the West Coast as a north-south erasure of boundaries, an anti-nation.

Speaking recently of 'Mythology and Landscape in Robinson Jeffers', Anne Tayler encouraged critics to apply her method of close reading in Jeffers's imaginary Big Sur to the larger task of describing a West-Coast poetics.[5] This paper takes up Tayler's invitation by briefly reading George Bowering's anti-historical novel, *Burning Water* (1980) and Charles Lillard's collection of poems, *A Coastal Range* (1984) for evidences of a Coastal poetics. From Bowering's and Lillard's considerable critical self-consciousness about what it means to be a poet on the West Coast, this paper also fashions a partial answer to the question: Is the West Coast really a literary region?

Since the partial answer is 'no' (contrary to the current literary-critical fashion of regionalist fracture), perhaps some mediation between the international critical situation and the peculiarly Canadian one is worthwhile. The general concentration of critical attention upon local or regional literatures is part of the centrifugal process by which the myth of a Great National Canon has been deconstructed. Necessarily, the process has drawn appreciation to the cultural works of ethnic, linguistic or racial minorities – to the words of speakers of under-languages or -dialects, to the ideas of groups *out* of cultural power. As viewed politically and sociologically, Canada seems to have undergone this process of regional deconstruction, right on schedule with the rest of the Europeanised world. Aside from longstanding grievances between the Periphery and the Centre (including complaints about the concentration of literary life in Toronto or Montreal), the process of regional fracture became more apparent after about 1965. A succession of federal governments added 'multiculturalism', contradictorily, to the historic and constitutional bilingualism of Canada. The rhetoric of politicians and journalists regularly alludes to 'the regions' and their aspirations, on the assumption that these are real divisions of the political confederation and of the national imagination. And academic critics and editors hve increasingly accorded significance to the geographical and linguistic differences within Canadian culture – despite the extra-Canadian supremacy of our two most internationalist critics, Northrop Frye and Marshall McLuhan. Two landmarks of Canadian literary regionalist deconstruction are the anthologies *Skookum Wawa: Writings of the Canadian Northwest*, edited by Gary Geddes (1975) and *Volvox: Poetry from the Unofficial Languages of Canada*, edited by Andreas Schroeder and Charles Lillard (1971).

Both Lillard and George Bowering have led lives apparently well-suited to the *regionalist* side of the dialectic with nationhood. Charles Lillard grew up in coastal Southern California and the Alaskan Panhandle; now he writes in Victoria, midway between those extreme limits of his earlier coastal life. George Bowering grew up in the semi-desert of the southern Okanagan Valley, where there are still only two significant geographical directions: the Interior and 'the Coast'. He came out to university in Vancouver, realigned himself, and has stayed within sight and smell of salt water. He was a founding member of the *Tish* group in the 1960s, which joined Vancouver and San Francisco – Bowering and Robert Creeley and Robert Duncan – along an axis of poetical theory and practice.[6] Of the reason for that connection, he recalls that

> when the whole *Tish* thing was happening, we were people who had been deracinated – we didn't get any Canadian writing at school in B.C. . . . I hadn't even thought about Canadian poetry. I didn't even think about thinking about Canadian poetry.[7]

The poets who influenced him were 'American. But that's not a matter of commitment, that's a matter of that I happened to be there. I found that the English poets were speaking to me from a foreign – even a hostile – situation.'[8] So were most Canadian poets, too.

Yet all of the apparent conformation of the Canadian situation to the general regionalist fracture does not make of the West Coast, in particular, a region. In a cultural, critical climate which favours regionalism, with personal histories which straddle the national boundaries, neither poet, as *critic*, defines the West Coast regionally. Both Bowering and Lillard have concentrated on what Bowering, following Charles Olson, has called 'locus' – the local situation of the poet, where he or she *is*.[9] Knowing that situation, on the West Coast, means not so much describing the place as inventing it, and inventing a sufficient syntax of place-in-time: *imagining* the history of the Coast, because, unlike the East, the Coast has no history. In his essay 'Searching for the Benchmark', Lillard affirms the connection between place and history, and admits the extreme difficulty of devising a syntax to join them:

> Anyone who will take the time to read the 2500 or so volumes of poetry about British Columbia will find one recurrent theme. . . . the attempt to define or to come to grips with B.C.'s landscape. . . .
> All of these poets have approached the landscape as historians, and almost every poem is dependent on history. This

approach falls into three categories: the European's view, the personal and the quasi-mythological. There can be no argument with any of the three; however, there is a fallacy built into each approach.

The European viewpoint cannot hope to define the landscape, because most of us long ago lost all feeling for the land, the soil....

All too often the personal approach fails to achieve its ends because we are only defining ourselves. Poem after poem is a self-portrait; the background is the landscape, and nothing more....

The quasi-mythological is ... the worst of all possible approaches. The west coast lacks a mythology, excepting the indigenous Indian mythology, and no writer can force a mythology on an area where the mythos did not arise from the local soil. To use the Indian mythology is impossible; the European writer cannot hope to understand it and use it fluently; even if he managed the task, he wouldn't find readers to share his knowledge.[10]

Guy Davenport reminds us of the origins of this mismatch, in his essay 'The Geography of the Imagination'. He glosses 'the Latin word for the sacredness of a place ... *cultus*, [as] the dwelling of a god, the place where a rite is valid', the root of cult and culture. Then he shows how *cult* and *culture* may become irrelevant:

When Europeans came to the new world, they learned nothing on the way, as if they came through a dark tunnel.... We new-world settlers, then, brought the imagination of other countries to transplant in a different geography.... We brought many things across the Atlantic, and the Pacific; many things we left behind: a critical choice to live with forever.[11]

The painter Emily Carr knew the meaning of this problem of transplantation for the West Coast artist, when she addressed a Victoria audience in 1930:

Misty landscapes and gentle cows do not express Western Canada, even the cows know that. I said to a farmer in Scotland once: 'That fence wouldn't keep out a Canadian cow.' 'You are right,' he replied, 'it would not. Your cows are accustomed to fighting their way through the bush. When they are shipped here it takes twice as many men and twice as high a fence to make them stay put.' So, if the country produces different cow-spirit, isn't it reasonable that it should produce different artist-spirit.[12]

What is different about this West Coast artist-spirit? Lillard answers in terms of cult and history, in terms of actual and ideal, in terms of poet and shaman, in terms of a half-discovered syntax:

> The shaman knew what lurked in those shadows; the gods were there. This is something that does not exist for us. Our poets do not see gods, nor do the rest of us. We live in the present; our existence is based on the spot of ground on which we stand. The shaman had no knowledge of the time as we do; he lived ... within time. ... We do not share his respect for the living and the dead; nor do we have his understanding of the *genius loci* – the spirit of place.[13]

Lillard concludes that the West Coast poet must fully form the intimate, acceptant spiritual connection with place which sustained and bound the shaman; must *become* 'the contemporary shaman'. The alternative is dislocation: 'Before 1970', he claims, 'B.C. poetry, the poetry of place, was an imitation of European or Asian poetry, and none of it worked.'[14]

George Bowering's sense of the West Coast as place has less to do with the soil than Lillard's, more to do with the specifically human activity of language-making. Bowering says: 'Locus, in that literal sense of place, I mean I know where I am now. So it's not a problem anymore.'[15] Yet, like Lillard's ideally shamanistic poet, Bowering's West Coast poet is convinced of the efficacy of word or *logos*. Because the history of a place is the tradition of using language that suits it, this conviction, too, like the shaman's penetration through time, leads the poet, leads Bowering, into history, and, ultimately, *through* history into a fully realised imaginative cosmos. When an interviewer in 1976 noted that Bowering 'did bounce around – Montreal, London, Calgary', Bowering replied:

> I'm not particularly located in a place. ... I believe in the

language.... To me, ... in the early sixties, those things ['a very rooted sense of place' and a concern 'with the linguistic landscape'] seemed ... to be co-determinant, that if you're a poet the only way you can find out about ... the configurations of the place in which you live, is with language.... now that that other sense of place is no longer in my work ... the language is the most important thing to me.[16]

Bowering has exactly marked this change in his sense of place. Of his time in Montreal, he writes:

my sojourn in the east took me out of place and took place out of my poetry. Since I discovered that there is no place east of Lake of the Woods, I had to look elsewhere to find poetry.... As I read the poems now I hear that I wasn't really there when I was writing.[17]

The difference between an eastern and a West Coast poetics is very clear, for Bowering: after the defunct lyric poem comes

a poem that is larger.... sometimes it tends toward epic, and other times it tends toward the cosmic.... in the east it tends toward something like the epic, a poem containing history. In Vancouver, particularly, it tends towards something that can contain a cosmos, or something that can contain clues to a cosmos.[18]

He describes a 'typical west coast book' of poems, in which 'you will find Hesiod', the cosmologist, 'and you will also find the cat that was walking around the house.... That is to say, make a world'.[19]

Bowering's sharpest expression of his sense of *locus* is his essay 'Reaney's Region', about his own puzzlement at the regional identity of the artists, such as James Reaney, whom he knew during his year in London, Ontario. Bowering argues that artists in old Canada, in Ontario, may be regionalists, but artists in British Columbia may not. Ontarians fully inhabit their place; the community and the history of the place seem co-extensive. On the West Coast, the place of habitation is still half-discovered; nothing about it can be assumed, and the inhabitant is an individual, alienated from both land and transitory society. Like Lillard,[20]

Bowering realises that the frontier newness of the West Coast is too disruptive, undigested: 'for us everything was new', he says.

> There wasn't even anything old to liken the new with.... Our Pacific Rim puts us inevitably among the exogamic; our 'Pacific Nation' is defined by a classic 'other,' the ocean.... Regionalist art happens when (a) the local people make or perform it, and (b) when the subject is local.[21]

'The work becomes for the reader or audience an environment, as the region has been for its creator.'[22] Regional environment and society are seamlessly one; in a region, nature is richly symbolic of man's presence in it. Bowering denies that any such conditions of familiarity or likeness between society and landscape apply to the West Coast poet's experience:

> 'The feeling of place is a power within us,' said Reaney.... I believe him but I don't *know* what he is saying, mainly because of that 'us.' When I visit my home towns I feel like an alien; though I know most of the roads, I know them privately. And what I like best, the mountain skylines with their scant trees, have not changed much since the retreat of the last glacier.[23]

In effect, Bowering negatively defines a West Coast poetics, by differentiating it from that of Upper Canada: the West Coast poetics doubts humanism; avoids simile and metaphor, documentarism and myth-making; treats nature as *other*, not as humanised correspondence or symbol; renders surfaces, instead of deep, dense, figurative structures. Mostly, Bowering emphasises the lack of domestication in West Coast art:

> We grew up without trust in household gods because we lived in so many houses, few of them older than ourselves. 'Nature' was for us not a human phenomenon, not intentional, but a place to live.[24]

Not a place to have, nor a place given, in the compositional sense.

This poetics utterly transforms the primal West Coast habitation stories, in Bowering's hands, deconstructing what might otherwise have become regional myth. The ostensible subject of his novel

Burning Water is the expedition led by Captain George Vancouver in 1792 to map the north-west coast of America and to test the possibilities of a passage through the continent. Yet the Prologue frames Bowering's real literary undertaking in an ironically disingenuous way, as if it were going to be a regionalist work of the kind Bowering denies for the West Coast:

> When I was a boy I was the only person I knew who was named George, but I did have the same first name as the king. That made me feel as if current history and self were bound together, from the beginning.
>
> When I came to live in Vancouver, I thought of Vancouver, and so now geographically involved my name too, George Vancouver. He might have felt such romance, sailing for a king named George the Third. What could I do but write a book filled with history and myself, about these people and this place?[25]

Against this apparent community of history and place, however, Bowering insists upon the artificiality of any history of this place: 'We are making a story, after all, as we always have been, standing and speaking together to make a history, a real historical fiction.'[26] Within the novel's shifting frame, this insistence continues. Here Captain Vancouver discusses the landscape he is charting, with his surgeon-naturalist nemesis, Archibald Menzies:

> 'It must be strange to live among such an extreme landscape', suggested Vancouver.
> 'Yet as we know, there are men who live upon the desert and in the snow,' said the surgeon.
> 'And in Scotland,' added the captain.
> 'It is we who come here and fancy it odd to live among mountains and so far from Mayfair. You fear it, then?'
> 'I have come to work here.'
> 'You imagine living here, and you fear the idea, then.'
> 'A peculiar verb of your choosing, Mr. Menzies.' Vancouver turned away from him.
> 'It is because you take a mountain for a god and a god for a father,' Menzies went on. 'The people who live here have conversed with me long upon this theme, and at my urging. They deem the mountains to be mountains, that and whatever advantage they can make of that. They are true Western man.'[27]

Menzies, a learned Scottish civilian among a mainly English naval crew, seems to understand how the primary, geographical mission alienates Vancouver and his men from the land that is their subject, just as he, as a naturalist, is fatally alienated from the mariner, his captain. The chief difference between them is like the difference between Eastern and West Coast poetics: Vancouver is an agent of domestic interests, trying, with 'a quarter million soundings',[28] to extend the grid of their rational control, or of their myths such as the convenient myth of the North-west Passage, over unknown, perhaps unknowable territory. He bridles when the land refuses to become familiar: one of his lieutenants complains of its convolutions. ' "The men have just come aboard after twenty-three days, during which time they rowed seven hundred miles. Now we are sixty miles farther up the coast." '[29] In contrast, Menzies is a gatherer, whose scientific rationalism is not so rigid as to prevent him from accepting that the West Coast of America is not even like the West Coast of Scotland. Menzies accumulates so many botanical specimens that the decks of the *Discovery* are nearly awash with them; he remakes the new, other-worldly cosmos of the West Coast on the decks of a floating outpost of European culture – and drives his commander crazy.

The title of Charles Lillard's *A Coastal Range* is at least a triple play on words. It encompasses the great spine of mountains, which spiritually and climatically faces the West Coast away from America, toward Asia. It encompasses the coastal territory of Lillard's own life, from southern California to the Alaskan Panhandle. And it implies an imaginative ranging along the coast, in order to 'make a world' of it for – and from – the otherwise unfulfilled self. Lillard immediately invokes the scepticism of West Coast poetics with an epigraph on islands, from Conrad's *The Secret Sharer*: 'Unknown ... to travel, almost to geography, the manner of life they harbor is an unsolved secret.'[30] In the opening poem, the mentor figure, Jenny, warns the poet: ' "You'll write your books, no doubt; / if you return to your dreaming, / to the landscape of your first living, / but don't tackle time; / none of us can hammer its warp flat / to the anvil bench." '[31] But he chooses to ignore her warning:

> I cannot forget the broken edges
> of this long narrow country;
> our phrases and fables,

> all the untitled subjects,
> those lives I call my own.
>
> Out north-northwestward of Jenny's distance
> I hear the rustle of my vocabulary
> growing infinitely louder
> than those worries that brought me here;
> it is a belonging I must bring home.[32]

He is also wary, however, of the temptation to use metaphor to smooth 'the broken edges / of this long narrow country': flying over islands of the Alaskan Panhandle, metamorphosing the land through metaphor, he none the less suspects the very process of flight – through air or through poetry – and the means that enable it:

> The wind slouches in the troughs of a dying tide.
> I have carves metaphors from these islands,
> today I must learn to meet the earth again.[33]

But meeting the earth means recognising and claiming as his own the illusion that a network of personal allusions or place-names or historical associations can realise it. As Bowering, following Olson, says, it means obeying the earth on which one finds oneself.[34] In 'Chart Work', Lillard admits the inadequacy of personal or common mythology, the dumbness of the language which is fit for other places:

> but now I need a fresh vocabulary
> for the inflections of this green rising beyond me,
> the blue boundaries, the accidents of history
> collapsing around me.
>
> .   .   .
>
> I must learn to fear this shoreline
> of restless companions and shaped voices,
> the nights' mysteries and their stories,
> a forest in the sea and a monologue at Orbea
> that enchanted me for weeks;
> this old west where
> a secret cove with an old house
> is called history,
> a raven crackling on a limb, mythology.[35]

The 'must learn' is significant. Fearing this shoreline, as some Eastern theorists tell us we should, is not natural for 'true Western man'. A poet 'must learn to fear' it. Though *A Coastal Range* is full of gatherings from the shallow detritus of memory and local legend and actual, physical ranging up the Coast, gatherings which may be accumulated into 'a real historical fiction', Lillard invariably returns, despite the seeming clarity of observation in his poems of coastal life, to the gulf between the West Coast and the poet's knowledge of it. In his newest book of poems, *Circling North*, a companion-piece to *A Coastal Range*, Lillard contrasts a companion's sureness about place with his own typical sense of indeterminacy in the syntax which tries to order the tangled coastline:

> The woman with me this weekend denies
> A site is more than sight
> The sand and sun are firm ground
>
> .   .   .
>
> I see the land spilling over into language
> And those shores crumbling
> The order of nature, disorder, ruthless
> Change, the infinite
> Lack of finality[36]

The West Coast poetics is acceptance of ephemerality and of a singular responsibility very like solitude; a style of drawing edges around images, edges which never fully enclose a shape;[37] a suspicious, ironical sabotage even of *personal* myth-making. The poems of *A Coastal Range* lovingly assemble the facts of lives spent between sea and shore, spent drilling 'the rock of ages' beneath the cliffs. Yet, when the drillers break from their labour and look up,

> Once again we knew
>   how far we were from our own voices.
>
> And the eagles were still there –
> three shadows streaking the palisades.
> They will be here forever
>   while men like ourselves
> come and go, and all our mauling
> will leave no more trace than a spray of sunbeams.

This is pain which cannot be wrung out in a freshet.
This is bedrock:
 eagles will dance forever in the unwinding wind.[38]

NOTES

1. Charles Lillard, *Seven Shillings a Year: A History of Vancouver Island* (Ganges, BC: Horsdal and Schubart, 1986) pp. 54–6.
2. Ernest Callenbach, *Ecotopia* (Berkeley, Calif.: Banyen Tree, 1975) and *Ecotopia Emerging* (Toronto: Bantam, 1981).
3. See editorial note to interview with Gary Snyder, *The New Catalyst* (Lillooet, BC) vol. II, no. 2 (Fall/Winter 1986) p. 11.
4. Proceedings of North American Bioregional Congress, *The New Catalyst*, vol. I, no. 2 (Fall/Winter 1986) p. 3.
5. Anne Tayler's paper 'Mythology and Landscape in Robinson Jeffers' was read to the 21st Annual Conference of the Canadian Association for American Studies, Royal Roads Military College, Victoria, BC, October 1985.
6. For a sympathetic, thorough insider's account of the San Francisco–Vancouver literary connection and the founding of *Tish*, see Warren Tallman, 'Wonder Merchants: Modernist Poetry in Vancouver During the 1960s', *Boundary 2*, vol. III, no. 1 (Fall 1974) pp. 57–89. See also Ken Norris, *The Little Magazines in Canada, 1925–80* (Toronto: ECW, 1984) pp. 97–131. George Woodcock responds to Tallman's account by arguing that Tallman overestimates the Californian influence upon Vancouver modernism. See Woodcock, 'Beyond the Divide: Notes on Recent Poetry in British Columbia', in *The World of Canadian Writing* (Vancouver: Douglas & McIntyre and Seattle: University of Washington Press, 1980) pp. 252–4. In her Preface to *West Window: The Selected Poems of George Bowering* (Toronto: General, 1982) [p. 10], Sheila Watson recalls her own interest in the San Francisco–California connection, as it applies to Bowering, and suggests another 'internationalist' influence:

> I knew that Marshal McLuhan had been a presence on the U.B.C. campus in May 1958 where he felt completely at home and where he elicited attentive interest. I knew from the published work of a poet of my own generation, who had grown up as I had and as Bowering had in what one critic has poetically described as the 'manifest reaches of humanly untouched space' that an ironic tension could exist between Pacific and Laurentian man. I did not know until 1967 when I read in a forward to *The New Writing in the USA*, edited by Donald Allen and Robert Creeley, that 'even Vancouver, B.C. [had] been colonized' by 'a whole new generation of American writers.' It was then that I began to collect

Bowering's work to see how he had survived not only colonization but the effects of the uncharacteristic 'national' outbursts that the new 'internationalism' seemed to provoke.

7. Interview with George Bowering, in *Outposts*, ed. Caroline Bayard and Jack David (Erin, Ontario: Press Porcepic, 1978) p. 81.
8. Ibid.
9. Ibid., pp. 79–80. See, for instance, Olson's explanation of projective verse in his letter to Elaine Feinstein (in *Charles Olson: Selected Writings*, ed. Robert Creeley [New York City: New Directions, 1966] pp. 29–30), and his dance-play *Apollonius of Tyana* (ibid., pp. 133–56). For a clear, extensive discussion of the differences between '*locus*' and 'region' see George Bowering, 'Reaney's Region', in *A Way with Words* (Ottawa: Oberon, 1982) pp. 38–9.
10. Charles Lillard, 'Searching for the Benchmark', in *Western Windows: A Comparative Anthology of Poetry in British Columbia* (Vancouver: CommCept, 1977) pp. 227–8.
11. Guy Davenport, 'The Geography of the Imagination', in *The Geography of the Imagination* (San Francisco: North Point, 1981) pp. 4–5.
12. Quoted by Gary Geddes in the Preface to *Skookum Wawa: Writings of the Canadian Northwest*, ed. Gary Geddes (Toronto: Oxford University Press, 1975) p. xiv.
13. Lillard, 'Searching for the Benchmark', pp. 228–9.
14. Ibid., p. 231.
15. Bowering, *Outposts* interview, p. 88.
16. Ibid., pp. 89–90. The interviewer's remark is Jack David's. Compare Lillard's autobiographical remark in the preface to his collection *Voice My Shaman* (Victoria, BC: Sono Nis, 1979): 'Either a poet is born with a landscape, or he spends his life searching for one. Happily, I count myself among the former. However, it is also true that I spend a great deal of time looking for a place to write' (p. 7).
17. George Bowering, 'Montreal', in *Craft Slices* (Ottawa: Oberon, 1985) p. 76.
18. George Bowering, 'Post Lyric', ibid., p. 92.
19. Ibid., p. 93.
20. Lillard, 'Searching for the Benchmark', p. 228:

> The truth is we are a frontier country. We have little history and less myth; we have shared the world's history in the 20th century, but we've not become part of it. We are as much a frontier today as we were in 1868 when Anderson published the first book of poems in B.C.... We may admire the landscape, but we do not love it.

21. Bowering, 'Reaney's Region', p. 47.
22. Ibid., p. 46.
23. Ibid., p. 48.
24. Ibid., p. 52. Bowering discusses simile in regionalist art on p. 47,

'density' on p. 46, regionalist humanism on p. 50, and regionalist deep structures on pp. 50–1.

25. George Bowering, *Burning Water* (1980; rpt. Toronto: General, 1983) [p. 8].
26. Ibid. [p. 9].
27. Ibid., p. 108.
28. Ibid., p. 242.
29. Ibid., p. 227.
30. Charles Lillard, *A Coastal Range* (Victoria, BC: Sono Nis, 1984) [p. 8].
31. Charles Lillard, 'Jenny', in *A Coastal Range*, p. 13.
32. Ibid., p. 14.
33. Charles Lillard, 'Flight', 'The Outside West', in *A Coastal Range*, p. 67.
34. Bowering, 'Reaney's Region', pp. 41–2.
35. Charles Lillard, 'Chart Work', 'The Outside West', in *A Coastal Range*, p. 89.
36. Charles Lillard, 'Kitsumkalum', in *Circling North* (unpublished MS).
37. Charles Lillard, 'Kispiox', in *Circling North*: 'In answer to the endless / A poem demands / More edge than shape, seeing / Honed to the quick / The circular motion of the eye over the nearby / The wrist of the mind flexing.'
38. Charles Lillard, 'One View from the Kynoch', 'The Outside West', in *A Coastal Range*, p. 78.

17

'Walloon Literature': Some Questions of Regionalism in a Bi-lingual Culture

PHILIP MOSLEY

'There aren't any Belgians, only Flemings and Walloons': so reads the key statement of Jules Destrée's 'Letter to the King' (1912), the celebrated reaction of a defiant Walloon to the continuing growth of Flemish power and influence in the country. Yet the name 'Belgium' has enjoyed longer currency than 'Wallonia' in the sense of a distinct geographical and political entity. Wallonia does not figure as a designated area until 1844, whereas modern Belgium came into being in 1830 as a direct result of strategic negotiations between the great European powers. However, 'Walloon' as an identity can be traced back to fifteenth-century chronicles and even to the fifth century as a spoken dialect of French. 'Belgian' may describe the Belgic tribes which inhabited the whole of the Low Countries in Roman times but usually refers, as a late eighteenth-century coinage, to the people of the area soon thereafter to be that of the new nation.

The imprecise notion of Wallonia gave rise to a number of ironies. For instance, before 1844 Belgian painters were described as Flemish but Belgian soldiers were always Walloon. Napoleon, too, should have known better. When his troops invaded the Walloon area, he ordered the appointment of Dutch-speaking interpreters in order to communicate with what turned out to be a one hundred per cent francophone population.

Given the uncertain uses of the terms 'Walloon' and 'Belgian' ('Flemish' less so, largely for reasons of longer cultural identity) it is unsurprising that the idea of Walloon and Belgian literature remains problematic to this day. My purpose here is to question the idea of 'Walloon literature', which I propose to consider on the basis of three categories for its possible identification. These

233

categories are: francophone Belgium, the region of Wallonia, and Walloon dialect. In each case, several geolinguistic and ideological questions also arise, since the categories depend for their validity on the application not only of specific literary criteria but also on the intrinsic meanings of such terms as 'francophone', 'region' and 'dialect'. The ideological implications of such semantics are by no means merely academic. Disputes between French- and Dutch--speakers have seriously threatened the continued existence of Belgium as a unified state. Having caused the collapse of the government in 1968, it is not for nothing that the language question in Belgium is often called the 'community problem' (cf. Wales, Gaelic-speaking Scotland).

BELGIAN FRANCOPHONE LITERATURE

In principle, 'francophone' is a neutral term solely identifying French language use. However, it may also be equated falsely with 'Walloon'. From the viewpoint of the more cosmopolitan francophone writer, there is a resistance to any association with an artificial ideology of Walloon literature. For many of these writers, 'francophone' invariably assumes an additional meaning. It suggests stronger links with Paris and mainstream French culture (or even with Brussels as a multi-lingual international community) than with Belgian national or provincial francophonism.

A major misconception of this category is that it presupposes a commonality of francophone interests, whereas the influence of French culture on Wallonia is ambiguous. From the viewpoint of the self-consciously Walloon writer, there is an undoubted allegiance to France, stemming from the period of her rule in the area from 1795 to 1815, when French language and culture were seen as the bastions of resistance to their despised equivalents in the kingdom of the Netherlands. Equally, there is little more affronting to Walloon pride than the supposed superiority of the *bruxellois*, that 'Franco-Flemish bastard of indeterminate speech'.[1]

Another problem with this category is that it cannot lay claim to geographical unity. Francophone writers are found throughout Wallonia but also in Flanders (including Brussels whose citizens are two-thirds francophone) where the francophone Flemings, descendants of the original bourgeois ruling class, remain a small but significant socio-cultural group. Such writers as Suzanne Lilar, Paul Willems and Guy Vaes testify to a continuity in Flemish francophone literature from the famous Flemish names of 'national' francophone literature in the nineteenth century, such as De Coster, Verhaeren and Maeterlinck.

Furthermore, this category must also refer to a *minority* literature since, in Belgium, francophones are outnumbered by Dutch-speakers. Yet 'minority' literature suggests that of a group of people with a body of common interests, which, as I have already argued, is a tenuous claim in this instance. There is rather more justification for it representing a large group of people whose everyday speech is other than that of the country's majority. 'Minority' literature also suggests considerable cultural and political subordination as well as relative unimportance. Such connotations are unwarranted in principle in a large area like Wallonia, where the minority in question is the whole population. Thus the 'minority' literature, that of the dominant native language, is produced anomalously in one of the widest-spoken languages in the world. In any case, there is no doubt that the contribution of the francophone writer to the history of 'Belgian' literature has been far too great to permit its relegation to a minority position on the basis of census alone.

LITERATURE OF THE REGION OF WALLONIA

What constitutes a region? What are the relationships between region and nation? Or those between literary and political notions of regionalism? Such questions, thematic of this conference, are especially relevant to the identity of Belgian literature, a problematic phenomenon deriving directly from the nationalist ideology of the nineteenth century. Belgian writers have consistently been troubled by the consequences of early attempts to establish a national literature, while such a concept has also inevitably compromised the interests and integrity of regional and linguistic variations, traditions and eccentricities.

As Raymond Williams says, 'a further effect of the dominant modern political meaning of "nation" is the specification of subordinate units of a "nation" as "regions". This term carries a linguistic irony, in that its root meaning relates to an "area of rule" (from Latin *regere* = to rule).'[2] As with 'minority' literature, so with 'regional' literature: it connotes subordination to the centralised nation-state.

Yet even if one considers Walloon literature as regional, in the rarer neutral sense of the native literature of the geographical area, the category still suggests a common interest based on the dominance of the French language. In my sense of a politico-cultural notion of Walloon literature, the category then remains exclusive of Belgian francophone writers in general. Furthermore, it invites the construction of a romanticised vision of Wallonia within a new regionalist ideology, based on a myth of the people and their history.

The presupposed commonality of regional interests isolates writers with broader concerns and obstructs or denies those potentially fruitful literary crossovers, such as might be expected to occur in bi- or multi-lingual communities dispersed within the geographical confines of a single nation. It also fails to account for the literary articulation of stark contrasts between urban and rural Wallonia; between, for example, the densely populated traditional industrial area of the Borinage and the agricultural remoteness of much of Luxembourg province. Wallonia (comprising the provinces of Hainaut, Namur, Liège, Luxembourg and part of Brabant) may be an economic, political and geographical unit in national terms but socio-culturally the region is highly varied, thus complicating the apparent straightforwardness of federalist solutions to the 'community problem'.

None the less, the region does have a literary tradition, going back to the late nineteenth century, to journals like *La Wallonie*, founded by Albert Mockel in 1886, and to regional novelists like Camille Lemonnier (one first finds 'Walloon' in literary titles at this time). In the main, however, these phenomena contributed either to ideas of national literary identity or to an international aestheticism, as in the case of the somewhat misleadingly titled *La Wallonie*, which became a platform for some of the leading Symbolist writers.

After its golden age (1890–1914), Belgian regionalist fiction survived in Wallonia alone after 1920, perhaps already indicating the turning tide in favour of more modern and progressive Flemish interests. It appeared to culminate in the work of Jean Tousseul, especially his cycles *Jean Clarambaux* (1927–36) and *François Stienon* (1938–9), but the tradition continued in the popular fiction of Arthur Masson, in such as his six works (1938–) based on the colourful figure of the *ardennais*, Toine Culot, and known collectively as the 'Toinade'.

The exclusivity of this category further implies that Walloon literature may be produced only by writers who live in the region and particularly those who see themselves as Walloon before Belgian. These writers typically feel out of place in Brussels, where to their ears a Dutch-sounding French is spoken and they feel writers are spiritually closer to Paris than, for instance, to Mons or Liège. By the same token, there are many writers originating from Wallonia who live in Brussels, Paris or elsewhere, who feel their attachment to the region is principally autobiographical, sentimental or even best ignored.[3]

Marc Quaghebeur has exposed the dangers of a new Walloon ideology, with its deliberate attachment to an artificial literature of mythical history and spirit, creating a 'cultural ghetto' based on a peculiar *mélange* of sub-French ethnicism and a defensive rejection of non-Walloon literary productions. Quaghebeur singles out two recent publications as examples of this dangerous position. One is the encyclopedia, *La Wallonie* (eds Lejeune and Stiennon, 1977–80), which he describes as the 'cathedral of the new rite' (r-i-t-e, that is!). The other (by Clotuche and Becquet, n.d.) is a guide for the benefit of librarians, presenting 366 'authentically Walloon' writers, characterised equally dubiously as 'Belgian citizens of French ethnicity'. Quaghebeur (himself a Brussels-based Walloon) also denounces what he sees as an unfair attack on Brussels-based writers and argues instead for a recognition of the complexity of Belgian writing, since

> the impossibility of an ill-considered homogenization of language, culture and nation ... effectively rules out all recourse to any notions of 'spirit of the people' as well as to a univocal participation in the 'eternalist' evolution of French literature.[4]

There is ample evidence of consciously Walloon writing. The writers of the 'Marie clap' Sabots' group, for instance, share a penchant for nostalgia and melancholia which links them with dialect literature. One of this group, Jean-Pierre Otte, is especially known for the grounding of his poetry and prose in an intensely personal vision of Walloon rural life. Yet Hubert Juin has expressed a less idyllic view of such life in his fictional series *Les Hameaux* (1958–68). However, Juin is first and foremost an international francophone writer and this broader identity informs the work of most other contemporary writers with Walloon backgrounds, such as Jacques Izoard, Eugène Savitzkaya, Christian Hubin, Jean Louvet and Jean-Pierre Verheggen. All these writers have national and, to lesser or greater degrees, French reputations, so it is inconceivable that they would wish their work to be known narrowly as either Walloon or regional.

Louvet is particularly important for his role in the politicisation of Walloon writing through the theatre; his influence may be seen on writers like Roland Hourez, Roland Thibeau and Michel Jamsin. There is also the radical position of such writers as José Fontaine and Michel Quévit, linked both to the establishment of magazines like the Liège-based *Carré*, and to a number of recent intellectual developments, such as the study of Walloon sociology and the publication of a book (1982) on Walloon literature at the University of Louvain-la-Neuve, or the seminars and study groups on Walloon writing there and at the University of Liège. As for Verheggen, he has successfully employed his knowledge of and feeling for the base idioms of Walloon dialect in the construction of his sophisticated textual strategies. Like many others, Verheggen has sought not a denial of his background but rather a balance between native affection and the attraction of an international francophone literature.

WALLOON DIALECT LITERATURE

This category again raises definitive questions. For instance, what is a dialect as opposed to a language? No necessary scientific distinction appears to exist. Definition thus comes down to a choice of criteria. Todorov and Ducrot (1972) identify a speech pattern with a dominant pattern, arguing to a historical but not necessarily genealogical relationship between the two, since the dominant language is often an extension or imposition, as in the case of French in modern Belgium. Williams (1981) again looks at etymology (Gk *diálektos* = discourse, that is, a particular way of speaking) noting again the growth of subordinate and inferior connotations. For Andrianne (1983), Walloon dialect valuably offsets the anonymity of standard French as the dominant language of the region. Lovelock (1980) points to the claims for

Walloon dialect as a language, not simply a patois or corruption of French, in view both of its derivation from Low Latin and mediaeval French, and of its distinctive and classified orthography. Literary production in this category thus presents familiar problems. Walloon dialect, of which the various forms are mutually intelligible only in theory, cannot pretend any more than francophone or regional categories to represent a linguistic or geographical unity. Beneath the banner of Walloon dialect literature, therefore, we may find language corresponding either to Gaume dialect (S. Luxembourg province), to Picard dialect (part of Hainaut and into France), or to Walloon dialect 'proper', subdivided into western (rest of Hainaut), central (Namur) and eastern (Liège) forms.[5]

This category is also exclusive in presupposing a kind of dialectal integrity. Traditional dialectology generally invites the false assumption that dialect speakers (and, by inference, writers too) never speak (or write) anything else. 'In reality' says David Graddol, 'their language is likely to include more standard features, which they will use to a greater or lesser extent according to the situation they find themselves in.'[6] In Wallonia, alternation between dialect and standard French is the spoken norm, though it may also produce conflicts between the two. According to the Walloon writer Willy Bal, dialect writing has only one generation to go before it dies out anyway, in consequence both of lack of young practitioners and of changing patterns in communication and leisure activities. Yet, in spite of this gloomy prognosis, sixty per cent of young people in Wallonia are exposed to dialect in their daily lives.

In the light of this figure, dialect literature is shown to be the most restrictive of my three categories of literary production. However, the emphasis on the spoken language is both under-standable and necessary, since it is common for many minority speakers to be unable to read or write their spoken language or to do so only with considerable difficulty. Although Walloon dialect literature has a 350-year history, it has only become conscious of its own identity in the last century.[7] Pre-sixteenth-century texts were basically French with added dialecticisms and do not therefore constitute a body of original literature. Since 'it has never been a written language even though one writes it' (Andrianne), Walloon dialect has never carried any official status in administrative, ecclesiastical or political affairs.

As it is, Walloon dialect literature is produced primarily by academics and intellectuals. Its activities are organised culturally around prizes (for example, Liège Biennial, Prix des Critique Wallons), associations (such as Les Scrîveûs du Cente, La Société de Langue et de Littérature Wallonnes) and magazines (for example, *El Mouchon d'Aunia, La Vie Wallonne, El Bourdon* and *Cahiers Wallons*). Two well-known writers, Albert Maquet and Louis Remacle, for example, are professors at the University of Liège; Géo Libbrecht is a distinguished poet in French too. This is not to denigrate their achievements in any way, nor to overlook the poor, self-taught backgrounds of earlier dialect writers like René Painblanc. However, it does point to an élitist practice (in sharp contrast to its popular oral forms) and to the limited nature of its diffusion and reception.

One might argue, then, that Walloon dialect literature is an artificial construct (cf. Lallans after MacDiarmid) and that the dialect is a natural expressive vehicle only in its spoken forms. Both its generical variety and its reception would seem to support this view. Its poetry, prose and drama betray a French influence, possessing a formal rigour and restraint which is uncharacteristic of popular dialect culture. Its minor genres – sketches, aphorisms, songs, tales – appear to have greater authenticity. Moreover, its audience appears to respond more enthusiastically to its role as entertainment within the framework of mass communication of popular culture, as in its popularity on radio and TV, than to its significance as a serious literary form.

As a result, dialect literature is generally treated as another source of nostalgia, as a folkloric cultural form, of relevance only to a popularised historical vision of the region. This perception is heightened by the cultivation (in the poetry, at any rate) of a wistful archaism, often in echo of Symbolist literature and of particular poets such as the 'rural' Verhaeren, Charles Van Lerberghe and Grégoire Le Roy.

In conclusion, it must therefore be said that 'Walloon literature' cannot pretend to represent a unified body of regional writing but must be viewed in the wider context of the complex and contentious nature of contemporary Belgian literature.

NOTES

1. René Andrianne, *Ecrire en Belgique* (Brussels, 1983) p. 125.
2. Raymond Williams, 'Review and Further Questions', in *Language in Use*, Educational Studies: E263 (block 6) (Open University, 1981) p. 10.
3. Andrianne notes the lack of interest in Wallonia shown by most of the 69 writers contributing to the reflective anthology, *La Belgique malgré tout* (Brussels, 1980). Exceptions are the pieces by the Brussels-based Françoise Collin ('bibliothèque paroissiale') and Jacques-Gérard Linze ('belgique s.a.'), and by Conrad Detrez ('le dernier des wallons') who lives in Paris.
4. Marc Quaghebeur, 'Littérature et fonctionnement idéologique en Belgique francophone', in *La Belgique malgré tout*, p. 520.
5. For this and related information, see Yann Lovelock (ed. and trs.), *The Colour of the Weather* (London, 1980).
6. David Graddol, 'Language Variation and Diversity', *Language in Use* Educational Studies: E 263 (block 1) (Open University, 1981) p. 103.
7. For a definitive work, covering writing in all the dialect forms from the seventeenth century to the present day, see Maurice Piron, *Anthologie de la littérature wallonne* (Liège, 1979).

18

'Lëtzebuergesch': a Dialect between Regional Tradition and National Vocation

JEAN-PIERRE CAMPILL

Luxembourg is a tiny country – from north to south it has a maximum length of 50 miles, and the maximum width from east to west is approximately 32 miles. It has about 365,000 inhabitants.

'Region' in the Luxembourg context does not mean the same as it would in a British perspective. For a student of the attitudes, manners and speech of the Luxembourg people, 'region' means something larger, geographically, historically, culturally and linguistically, than the present national territory, which is only about one quarter of the area covered by the original Duchy of Luxembourg before successive cessions to France, Prussia and Belgium, from 1659 to 1839, reduced it to its present size. The vaster region survives as a kind of vague historic, cultural and linguistic entity which has its roots in a very distant past, possibly beyond even the Middle Ages, and the language, Lëtzebuergesch, is still understood and occasionally used by a number of people in some of those formerly Luxembourgish territories in Belgium, Germany and France.

Lëtzebuergesch is a Moselle (that is, Central West) Franconian dialect situated half-way, on a south to north axis, between High German and Low German. Phonologically, its intermediate character is marked by its having undergone the High German Sound Shift only partly.

The other axis along which Lëtzebuergesch is situated, the one linking east and west, the Germanic and the Romance languages, may well be a more important one, as its effects are not only linguistic, but psychological and cultural, too.

242

Luxembourg has always been a border country. It is situated in that part of the Continent which, when Caesar conquered Gaul, was inhabited by the Treveri, a people partly Celtic and partly Germanic. Between the third and the sixth centuries, Frankish invaders twice overran the country, first from the east, then from the west. According to the Luxembourg linguist Robert Bruch this two-stroke Frankish invasion has been a decisive factor in the shaping of the mental outlook and, indirectly, of the language habits of the Luxembourg people. Trying to survive between West and East, between France and Germany, they depend on both, they intimately communicate and deal with the two, but they never feel quite identical with either. Ever since the days of the Merovingian kings, this instinctive search for balance has marked the fate of the country and the behaviour of its people.

In 1239, Luxembourg being then part of Germany, the Countess Ermesinde of Luxembourg granted a charter to one of her German-speaking boroughs, Diedenhofen. The charter was formulated in French. In the fourteenth century Duke Wenceslas of Luxembourg received Jean Froissart and Eustache Deschamps at his court (he may have met Chaucer), and he composed French poems himself. At the same time, his half-brother, the Emperor Charles IV, founded the first University of German expression, at Prague. In the eighteenth century, under the Habsburg rule, the administrative language used between the regional authorities at Brussels and Luxembourg was predominantly French. At the local level, however, the inhabitants of the Duchy wrote French or German, as suited them best, and they probably already spoke their own dialect speech when among themselves.

After the Belgian Revolution of 1830 King William I of the Netherlands, who was also Grand-Duke of Luxembourg, tried to germanise schools and public services in Luxembourg in order to stop the spreading of French-speaking pro-Belgian propaganda. This provoked such resistance in Luxembourg that he soon gave up the attempt. In 1848, a proclamation of the Luxembourg Government in favour of a union with the short-lived liberal Germany of the Frankfurt Parliament was strictly bilingual (German and French).

In 1941 the Nazi occupants staged a census in Luxembourg to induce the people to declare themselves German. But an overwhelming majority stated that their country, nationality and language were Luxembourg, Luxembourgish and Lëtzebuergesch.

Thereupon the Germans decided to call off the experiment. Even in the jubilant first weeks of the liberation of the country by American forces, in September 1944, the press almost immediately reverted to the traditional pattern of the mixed use of German, French and Lëtzebuergesch.

The divided attitude of the national psyche is reflected in the dialect: the basic structures of Lëtzebuergesch are undeniably German, but the French influence is important, especially in the lexical domain. As in English, this is particularly true for that vocabulary which pertains to a more refined way of life. Luxembourgers say 'bonjour', 'bonsoir', 'au revoir', 'merci', 'pardon', and so on. Altogether, reference to familiar objects and the expression of elementary feelings tend to rely on Germanic vocabulary, whereas an abstract style will often use more words adopted from French. Phonetically, the feature which most unmistakably distinguishes the dialect from High German is the absence in Lëtzebuergesch of the glottal stop which gives High German its characteristic clipped quality. Like French and English, Lëtzebuergesch allows words to pass into one another by phonetic links or 'liaisons'. French also influences the grammatical gender of certain dialect words which have the gender of their French synonym rather than that of the High German equivalent (for example: G. *Dach*, n., but L. *Daach* and F. *toit*, m.; G. *Butter*, f., but L. *Botter* and F. *beurre*, m.; G. *Kinn*, n., but L. *Kënn* and F. *menton*, m.)

Professor Fernand Hoffman, our greatest living expert in this domain, believes that a native Luxembourger, far from being bilingual or trilingual, has only one native language, namely Lëtzebuergesch, and that the language situation in Luxembourg is one which could be defined by the concept of triglossia. Perhaps an illustration of the state of triglossia ought to begin by a short note on names in Luxembourg.

Official statistics published in 1984 indicate that the ten most frequent family surnames in Luxembourg are: Schmit, Weber, Muller, Thill, Hoffman, Wagner, Klein, Schroeder, Welter, Kremer. These are all German names. The first surname of French origin is, rather ironically, Flammang (Fleming). It comes only thirty-first on the frequency list. Do not, however, expect these Schmits and Mullers to have German Christian names as well: characteristically, they will have such names as François, Jules, Nicole, Pierre, Roger, Martine, Fernand, Raymond . . . while their relatives and friends

may call them by a Lëtzebuergesch version of their official
Christian name (Pitt for Pierre, Rosch for Roger), none of them
would dream of using the High German equivalent.
  Imagine, then, an average Luxembourger called Pierre Welter
(Weltësch Pitt for his friends). He will speak nothing but
Lëtzebuergesch when he speaks to other Luxembourgers. This
practice is subject to no social or educational register – Pierre
Welter started learning German when, at the age of six, he went to
primary school. But, unless he be a writer or a journalist, his
practical use of German will, on the whole, be a passive or
receptive one. In his daily paper, for instance, most news and a
great number of commercial advertisements will be conveyed to
him in German. As he finds it somewhat easier to understand
spoken German than French, he will more naturally switch on to a
German-speaking radio or television programme than to a French
one. He may also preferably buy German magazines, and his
children will probably read most of their comic strips and novels of
adventure in the German translation. On the active side, he and
his wife may draw up their shopping list in German, or send a
letter to the editor of their daily paper in that language. But they
may also use French or Lëtzebuergesch for these purposes – our
friend started learning French from his second primary school year
onward. In his daily papers he expects to read some news and
commentaries (not the leader, though) and a great number of
advertisements in French. The mail he gets from government
departments will be either just French, or bilingual, French and
German (forms to be filled out and returned tend to be bilingual).
Letters from his children's grammar school and from his bank will
be in French. Cheques, money orders, invoices and bills are mostly
French. French predominates in the telephone directory and the
railway guide. He must be able to understand French explanations,
instructions and directions on tins and packages, on road signs and
public notices, at bus stops and in railway stations. Addresses and
place names are usually indicated in French. Shop signs are
practically always French. Public buildings are marked by French
door plates. As for the active use of French, one could state that the
higher and more responsible Pierre Welter's job, the more often he
will have to write letters and reports in French. However, he will
actually speak French only to French-speaking visitors from abroad
and to the great number of foreign residents and immigrant
workers in the country, for many of whom French has become a

kind of *lingua franca* on the Luxembourg market. At school, German and French are both used as teaching languages, with French becoming more common in the upper forms of secondary schools and at university level.

A certain number of changes have taken place over the last twenty or thirty years and go on operating. Again, however, these changes seem to confirm the inherent Luxembourgish tendency towards balancing German and French. Thus, today, mainly because of the powerful appeal of television programmes in German, this language is quite noticeably influencing both the grammar and the vocabulary of many Luxembourgers. However, rather incongruously, the High German distinction between velar or 'thin' 'ch' (as in 'lächerlich') and palato-alveolar or 'thick' 'sch' (as in 'schön' and 'Busch'), which used to be a feature of the Lëtzebuergesch spoken by a majority of native speakers, nowadays seems to be observed less and less, particularly among the young. Whatever the explanation of this puzzling phenomenon may be, the simultaneous appearance of two contrary linguistic trends, the one towards German, the other away from it, is typically Luxembourgish.

It is worth noting, too, that the dialect seems to be invading domains nowadays from which it was formerly barred. In some places the names of streets are nowadays indicated not only in French but also in Lëtzebuergesch. Until about twenty years ago, staff meetings at grammar schools were held in French. These days one hears only Lëtzebuergesch at such conferences. Until about ten years ago Pierre Welter, wishing to announce some important family event in the papers – a birth, an engagement, his father's death – would almost certainly have used French. Today he may use either French or Lëtzebuergesch.

On counting and analysing one sample week's obituary notices in the most widely circulated daily paper, the 'Luxemburger Wort' over a period stretching from 1900 to 1986, one finds that before 1914, German and French were almost equal competitors in this special field. French then became absolutely predominant till May 1940 when the Nazis occupied the country and soon prohibited the use of any language but German in the papers. Lëtzebuergesch was first used for obituary notices amidst the outbursts of patriotic fervour in September 1944, but very soon gave way to French again. After what had happened during the time of the German occupation, the use of German had become quite impossible in this domain, and that language still has not recovered from the setback. Interestingly, however, since the late 1970s, obituaries in Lëtzebuergesch have become more and more common, and today their number tends to pass that of the French ones. The application of what one might term 'obituarology' can thus lead to rather interesting insights into certain trends and uses in a polyglossal country.

A last puzzling development ought not to go unmentioned. At a time when the massive immigration of Portuguese workers makes it increasingly necessary for native Luxembourgers in their own country to use French when communicating with these immigrants, there has arisen, outside Luxembourg on the French side of the border, a rather vociferous movement aiming at a revival of the 'Francique' (that is, Frankish or Franconian) culture and languages, including Lëtzebuergesch, as opposed to Central French. The regional past here seems to rise across national borders against the levelling and unifying structures of the political present.

In February 1984 Lëtzebuergesch was officially acknowledged by an Act of Parliament to be the national language of the Luxembourg people. Nevertheless, French and German go on being the administrative languages, and a more radical proposal tending to make Lëtzebuergesch a compulsory means of official correspondence was rejected by a majority of the Members.

So far, then, Lëtzebuergesch has enjoyed the status of being the universally accepted instrument of oral communication of all native Luxembourgers. The Act of 1984 merely confirmed the existing status of a language whose national vocation had never been seriously challenged since the nineteenth century, except for the four years of Nazi occupation during the Second World War. Yet it is difficult not to worry about the future. For irrefutable official surveys tell us that already in 1981, of a total population of 364,000 inhabitants, only 268,000 were of Luxembourgish origin. Almost 100,000 were foreign residents or immigrants, some 30,000 of these from Portugal and her ex-colonies. The current birthrate of the native Luxembourgish population is disastrously low. From the constant proportional decline of the native population there ensues its growing inability to assimilate the immigrants socially, culturally and linguistically. Finally, one must also take into account the ever-increasing number and weight in Luxembourg of supra-national organisations, agencies and businesses whose senior staff are not primarily native speakers of Lëtzebuergesch.

It must be assumed that a language will survive in a community only as long as its native speakers represent a dominant, or at least a very significant, part of that community, either by sheer numbers, or by their economic, professional, social, political or military importance. Without such support, it will soon decline to the level of a local dialect or evaporate into the misty realms of nostalgic folklore and academic antiquarianism. No Act of Parliament can change this truth. Applying the rule to the situation in Luxembourg, one could say that as long as a majority of employers, superiors and decision-makers are native speakers of Lëtzebuergesch, the language will survive. If this balance were to be upset, and that is exactly what the current demographic evolution seems to be leading to, the fate of Lëtzebuergesch would be sealed, and it would probably die within one or two generations.

19

Literature in 'Lëtzebuergesch' in the Grand Duchy of Luxembourg

SEPP SIMON

In effect, the Grand Duchy has a trilingual literature: we have had, and still have, authors writing in French, German or 'Lëtzebuergesch'. The reasons that may have motivated a writer when opting for French or German are usually quite personal (education or war experiences for instance); choosing 'Lëtzebuergesch', however, was in the nineteenth century and the first half of our century a conscious political act, that could not possibly be compared with, say, a Bavarian expressing himself in his own dialect. A Luxembourg author, by choosing his own language, insists on its peculiarity and insists on its being quite different from standard German (*Hochdeutsch*); his choice is a separatist's action.

Such ninteenth-century authors as Edmond de la Fontaine, Michel Lentz and Michel Rodange[1] were fully aware of this and their success has been, and is, an obvious proof of a conscious nationalistic delimitation from powerful neighbours on their readers' part. From the early twentieth century onwards our literature has been largely nationalistic in tone and contents (Lucien König, 1888–1961), sometimes aggressively so, without ever reaching that degree of popularity the three nineteenth-century authors mentioned above still have. Writers had to face a double threat to our national identity: (a) the aftermath of the First World War led some left-wing intellectuals to openly show their scepticism as to a small nation's viability and made them look towards France, thereby, however unconsciously, increasing our language's magpie quality of absorbing words from other languages; (b) much more directly dangerous to the nation's survival was the rise of Nazism and German claims of annexation though, ironically enough, this direct menace brought the Grand Duchy's inhabitants closer together than ever before and, on the occasion of a census (1941) organised with the aim of giving a varnish of legitimacy to the annexation, the Luxemburgers, when asked to give their native language, answered 'Lëtzebuergesch' to a man.

After the Second World War, with anti-German feelings running high the Civil Service, the Church authorities (to some extent) and our best authors switched over to French, and the French language for a while influenced Lëtzebuergesch, considerably expanding its vocabulary, unequivocally differentiating it from nearby (Eifel and Hunsrück) German dialects. Nevertheless, two outstanding authors resisted the social and political pressures of the time: Tit Schroeder (1911–86) who managed to innovate on the stage with a socially critical play (t'*Döltchesfamill*), illustrating the humdrum life of a family belonging to the lower middle class; and Marcel Reuland (1905–56), a fine lyricist, who also adapted both Molière and Shakespeare's comedies to Lëtzebuergesch.

As memories of the war faded away and rancour abated, the following generation became ripe in the 1960s for a second wave of cultural annexation which one may feel anxious about: the growth and influence of German television programmes, popular daily papers and magazines has been and still is seriously underestimated by politicians, educators and writers alike. As German TV channels have become the undisputed favourites with the vast majority of households, the cultural spectrum for which we could have been envied in the 1950s and early 1960s has certainly been impoverished.

France and French culture is becoming more and more alien to our pupils, among them our future writers, and to the nation as a whole. French, as a language, has lost its impact, and some reading material that would have been a normal part of a child's 'baggage' about twenty years ago, has quite simply vanished from the market, for example, *Poil de Carotte*, *Le Petit Chose*, *La Foire aux Cancres* (the French equivalent to *1066 and All That*). Much worse – this ought to leave us rather thoughtful – young people's magazines and comic-strips such as *Tintin et Milou* or *Asterix* are now being read in German (*Tim und Struppi*). The numbers of these magazines sold in French on our market has become statistically insignificant. French has disappeared as an auxiliary language with some subjects at secondary schools and thus, the receptivity of

Lëtzebuergesch, with its subtle ways of adopting and adapting words from neighbouring languages, has been considerably weakened, and our language is moving dangerously close to being no more than one German dialect among others.

On the other hand, our writers could not have been unaware of the development of dialectal literature throughout Europe; and one consequence of this is that an increasing number of our students studying abroad, especially at the more recently founded German universities, have come to learn from other minorities, numerically far more important, a new pride in their own language. This has brought us a new social and political awareness thanks to the talented endeavours of a group of young writers who are taking a much more critical look at their native country and its inhabitants than their predecessors did (with the exception of Michel Rodange), and the subjects they discuss and scrutinise are the best evidence that we do have a separate identity, with problems very much our own. We are no longer, parochially enough, fed with patriotic fervour; that social and cultural identity can now be taken for granted, and even dissected, and we, the readers, are able to discover the power of the written and the spoken word in Lëtzebuergesch with an intensity so far unknown in the literary history of the Grand Duchy.

The new generation of writers – Jos Braun, Paul Greisch, Nico Helminger, Guy Rewenig and Guy Wagner, to name but a few – nearly all belong to the political left; they have taught us that our language can be not merely a cosy refuge or a harmless tool for a vaudeville show, but a stimulating and sometimes even a shocking weapon, though they are sometimes all too clumsily didactic or biased, and often reveal (yet again) the powerful influence of the German 'Greens' and their supporters. The position of immigrants in Luxembourg, the power of the Roman Catholic Church, birth control, drugs, the problems of growing old in a wealthy place, and, much more recently, ecological problems and the threat of a nearby nuclear power station – these were topics that we used to think could only be decently discussed and written about in French, German or Dutch. But this attitude has been radically changed by our present-day writers.

And yet, no matter how profoundly justified some of these vitriolic texts may be, our writers seem to write for other fellow-writers only; they move within an incestuous coterie, rarely touching a larger audience, and only then with the help of the stage or the cinema. In other words, the potential reader tends to shrink from Lëtzebuergesch in print, unless it is used for strictly social or downright commercial purposes. Why is this? There are several possible reasons: the spelling system is forbidding, and all too often seen as a contrived handicap; as a language, Lëtzebuergesch is not systematically taught at school; and, above all, there is no established publishing industry. Printer, publisher and editor are likely to be one and the same person or group. Independent publishers as such are very rare and strictly marginal, though they deserve support and respect for their courage to publish for an exceedingly small market.

A last point, and a gloomy forecast: *because* these authors are successful and (rightly) conscious of their talent, they will ask for a larger readership, and, what with the powerful attraction of *Hochdeutsch* and the fact that our own language is fast losing its earlier receptivity, it is to be feared that the best of them will switch from Lëtzebuergesch to German, as their koine, thereby destroying the new aesthetic power they themselves have given to their own language.[2]

NOTES

1. Edmond de la Fontaine, 'Dicks' (1823–91) for the stage, Michel Lentz (1820–93), poet and author of the national anthem, and Michel Rodange (1827–76), author of 'De Renert', a still highly satirical animal epic poem influenced by Goethe's 'Reineke Fuchs'.
2. For further information on the trilingual literature in the Grand Duchy see: 'Fernand Hoffman: Das Erwachen, Aufblühen und Erstarken des luxemburgischen National gefuhls in der luxemburgischen Literatur', in *Nos Chaier, Letzeburger Säitschreft fir Kultur*, 2/84 (Luxembourg: Imprimerie (St Paul)) pp. 127–74.

Appendix

International Conference on the Literature of Region and Nation, University of Aberdeen, 19–23 August 1986

LIST OF PAPERS

J. H. Alexander, 'Wordsworth, Regional or Provincial? The Epistolary Context'.

James Booth, 'Wole Soyinka: Imitator of Europe or Yoruba Original?'

Jean-Pierre Campill, 'Lëtzebuergesch': a Dialect between Regional Tradition and National Vocation'.

R. H. Carnie, 'The Scottish Contribution to Nineteenth-Century Canadian Poetry'.

Robert Crawford, 'Robert Frost: Scotsman'.

Thomas Crawford, 'The View from the North: Region and Nation in *The Silver Darlings* and *A Scots Quair*'.

Edmund Cusick, 'Highland Folklore in the Work of George MacDonald'.

Gerald Dawe, 'Beyond *Across a Roaring Hill*: the Protestant Imagination in Modern Ireland'.

R. P. Draper, 'Philip Larkin: Provincial Poet'.

Joris Duytschaever, 'The Rhetoric of Ethnic Nationalism: Flemish Literature'.

Robin Gilmour, 'Regional and Provincial in Victorian Literature'.

Barbara Hardy, 'Region and Nation: R. S. Thomas and Dylan Thomas'.

Seamus Heaney, 'The Regional Forecast'.

David Hewitt, 'Scoticisms and Cultural Conflict'.

Lindsay Hewitt, 'Sociolinguistic Implications of the Use of Dialect in Galt's Scottish Novels'.

Gary Kelly, 'Print, People and Nation: Literacy and Literature, Self and Nation in British Fiction, 1780–1830'.

Robert Lawson-Peebles, 'The Local Is the Universal: William Carlos Williams and Neil Gunn'.

A. Walton Litz, 'Williams and Stevens: the Quest for a Native American Modernism'.

Index